EXPERIENCING OLMSTED

The Haseltine Building
133 S.W. Second Avenue, Suite 450
Portland, Oregon 97204-3527
timberpress.com

Printed in China
Cover design by Vincent James
Book design by Jason Arias
ISBN 978-1-64326-036-5
A catalog record for this book is available from the Library of
Congress and the British Library.

Furthermore:
a program of the J.M. Kaplan Fund

Publication of this volume was assisted by a grant from
Furthermore: a program of the J. M. Kaplan Fund.

EXPERIENCING
OLMSTED

The Enduring Legacy of Frederick Law Olmsted's
North American Landscapes

THE CULTURAL LANDSCAPE FOUNDATION

CHARLES A. BIRNBAUM, ARLEYN A. LEVEE, AND DENA TASSE-WINTER

TIMBER PRESS
PORTLAND, OREGON

CONTENTS

Introduction   10
Acknowledgments   14

ALABAMA

Birmingham City Parks Plan   17
Alabama Educational Institutions   19
University of North Alabama, Florence   19
Huntingdon College, Montgomery   21

CALIFORNIA

California State Park System   23
Yosemite National Park and
      Mariposa Grove   27
Mountain View Cemetery, Oakland   29
Stanford University Campus, Palo Alto   31
St. Francis Wood, San Francisco   34
Palos Verdes Syndicate, Palos Verdes   37
Palos Verdes Parkway, Los Angeles   40

COLORADO

Boulder Park System   43
Denver Park and Parkway System   45
Denver Mountain Parks System   47

CONNECTICUT

Beardsley Park, Bridgeport   51
Hartford Parks System   52
Goodwin Park, Hartford   53
Keney Park, Hartford   54
Pope Park, Hartford   55
Bushnell Park and Connecticut State
      Capitol Grounds, Hartford   56
Walnut Hill Park, New Britain   58
Waveny Park, New Canaan   59
Hillside Cemetery, Torrington   60

DISTRICT OF COLUMBIA

United States Capitol Grounds   63
White House Grounds
      (President's Park)   64
Rock Creek Park   65
McMillan Plan   67
Thomas Jefferson Memorial   68
Lincoln Memorial Grounds   70
Washington Monument   71
Theodore Roosevelt Island
      National Memorial   72
National Cathedral Grounds   74

DELAWARE

Brandywine Park, Wilmington   76
Kentmere Parkway, Wilmington   76

FLORIDA

Memorial Park, Jacksonville   79
Mountain Lake, Lake Wales   80
Bok Tower Gardens, Lake Wales   81
Pinewood Estate, Lake Wales   82

GEORGIA

Druid Hills, Atlanta   84
Grant Park, Atlanta   88
Piedmont Park, Atlanta   90
Bradley Olmsted Garden, Columbus   92

IDAHO

University of Idaho, Moscow   95

ILLINOIS

South Park System, Chicago   97
Riverside Community, Riverside   99

INDIANA

Indiana University, Bloomington   101
Oldfields, Indianapolis   102

KENTUCKY

Bernheim Arboretum, Clermont   105
Kentucky State Capitol
    Grounds, Frankfort   106
Ashland Park, Lexington   107
Parks and Parkways System, Louisville   109
University of Louisville   111

LOUISIANA

Audubon Park, New Orleans   114
Louisiana State University, Baton Rouge   116

MAINE

Acadia National Park, Mount Desert   119
Maine State Capitol Grounds, Augusta   121
University of Maine, Orono   122
Portland Parks, Eastern and
    Western Promenades   123

MARYLAND

Parks and Parkways System, Baltimore 127
Roland Park, Baltimore 129
Sudbrook Park, Baltimore County 130
Guilford Park, Baltimore 131
Homeland Park, Baltimore 132
Johns Hopkins University, Baltimore 133

MASSACHUSETTS

Metropolitan Park Commission, Boston 136
World's End, Hingham 140
Amherst College, Amherst 141
Phillips Academy, Andover 142
Moraine Farm, Beverly 144
Emerald Necklace Park System, Boston 146
Frederick Law Olmsted National
    Historic Site (Fairsted), Brookline 149
Harvard University, Cambridge 151
Middlesex School, Concord 153
Parks of Fall River 155
Newton City Hall 157
North Easton Town Complex 158
Stonehurst, Waltham 159
Williams College, Williamstown 160

MICHIGAN

Belle Isle Park, Detroit 162
Barton Hills, Ann Arbor 164
Washtenong Cemetery, Ann Arbor 165

MISSISSIPPI

Alcorn State University, Alcorn 167
University of Mississippi, Oxford 169

MISSOURI

Liberty Memorial, Kansas City 171

NEW HAMPSHIRE

Phillips Exeter Academy, Exeter 174
Swasey Parkway, Exeter 176

NEW JERSEY

Essex County Park System 178
Branch Brook Park, Newark 179
Eagle Rock Reservation,
    West Orange-Verona-Montclair 183

South Mountain Reservation,
Maplewood-Millburn-West Orange 184
Lawrenceville School, Lawrenceville 186
Cadwalader Park and Cadwalader
Heights, Trenton 187
Union County Park System 188
Warinanco Park, Elizabeth 190
Echo Lake Park, Mountainside 190
Rahway River Parks, Rahway 190
Watchung Reservation, Mountainside 192

NEW YORK

Buffalo Park and Parkway System 195
Niagara Reservation, Niagara Falls 198
Brooklyn Park and Parkway System 200
Prospect Park, Brooklyn 201
Fort Greene Park, Brooklyn 204
Ocean and Eastern Parkways, Brooklyn 205
Brooklyn Botanic Garden, Brooklyn 207
Central Park, Manhattan 209
Morningside Park, Manhattan 211
Riverside Park, Manhattan 213
Fort Tryon Park, Manhattan 215
Forest Hills Gardens, Queens 217
Gold Coast Estates, North Shore of
Long Island 218
Rochester Parks System 220
Highland Park, Rochester 222

Genesee Valley Park, Rochester 223
Seneca Park, Rochester 224
Thompson Park, Watertown 225

NORTH CAROLINA

Biltmore, Asheville 228
Duke University, Durham 231
Village of Pinehurst 232
Capitol Square, Raleigh 233

OHIO

Fine Arts Garden, Cleveland Museum
of Art 237
NCR Projects, Dayton 239
Denison University, Granville 241

OREGON

Elk Rock Garden at the Bishop's
Close, Portland 244
Portland Park System 246
Terwilliger Parkway, Portland 248

PENNSYLVANIA

FDR Park, Philadelphia   251
Vandergrift Town Plan   252
Stoneleigh, Villanova   254
Kirby Park, Wilkes-Barre   256

RHODE ISLAND

Newport City Plan   259
Newport Estates, Newport   260
Blackstone Boulevard, Providence   263

SOUTH CAROLINA

Yeamans Hall Club, North Charleston   265

TENNESSEE

Laura Spelman Rockefeller
      Memorial, Gatlinburg   268
Woodmont Estates, Nashville   271
Fisk University, Nashville   271

UTAH

Utah State Capitol Grounds, Salt
      Lake City   274

VERMONT

Shelburne Farms, Burlington   277

VIRGINIA

Masonic Memorial to George
      Washington, Alexandria   280

WASHINGTON

Thornewood, American Lake   283
Washington State Capitol,
      Olympia   285
Dunn Gardens, Seattle   286
Seattle Parks and Boulevard System   287
Seward Park, Seattle   290
Volunteer Park, Seattle   290
Lake Washington Boulevard, Seattle   291
Washington Park Arboretum, Seattle   292
University of Washington, Seattle   293
Park System of Spokane   295

WISCONSIN

Town of Kohler   298
Washington Park, Milwaukee   300
Lake Park, Milwaukee   302

CANADA

Capilano Estates, Vancouver   304
The Uplands, Victoria   307
Mount Royal, Montreal   309

Olmsted Firms   313

Selected Biographies of Principals and
    Members of Olmsted Firms   316

Selected Bibliography   328
Photography and Illustration Credits   332
Index   334

INTRODUCTION

EXPERIENCING OLMSTED
—Charles A. Birnbaum, FASLA

Experiencing an Olmsted landscape can alter your mood, calm your spirit, and provide lifelong memories. Distinct from fine art, architecture, music, and dance, a great work of landscape architecture—from a meticulously planned and designed park or garden to an expansive open space preserved as a natural or scenic reservation—is uniquely multisensory and utterly transporting.

In her 1893 treatise *Art Out-Of-Doors* (written just two years before Frederick Law Olmsted Sr.'s retirement from practice), Mrs. Schuyler Van Rensselaer reflected on designed landscapes as an art form, noting, "The Arts of Design are usually named as three: architecture, sculpture and painting. It is a popular belief that a man who practices one of these is an artist, and the other men who work with forms and colors are at the best but artisans. Yet there is a fourth Art of Design which well deserves to rank with them, for it demands quite as much in the way of aesthetic feeling, creative power, and executive skill. This is the art which creates beautiful compositions upon the surface of the ground. . . . The mere statement of its purpose should show that it is truly an art."

Van Rensselaer goes even further in her preface, proclaiming, "It is one which has produced the most remarkable artist yet born in America; and this is reason enough why Mr. Olmsted's fellow-countrymen ought to try to understand its aims and methods."

Following Olmsted Sr.'s death in 1903, during the next half century, the firm he founded was led by his nephew and stepson, John Charles Olmsted (1852–1920), and his son, Frederick "Rick" Law Olmsted Jr. (1870–1957). After John Charles Olmsted's death in 1920, Rick ran the firm until his retirement in 1949, and remained a partner until his death (see selected staff biographies of the Olmsted firms at the end of this book). While the thousands of projects undertaken in these years—a cross section of which are included in this volume—were produced under the mantle of the firm name, here we have endeavored to illuminate the involvement of the individual talented practitioners employed by the firm, whose creative interpretations enhanced each landscape. Although the Olmsted firm remained active until 1979 under the leadership of Artemas Partridge Richardson II and Joseph George Hudak, the projects during that period reflected contemporary realities such as limited acreage and more demanding recreational needs, a different set of circumstances than the firm encountered in the late nineteenth and early twentieth centuries.

In the postwar era, a lack of appreciation for the historic built legacy of the earlier century of practice led to neglect, subdivision, or at worst, erasure.

Fortunately, during the last forty-plus years, much has been done to make Frederick Law Olmsted Sr.'s pioneering approach to the art of landscape architecture—namely, planning, design, and stewardship—more visible and publicly accessible. The result is a *new* golden age for Olmsted.

This new era is marked by the founding of a dedicated non-profit, the National Association for Olmsted Parks, and the designation of Fairsted, the Frederick Law Olmsted National Historic Site (FLONHS) in Brookline, MA, as a unit of the National Park Service. Both events took place in 1980, the same year that the Central Park Conservancy was created in New York City. Fundamental to the work of these entities, and the rediscovery of the Olmsted design legacy, are the extraordinarily rich Olmsted archives.

Fairsted houses what is probably the most significant landscape architectural archive in the country, if not the world. Spanning the 1850s to 1980, the collection of professional office records of the Olmsted firms includes more than 6000 projects and contains approximately 138,000 plans and drawings. The collection also includes 100,000 photographs and lithographs, 70,000 pages of plant lists, numerous files of project correspondence, business records, and other ephemera. Essential complementary collections are the Frederick Law Olmsted Papers and the Olmsted Associates Records at the United States Library of Congress. These collections (the latter as of yet only partially digitized) contain more than 173,000 items, including business correspondence and reports, newspaper clippings, drawings, photographs, and more, all illuminating the design intent and historical context for both the landscape architects and their patrons.

Buoyed and enabled by these unrivaled archives (noted in the bibliography of this book) is a treasure trove of publications created for many different audiences: in-depth scholarship (for example, the twelve-volume series of the Frederick Law Olmsted Papers project started in 1972 and completed in 2020), and numerous articles and analyses in academic journals and collections; site-specific publications for myriad Olmsted landscape typologies, including parks, subdivisions, institutional grounds, and much more (including *Fresh Pond: The History of a Cambridge Landscape*, Jill Sinclair, 2012, and *San Francisco's St. Frances Wood*, Richard Brandi, 2012); exhibitions at museums, universities, historical societies, and other institutions (*Art of the Olmsted Landscape*, Metropolitan Museum of Art, New York, NY, and elsewhere, 1981–1983, and *Viewing Olmsted: Photographs by Robert Burley, Lee Friedlander and Geoffrey James*, Canadian Centre for Architecture, Montreal, Canada, 1996 to 1997); documentaries (*Frederick Law Olmsted: Designing America*, 2014, and *Olmsted and America's Urban Parks*, 2011), park and open space surveys conducted at statewide, regional, and municipal levels (including Dayton, OH; Rochester, NY; Massachusetts, and Maine); popular histories about Olmsted Sr. or where he appears as a central character (*A Clearing in the Distance*, Witold

Rybczynski, 1999, and *Devil in the White City*, Erik Larson, 2003); coffee table books (*Frederick Law Olmsted: Designing the American Landscape*, Charles E. Beveridge and Paul Rocheleau, 2005); and even books for children (*Parks for the People: Frederick Law Olmsted*, Julie Dunlap, 1994). Online databases have been developed to enable easier exploration for both scholars and travelers of this extensive nationwide legacy of designed spaces. The name "Olmsted" has achieved such currency that even real-estate advertisements include it in a property's provenance as a client enticement. And let's not forget that both Olmsted Sr. and Jr. wrote and published extensively, providing a deep and wide historical record that documents their design philosophies, ambitions, and often site-specific design intentions.

With this expansive primary and secondary resource knowledge base facilitating greater attention to the Olmsted firms' design legacy, a body of research, analysis, and revitalization project work followed, ushering in an ever-expanding Olmsted renaissance. Landscape histories and historic-cultural landscape reports undertaken by leading landscape architects and historians, aided by federal and state government agencies, conservancies and friends' groups, and local residents and funders continued for the next decades, establishing a planning and design approach not just for Olmsted-designed landscapes, but for the broader emerging landscape preservation discipline in search of such strategies and tools.

There has been a renewed appreciation for and attention to Olmsted-designed landscapes following decades of neglect and deferred maintenance, including the pioneering work of the Central Park Conservancy, which stimulated similar efforts in cities across the country. The public's recognition for these landscapes can be measured further by the more than 200 Olmsted firm–designed projects that are listed in the National Register of Historic Places (including the Louisville Park System, KY, 1982; Denver Mountain Park System, CO, 1990; and Acadia National Park, Mount Desert, ME, 2005), and as National Historic Landmarks (for example, Lawrenceville School, NJ, 1986). It is safe to say that there is no other landscape architectural practice that could come close to this level of recognition.

With this as a foundation, and the close to 200 projects spread across thirty-three states, plus the District of Columbia and Canada explored in this volume, experiencing an Olmsted-designed landscape today may be easier than you think. In some cases, these experiences might be at landscapes designed by firms that are below the radar (for instance, Kirby Park, Wilkes-Barre, PA; Thompson Park, Watertown, NY; and University of North Alabama, Florence, AL). The last four decades have also yielded a broader understanding of (1) Olmsted beyond his best-known and most iconic parks, and especially (2) the generations of others connected with the firm who contributed to a great typological and geographical diversity of designed landscapes. The age-old academic notion that one should *publish or perish* has paid off not only with a deeper understanding of Olmsted, but the possibility to experience his work as he intended.

As this book demonstrates, the Olmsted firm literally shaped the nation from coast to coast, from park systems (such as Seattle, WA, and Birmingham, AL), to State Capitol Grounds (including Salt Lake City, UT; Hartford, CT; and Olympia, WA), among others. We also learn that relationships with clients and patrons spanned multiple generations. Examples include family patronage that encompassed other Vanderbilt projects beyond the well-known Biltmore estate, as well as various generations of Rockefeller projects (Laura Spelman Rockefeller Memorial, Gatlinburg, TN; Acadia National Park, Mount Desert, ME; Fort Tryon Park and the Cloisters, New York, NY). Bok Tower Gardens in Lake Wales, FL, was for philanthropist Edward Bok, and was followed by numerous civic projects for his widow in the Camden, ME, area. A variety of patronage projects were built out by the Olmsted firm by way of Walter Kohler Sr. in Wisconsin; these projects spanned a quarter century and ranged from entire neighborhoods and memorial highways to parks, plazas, and even family burial plots. Most of these places are covered within this volume.

Additionally, it is worth noting that many of the landscape typologies that we take for granted today were literally invented and promoted by the Olmsted practice, including the very idea of the comprehensive park system (in Boston, Louisville, Seattle, and Rochester), parkways (Brooklyn's Eastern Parkway, at 6600 linear feet, was the first), and performative, ecologically driven design (the Back Bay Fens in Boston). Olmsted expanded our notion that the landscape itself can serve as memorial (Memorial Park, Jacksonville, FL, and the National World War I Memorial, Kansas City, MO).

Finally, as this publication has been prepared by The Cultural Landscape Foundation, whose mission is to "connect people to places," it is important that we recognize that in the twentieth century, the Olmsted firm was among the first to place value on a landscape's historic extant fabric. Historic and cultural values were acknowledged by the firm as assets, much the same as scenic and natural resources were valued, protected, and leveraged in the planning and design process. This ranged from the White House Grounds, where the in-depth analysis of the site's history informed the 1930s planning efforts undertaken by Rick Olmsted, to larger scale planning efforts such as the 1913 Newport City Plan in Rhode Island, where historic fabric was weighed alongside scenic and natural resource values, as well as the ambitious and pioneering California State Park System, which began in 1927 and spanned multiple decades. The latter resulted in the preservation and protection of many of California's most treasured scenic and native horticultural resources, from its coastline to desert landscapes; of which 125 now owned and operated by the state were based on Olmsted firm recommendations.

The bicentennial of Olmsted's birth provides an opportunity to reflect on this extraordinary and influential legacy and on how it is distinct from others. Indeed, the past decade has seen milestone anniversaries for other great artists, architects, and landscape architects: the 400th anniversary of André Le Nôtre's birth (2013), the 300th anniversary of Capability Brown's birth (2016), and the 150th anniversary of Frank Lloyd Wright's birth (2017) among them. Unlike those three, whose work was largely created for private clients, much of the Olmsted firms' work was created to be free and open to the public. These places were designed with democracy and democratic values in mind and their benefits were available to everyone.

> "The enjoyment of scenery employs the mind without fatigue and yet exercises it; tranquilizes it and yet enlivens it; and thus, through the influence of the mind over the body gives the effect of refreshing rest and reinvigoration to the whole system."
>
> —Frederick Law Olmsted Sr.

ACKNOWLEDGMENTS

The creation and publication of this book would not have been possible without many people who were giving of their time and talents.

First and foremost, thanks are due to my coeditors, Arleyn A. Levee and Dena Tasse-Winter. From the initial whittling of hundreds of Olmsted prospective projects down to the written and illustrative content for the approximately 200 landscapes that you will find within these pages, Arleyn and Dena saw this project through to its final form, managing its smooth execution and contributing countless hours of research, writing, and refining.

At Timber Press, we would like to extend our thanks to Stacee Lawrence, executive editor, who originally suggested the idea and has provided steadfast support throughout the process, and to Julie Talbot, project editor, who shepherded this book through the editing process with her keen review. Collectively, their thoughtful feedback and professional guidance were crucial in shaping this project into its final form.

Also instrumental to this endeavor were the employees of The Cultural Landscape Foundation, for their efforts as writers, administrators, and so much more: Nord Wennerstrom, Scott Craver, Justin Clevenger, Aileen Beringer, Ayla Mangold, Barrett Doherty, Eduard Krakhmalnikov, Ranjani Srinivasan, Brendan Ayer, and Suehyun Choi.

Beyond the written content created by the aforementioned individuals, several freelance writers shaped key texts. In particular, special thanks to Piera Weiss and Kevan Klosterwill, along with Olivia Lott and Debbie Siegel for their contributions.

We are grateful to Hubbard Educational Foundation; Furthermore grants in publishing, a program of the J. M. Kaplan Fund; and the National Endowment for the Arts Art Works program, for the generous funding that they provided in support of the production of this book.

And to the dozens of photographers who lent us their creativity and discerning eyes, capturing the beauty of the hundreds of Olmsted-designed landscapes found within the pages (and, in the case of Ngoc Minh Ngo, on the front jacket) of this volume, including Brendan Albolins, Nick Allen, Marc Ancel, David Basanta, David Berkowitz, Madeline Berry, Alex Bevk, Lucas Blair, Ted Bobosh, Don de Bold, Ted Booth, Hallie Borstel, Tod Bryant, Trey Bunn, Steve K.C., Kim Carpenter, Ani Od Chai, R. Chappo, Lawrence Chernin, Java Colleen, Abele J.E., Jacob Y. Elrod, Roman Eugeniusz, T.J. Flex, Franco Folini, Jennifer Franklin, Nancy Fuentes, Jayson de Geeter, Joe Goldberg, Josh Graciano, Robin Grussling, Steve Guttman, Billy Hathorn, Asher Heimermann, Adam Hill, Josh S. Jackson, Kristina Hoeppner, Tom Klein, Jennifer Kowatch, Alex Leung, Brian Logan, Daniel J. Ludwig, Joe Mabel, Scott McDonough, Andreas Metz, Sara Cedar Miller, Fred Moore, Orah Moore, Ngoc Minh Ngo, Erin O' Toole, John Roger Palmour, Daniel Penfield, Jason Persaud, Joe Phebus, John Phelan, Radio Raheem, Daniel Ramirez, Bill Reynolds, Beau

Rogers, M.E. Sanseverino, Thomas Shahan, Courtney Spearman, James Spearman, Leslie Sherr, Maria Stenzel, Michael Stewart, Corey Templeton, Brian Thomson, Matthew Traucht, Sarah Vance, Guilhen Vellut, Regan Vercruysse, Aniko Nagyne Vig, Marshall Webb, Liz West, and Christian Zimmerman.

Olmsted-designed landscapes throughout the country benefit from the unwavering mission of nonprofits and friends' groups dedicated specifically to their ongoing stewardship and interpretation and will continue to do so into the future. Many stalwart individuals from within these organizations have also helped bring this book to fruition. We would like to thank the Blue Garden (Newport, RI), Brooklyn Botanic Garden, Buffalo Olmsted Parks Conservancy, Central Park Conservancy, E. B. Dunn Historic Garden Trust, the Emerald Necklace Conservancy, Friends of Blue Hills, Friends of Maryland's Olmsted Parks + Landscapes, Friends of Seattle's Olmsted Parks, Louisville Olmsted Parks Conservancy, Prospect Park Alliance, Olmsted Linear Park Alliance (Atlanta), and Stonehurst, the Robert Treat Paine House, for supporting our efforts and for being such steadfast stewards of these sites.

Additionally, thanks are due to the various government agencies, academic institutions, museums, archives, and special collections that have contributed knowledge and historical documentation to this endeavor: above all, the Olmsted Archives at Fairsted, Frederick Law Olmsted National Historic Site, National Park Service; and the Frederick Law Olmsted Papers at the Library of Congress—this project would not have been at all possible without the critical and comprehensive resources that these collections provide. Additionally, the Archives + Special Collections at the University of Louisville, The Columbus Museum (GA), Dayton History, Denver Public Library Special Collections, Harvard University Graduate School of Design Frances Loeb Library—Special Collections, National World War I Museum and Memorial (Kansas City), New York City Department of Parks and Recreation, Oheka Castle Hotel and Estate, Parks and Nature (Montreal), Planting Fields Foundation, Seattle Parks and Recreation, Stanford University—Special Collections and University Archives, TIA International Photography, U. S. Fish and Wildlife Service, Washington State Department of Transportation, Weequahic Park Association, and Williams College—Special Collections were all supportive and critical to the realization of the visual campaign for this book.

Finally, thank you to those landscape architects, horticulturalists, architects, engineers, arborists, and other experts that served in the various Olmsted firms for over a century of time, who collectively advanced, refined, and brought Frederick Law Olmsted Sr.'s vision to life, adapting his aesthetic to the changing needs of new eras, and in doing so, shaped many of the cherished landscapes—both public and private—that many of us have the good fortune to experience every day.

ALABAMA

Birmingham City Parks Plan   17   University of North Alabama, Florence   19
Alabama Educational Institutions   19   Huntingdon College, Montgomery   21

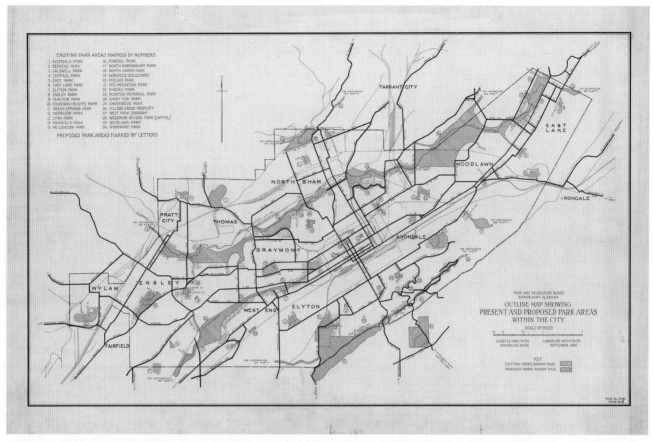

Birmingham's park system plan, 1924.

🛋

BIRMINGHAM CITY PARKS PLAN

Founded in 1871, the city of Birmingham had become one of the South's largest industrial centers by 1925, with 200,000 residents but only 600 acres of parkland. The city leaders of the time deemed this amount of park space inadequate. To address the perceived need, the Birmingham Park and Recreation Board was created in 1923, and they contracted with the Olmsted Brothers firm the following year. The report of Olmsted Brothers' efforts, published by the park board in 1925, was titled *A System of Parks and Playgrounds for Birmingham: Preliminary Report Upon the Park Problems, Needs, and Opportunities of the City and Its Immediate Surrounds*. It set the stage for landscapes to come.

The Birmingham work was supervised by Frederick Law Olmsted Jr., with Edward Clarke Whiting serving as project manager. The report put forth proposals both for active and passive neighborhood parks within easy walking distance for residents of all socio-economic and racial groups.

The report's opening statement, signed by the park board on May 1, 1925, made a plea "To the Citizens of Birmingham," recognizing that little money had been invested in parks and playgrounds and that, as a result, the city was "far behind other progressive cities of the South" and that "it is imperative that citizens cooperate in the granting of adequate funds."

Linn Park, Birmingham.

With work already underway by the Olmsted firm to prepare plans for Birmingham's Linn, Rushton, and Underwood Parks, and while the company also served as an advisor for Green Springs (now George Ward), Avondale, and Ensley Parks, a number of these acquisitions and recommendations would be carried out, thanks to a Bond Issue (1931) and Depression-era funds that followed.

In addition to the parks and playgrounds, the firm proposed parkways along the crests of mountains and ridges that afforded spectacular views and viewsheds. Of those proposed, the Shades Mountain Parkway (now Shades Crest Road) was realized and survives today, as do segments of the Red Mountain Parkway (including Altamont and Crest Roads, and Clairmont Avenue in Crestwood South) which similarly offer scenic views and overlooks.

Moving beyond the more urbanized part of the city, the Olmsted firm urged for the preservation and protection of natural scenery associated with outlying parks and scenic reservations that were still "unspoiled." Specifically, in the area to the north of Shades and Red Mountains, such an approach would take hold, protecting the floodplain and the creeks as part of the 1920s planning for Mountain Brook and Homewood. Today, several areas are held in trust for the public's benefit. These include the Mountain Brook reservation; Homewood's sixty-five acres of old growth, which has been recognized as a forest preserve; the Freshwater Land Trust's stewardship of areas around Five Mile Creek and Tarrant Springs Branch; and Butler Mountain's roundish hills northeast of Pinson (the Crosby and Shadow Lake area today). When taken together, one can suggest that the Olmsted firm's recommendations for future use of reservation lands for "perpetual use and refreshment" took hold.

ALABAMA EDUCATIONAL INSTITUTIONS

After his 1926 election, Governor Bibb Graves, a controversial figure due to his early Ku Klux Klan involvement, embarked on an ambitious program to upgrade Alabama's educational institutions, to raise teaching standards and make capital improvements. In 1928 the Alabama Board of Education voted to engage Birmingham architects Warren, Knight, and Davis along with the Olmsted Brothers firm to evaluate campus needs, developing general and construction plans. From the late 1920s into the 1960s, the Olmsted firm and its architects were involved in campus planning for over twenty colleges, universities, and high schools—both public and private—throughout the state, in Auburn, Birmingham, Florence, Huntsville, Jacksonville, Livingston, Marion, Mobile, Montgomery, Troy, and Tuscaloosa. Although Frederick Law Olmsted Jr. was involved in a few of these projects, this considerable body of work was mostly supervised by James F. Dawson, Edward Clark Whiting, and Carl Rust Parker, providing a matrix to shape future growth for these institutions.

UNIVERSITY OF NORTH ALABAMA, FLORENCE

The University of North Alabama at Florence has a history that dates to 1830 when it first opened as LaGrange College, a Methodist school open to all denominations. Deeded to the state in 1872, the college then became one of the first state-chartered normal schools, admitting women by 1874. In 1929 it became a state teachers college with a four-year curriculum in secondary education.

The Olmsted Brothers firm was involved in campus planning on the 130 acres beginning in 1928 and continuing through the 1950s, producing nearly 200 plans in collaboration with Warren, Knight, and Davis.

The 1929 Olmsted General Plan of Campus gave coherence to a gently rolling site, which at the time was split into sections by two roads (Wesleyan Avenue and Morrison Road). At the junction, they designed a circular plaza faced by an angled academic building (Bibb Graves Hall, 1930), designed by the architects. To the north were the main academic buildings and a library surrounded by green space, where natural bowl-shaped topography became an amphitheater, dedicated in 1934 to WWI veterans.

The campus has grown substantially since this period, now encompassing more than 200 acres with major athletic facilities. Integrated in 1963, the school became the University of North Alabama in 1974. During the 1990s, the university embarked on a massive multidecade campus renovation to anticipate 10,000 students and numerous graduate programs. Reflecting Olmsted Brothers' design, the historic core was retained as a pedestrian way, Wesleyan Avenue became an undulating brick path to evoke the nearby Tennessee River, and the plaza was enlivened by a fountain. Necessary new structures are accompanied by spacious lawns and tree-shaded walks, further respecting the Olmsted design intent. Abutting the Seminary–O'Neale National Register Historic District, the University's current master plan embraces its historical landscape and architectural context while adapting to a sustainable, diversified, yet coherent vision.

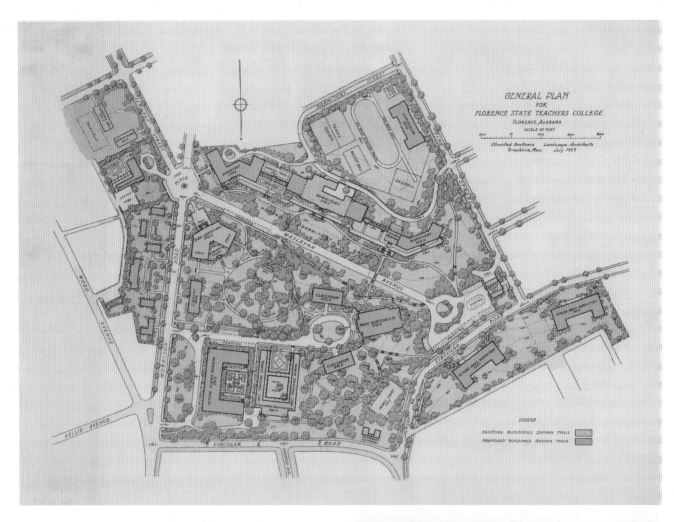

The original sketch **(lower left)** for an amphitheater at what is now the University of North Alabama, in Florence, was realized and still stands today at the intersection of graceful radial paths at the center of campus.

Responsibility for the Tuskegee Female College, founded in 1854, was assumed by the Methodist Church after the Civil War. It was renamed the Woman's College of Alabama and eventually relocated to a sloping, fifty-three-acre property in the Cloverdale section of Montgomery, abutting the Montgomery Country Club. After an October 1908 visit to the campus in conjunction with other work in the area, Frederick Law Olmsted Jr. wrote a lengthy report punctuated with sketches in which he recommended distinguished yet functional architecture and wise planning for future growth (the college then specified 500 students). After a devastating fire, the college turned to Olmsted's recommendation: H. Langford Warren, then Dean of Harvard's School of Architecture, to design the main college building, Flowers Memorial Hall (1910). Using the Collegiate Gothic style and locating this building as Olmsted had suggested, Warren's Harvard team set the tone and shape for the college's future.

After WWI, the college admitted its first male student. It also expanded its academic offerings and its campus, adding numerous buildings in the 1920s. Reflective of its coeducational status it again changed its name in 1935 to Huntingdon College. The growth that Olmsted Jr. had anticipated decades earlier occurred after WWII, to service the needs of returning veterans, financed by the GI Bill. In 1945 the college contacted the Olmsted Brothers firm, seeking plans for coherent expansion. Associate Carl Rust Parker, then handling many academic projects in the south, responded with a plan that placed buildings around the sloping green, with an outer ring of athletic facilities and dormitories. The main drive enters the compact campus on the north side of Flowers Hall, encircling the multifunctional building (it also contains the chapel) and defining the central green. The large amphitheater intended for this space was not constructed, but the lawn, punctuated by tree groves, a pond, and a small stage, reflects a characteristic Olmsted campus feature—a green space for congenial gatherings.

The school now hosts over 1000 students with resultant new buildings and parking lots as anticipated by Parker. In 2000 the Huntingdon College Campus Historic District was listed in the National Register of Historic Places.

CALIFORNIA

California State Park System 23

Yosemite National Park and Mariposa Grove 27

Mountain View Cemetery, Oakland 29

Stanford University Campus, Palo Alto 31

St. Francis Wood, San Francisco 34

Palos Verdes Syndicate, Palos Verdes 37

Palos Verdes Parkway, Los Angeles 40

Surveying California's desert land; a Joshua tree this large was notable even in earlier times.

CALIFORNIA STATE PARK SYSTEM

In 1927 the California State Legislature, spurred by the Save the Redwoods League, formed a commission to create a centralized state park system. The California State Park Commission hired Frederick Law Olmsted Jr. of the Olmsted Brothers firm, who partnered with regional landscape architects including Emerson Knight, Daniel Hull (who had recently ended his relationship with the National Park Service, or NPS), and Harry W. Shepherd, to create a survey identifying potential park sites that would represent the state's wide-ranging ecology.

The report, regionalized in twelve districts, highlighted specific areas in urgent need of preservation and protection, including the coastline, desert landscapes, and both the redwood and sequoia groves. The report also provided suggestions on how to preserve the state's scenic highways and tidelands, and consideration was given to significant historical and cultural sites. In 1928 California passed the State Park Bond Act, allowing for the implementation of Olmsted Brothers' park system. Under the leadership of Newton Drury, the park system's land acquisition officer and executive director of the league, the total number of state parks grew to 150 by 1959. A second bond act in 1964 ensured the continued growth of the park system into the late twentieth century. Today, the California Department of Parks and Recreation manages 280 state parks, 125 of which were recommended by Olmsted. Other suggested sites including Lost Horse Valley and Kings Canyon were either integrated into other state parks or were later preserved by the federal government.

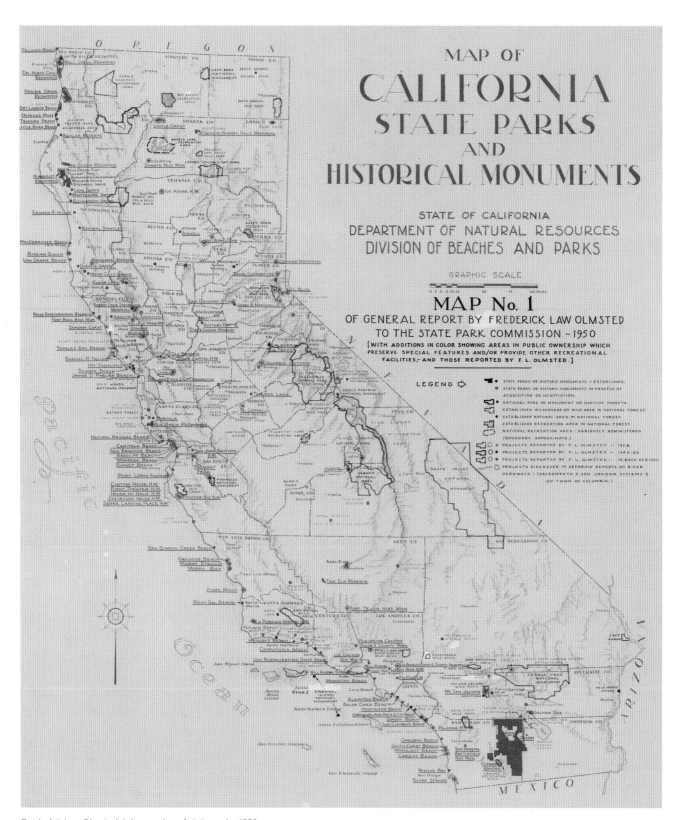

Frederick Law Olmsted Jr.'s mapping of state parks, 1950.

Many natural locations were recommended by Frederick Law Olmsted Jr. to be preserved and protected. **Clockwise from top:** Bodega Bay, Lake Tahoe, and the Humboldt Redwoods.

More locations in the California state park system shaped by the Olmsted Brothers firm. **Clockwise from top:** Castle Crags, scenic State Route 1, and Point Lobos.

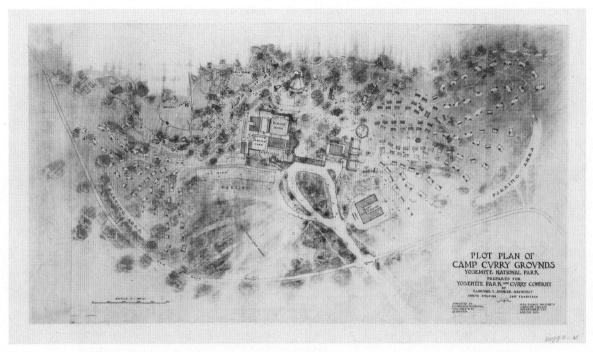

Plans for the Camp Curry cabins and tented accommodations, 1929. The area, now known as Curry Village, still hosts visitors.

YOSEMITE NATIONAL PARK AND MARIPOSA GROVE

The granting of the 3600 acres of Yosemite Valley and 2500 acres of the Mariposa Big Tree Grove to the state of California by the federal government in 1864 constitutes the first-in-the-world efforts of a central government to set aside land for nonutilitarian purposes. It set a precedent for the National Park Service in the United States. When California accepted the grant in 1864 and appointed an eight-person Board of Commissioners, Frederick Law Olmsted Sr. became the chairman. The following year, Olmsted authored *Yosemite and the Mariposa Grove: A Preliminary Report, 1865*, suggesting that this pristine landscape could provide visitors with a place for "refreshing rest and reinvigoration," and the national park ideal took hold.

Through the efforts of John Muir and other like-minded activists, Yosemite became a national park in 1890 during the same week that Glacier National Park in Montana and Rock Creek Park in Washington, DC, were established. Yosemite extends from the Mariposa Grove at the southern tip northward through the upper Merced River watershed, which includes Yosemite Valley and Little Yosemite Valley, through the upper Tuolumne River watershed. Olmsted specifically noted that a visitor could find "unusual trees and shrubs of the western slope of the Sierra Nevada" and "about six hundred mature trees of the giant sequoia." The northern portion of the park is also home to the flooded Hetch Hetchy Valley and its reservoir, which supplies San Francisco, 190 miles west.

In the 1930s the Olmsted Brothers firm was involved in a number of the park's projects. This included design revisions to the Ahwahnee Hotel environs in 1930, including regrading around the hotel's primary terrace, a new parking area for 100 automobiles, modifications to its approach road, and planting enhancements along the property's southern edge. Later in the decade, the firm consulted on the design and layout of village housing for employees and the environs of the Yosemite Lodge.

The boundaries of the park continued to evolve through the Mission 66 era, eventually encompassing 1169 square miles. In 1984 Yosemite was recognized as a World Heritage Site.

One of America's truly iconic places, Yosemite National Park, seen here with El Capitan at left, was marked for preservation by Olmsted Sr. in 1865 and became one of the first national parks in 1890.

The scale of the 500 giant sequoias in Mariposa Grove is difficult to capture without a human-introduced element for comparison, such as this historical cabin.

Formal plots arranged to take advantage of the hillside site.

MOUNTAIN VIEW CEMETERY, OAKLAND

In 1863 prominent citizens of Oakland established a rural cemetery north of the city and hired Frederick Law Olmsted Sr. to create the layout for an arid, windswept, 209-acre hillside site. This would be Olmsted Sr.'s first design in California and his only cemetery. His intention was to provide a restorative place for mourners of several faiths to honor the dead.

Olmsted, with the assistance of surveyor and engineer Edward Miller, created an initial plan in 1864 with further refinement over the next two years. Olmsted carefully selected a drought-resistant planting scheme that opened to extensive views and screened the site from heavy winds. Seeking to create a harmonious plant palette, Olmsted selected dark-foliaged evergreens, including columnar Italian cypress complemented by the horizontal canopies of Italian stone pine, Monterey cypress, cedar of Lebanon, and live oaks. Finding that cemeteries by nature cannot fully emulate the Picturesque style, Olmsted ran a formal, tree-lined avenue of Chinese cypress on a flat plane that bisected the otherwise hilly site. Connecting to the avenue at a series of roundabouts ornamented by fountains, several serpentine drives and pathways trace natural contours, curving uphill to reveal panoramic views of the Bay Area.

The cemetery has since been expanded to 226 acres, with additions not found in Olmsted's original plan, including a Gothic Revival chapel and mausolea, three small reservoirs, and a greater variety of tree species. Other features such as twin avenues that radiated out from the entrance were never constructed. In the 1940s the Olmsted Brothers firm along with former Olmsted associate landscape architect Prentiss French proposed a road layout, grading plan, and a drainage scheme uphill from previously developed plots. Rehabilitation efforts in 2006 included a new entry and improvements to fountains and plantings. In 2017 more than 6000 new burial sites were approved within undeveloped portions of the site. New work was predicated on the sensitive treatment of Olmsted's design and preserving the cemetery's live oaks.

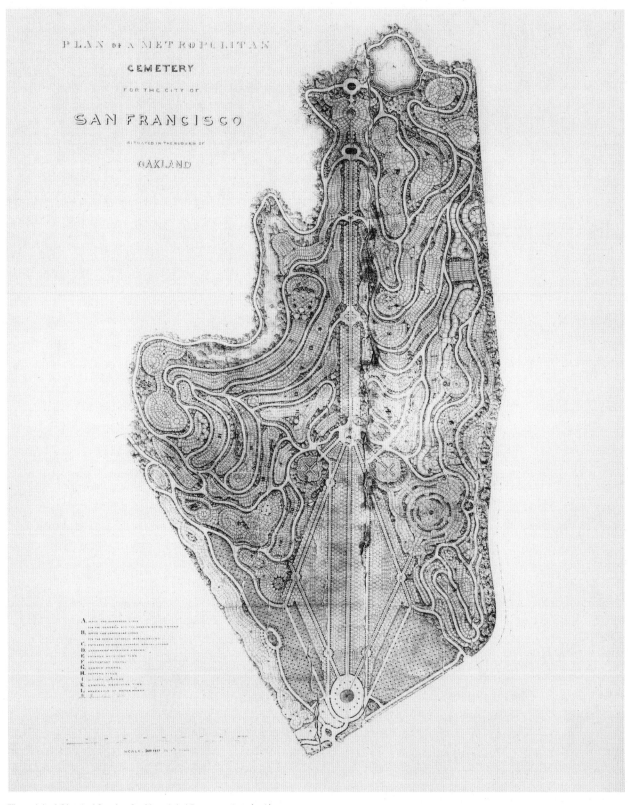

The original Olmsted Sr. plan for Mountain View cemetery (n.d.).

Mile-long Palm Drive, seen here in both 1920 and today, was originally a dirt road; it still creates a stately entrance to the campus.

STANFORD UNIVERSITY CAMPUS, PALO ALTO

Founded in 1885, this 8180-acre university was underwritten by railroad magnate Leland Stanford and his wife, Jena Lathrop Stanford. Placed on the Stanfords' Palo Alto stock farm, featuring both hills and flatlands, the institution was designed by Frederick Law Olmsted Sr. and Leland Stanford, assisted by the architectural firm Shepley, Rutan, and Coolidge.

Olmsted felt that certain design aspects were critical to campus design: climate and water supply, and the arrangement of the main quadrangle to direct views and take advantage of vistas. He would have liked to locate the campus on the hills, looking out over the landscape, but was unable to convince Stanford of the desirability of that approach. Olmsted also urged Stanford to consider a new style of landscape design better suited to the climate of California rather than the traditional green lawns found on East Coast campuses, where water was plentiful. Olmsted laid out eight fifty-foot-diameter circles filled with palm trees, smaller trees, and ground cover in the main quad, all of which could be efficiently watered. He

THE
LELAND STANFORD JR UNIVERSITY·
PALO ALTO CAL

An early drawing showing the integration of the landscape plan with the architectural plan.

proposed interlocking quadrangles on an east–west axis from the main quad, which faced north–south, the interlocking quads connected by arcades typical of Mediterranean architecture. Outside the rectilinear quads, neighborhood roads extended straight but grew curvilinear as the topography became more rolling. The central green space, the Oval, looked north to the wooded area. James Dawson and Frederick Law Olmsted Jr. continued to provide advice and drawings from 1914 until 1937 for campus improvements, the location of athletic facilities, and grading.

Today, the historical core of the campus consists of a three-acre main quadrangle with eight inset circles containing native flora. On this quad, twelve Mission Revival–style buildings are linked to other quads along strong axes in all four cardinal directions. Forming the main, northern entrance is the Memorial Court, a partially enclosed courtyard with a long vista that begins at a four-acre, tear-drop-shaped lawn and culminates in Palm Drive, a tree-lined road designed by Olmsted Sr. that stretches one mile into the horizon.

A 1913 drawing of the entrance sequence to the neighborhood, showing stately loggias and fountains.

ST. FRANCIS WOOD, SAN FRANCISCO

In 1911 as the city was rebuilding after the devastation of the 1906 earthquake, the Mason-McDuffie Company purchased 175 acres of wooded land for a new residential neighborhood in southwest San Francisco, an area made accessible by construction of the Twin Peaks Tunnel and new streetcar lines. The vision of real estate developer Duncan McDuffie was for a "rus in urbe," a garden suburb with larger lots, planted streets, and parks, all with good access to the city center.

McDuffie, responsible for numerous developments around the Bay Area, hired the Olmsted Brothers firm to achieve his vision. Led by James F. Dawson, the firm laid out curvilinear streets, fit to the steeply sloping topography to retain good views. He convinced McDuffie to widen the main ascending road, St. Francis Boulevard, to enable a substantial central concourse lined by a double row of bordering trees and plantings. This residential community, with varied Mediterranean-style houses (many designed by architect Henry Gutterson), was planned with

Decorated sidewalks, a broad concourse lined by lush plantings, and Mediterranean- and Tudor-style homes still mark Saint Francis Wood as a neighborhood of distinction.

generous streets, buried utilities, patterned sidewalks, and textured herbaceous borders in the strip between walk and street. To strengthen the allusion to its namesake, Saint Francis, supervising architect John Galen Howard established the Italian Renaissance design idiom with his distinctive loggias and gardens flanking the

The Mason-McDuffie plan for the neighborhood.

main entrance at the western end of the boulevard, augmenting this theme with a fountain plaza at the boulevard's midpoint. To delineate the eastern end of the boulevard, Gutterson designed a terrace with another Italianate fountain with steps leading up to the hilltop woods of St. Francis Park, all of which took advantage of sweeping vistas to the Pacific Ocean. The distinctive character of the neighborhood today remains much as it was originally intended, as an artful residential enclave.

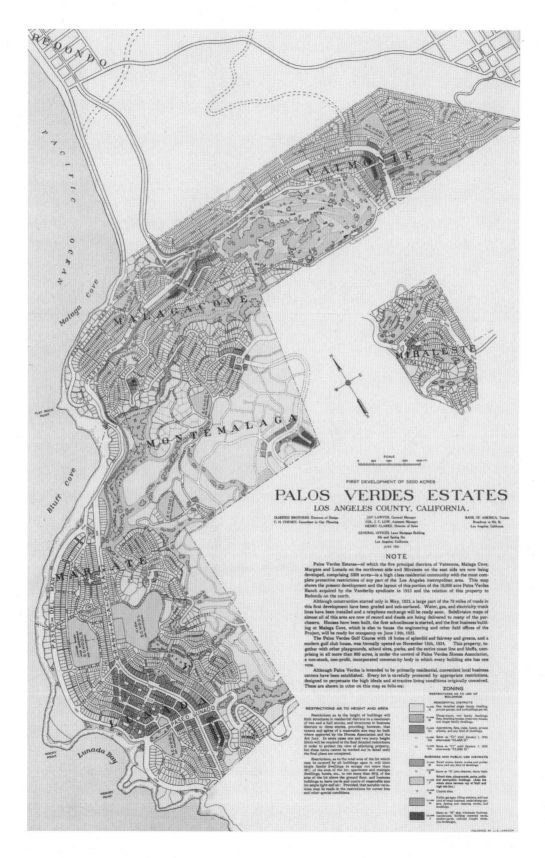

FIRST DEVELOPMENT OF 3200 ACRES

PALOS VERDES ESTATES
LOS ANGELES COUNTY, CALIFORNIA.

OLMSTED BROTHERS, Directors of Design   JAY LAWYER, General Manager   BANK OF AMERICA, Trustee
C. H. CHENEY, Consultant in City Planning   COL. J. C. LOW, Assistant Manager   Broadway at 6th St.
                                                HENRY CLARKE, Director of Sales   Los Angeles, California

GENERAL OFFICES, Lane Mortgage Building
9th and Spring Sts.
Los Angeles, California
JUNE 1925

NOTE

Palos Verdes Estates—of which the five principal districts of Valmonte, Malaga Cove, Margate and Lunada on the northwest side and Miraleste on the east side are now being developed, comprising 3200 acres—is a high class residential community with the most complete protective restrictions of any part of the Los Angeles metropolitan area. This map shows the present development and the layout of this portion of the 16,000 acre Palos Verdes Ranch acquired by the Vanderlip syndicate in 1913 and the relation of this property to Redondo on the north.

Although construction started only in May, 1923, a large part of the 70 miles of roads in this first development have been graded and sub-surfaced. Water, gas, and electricity trunk lines have been installed and a telephone exchange will be ready soon. Subdivision maps of almost all of this area are now of record and deeds are being delivered to many of the purchasers. Houses have been built, the first schoolhouse is started, and the first business building at Malaga Cove, which is also to house the engineering and other field offices of the Project, will be ready for occupancy on June 15th, 1925.

The Palos Verdes Golf Course with 18 holes of splendid sod fairway and greens, and a modern golf club house, was formally opened on November 15th, 1924. This property, together with other playgrounds, school sites, parks, and the entire coast line and bluffs, comprising in all more than 800 acres, is under the control of Palos Verdes Homes Association, a non-stock, non-profit, incorporated community body in which every building site has one vote.

Although Palos Verdes is intended to be primarily residential, convenient local business centers have been established. Every lot is carefully protected by appropriate restrictions, designed to perpetuate the high ideals and attractive living conditions originally conceived. These are shown in color on this map as follows:

RESTRICTIONS AS TO HEIGHT AND AREA

Restrictions as to the height of buildings will limit structures in residential districts to a maximum of two and a half stories, and structures in business districts to three stories, providing, however, that towers and spires of a reasonable size may be built where approved by the Homes Association and the Art Jury. In some cases one and two story height limits will be required in the final detailed restrictions in order to protect the view of adjoining property, but these items cannot be worked out in detail until the final plans are completed.

Restrictions, as to the total area of the lot which may be covered by all buildings upon it, will limit single family dwellings to occupy not more than 35% of the area of the lot; apartments and multiple dwellings, hotels, etc., to not more than 50% of the area of the lot where the ground floor, and business buildings to leave yards and courts of reasonable size for ample light and air: Provided, that suitable variations may be made in the restrictions for corner lots and other special conditions.

ZONING

RESTRICTIONS AS TO USE OF BUILDINGS

RESIDENTIAL DISTRICTS

One detached single family dwelling, private garage, and outbuildings per lot.

Three-fourths, two family dwellings, flats, boarding houses, fraternity houses, and single family dwellings.

Apartments, flats, clubs, hotels, private schools, and any kind of dwellings.

Same as "C1" until January 1, 1931, afterwards "CLASS D."

Same as "C1" until January 1, 1931, afterwards "CLASS D."

BUSINESS AND PUBLIC USE DISTRICTS

Retail stores, banks, trades and professions, and any kind of dwellings.

Same as "F" plus theatres, dance halls.

School sites, playgrounds, parks, public and semi-public buildings. (Also the ones which share between top of bluff and high tide line.)

Church sites.

Public garages, filling stations, and any kind of retail business, undertaking parlors, dyeing and cleaning works, and dwellings.

Same as "H" plus wholesale business, warehouses, building material yards, lumber-yards, railroad freight sheds. (no dwellings).

PREPARED BY: J. D. LANGDON

PALOS VERDES SYNDICATE, PALOS VERDES

In 1913 banker Frank Vanderlip and a group of East Coast investors purchased 16,000 acres on the Palos Verdes Peninsula, situated along the southwestern border of Los Angeles County. Vanderlip, familiar with the Olmsted Brothers from previous projects, hired the firm to develop this scenic but challenging coastal landscape, reminiscent of the Italian Amalfi Peninsula, into a series of resort colonies. Exploring the property on horseback in 1914, John Charles Olmsted appointed then associate James Dawson to be the leading planner. This was residential and regional planning by a private group at a far vaster scale than had previously been accomplished. Initial considerations to connect this immense area by railroad, street cars, and parkways to cities to the north and south were all put on hold due to World War I.

Resuming after the war and the 1920 death of John Charles Olmsted, Frederick Law Olmsted Jr. took charge of the project, with Dawson still serving as the chief planner on-site, setting up a West Coast office in nearby Redondo Beach. Olmsted Jr., Dawson, and many of the firm's associates established residences in the developing community to oversee the work. Consultants included scientists, engineers, and horticulturalists to transform these twenty-five square miles from treeless, hilly, lime-shale terrain crisscrossed by ravines to land suitable for several distinct communities. Amenities such as varied parkland, golf courses, country clubs, and resorts, all with scenic coastal vistas, graced neighborhoods mixing modest homes and luxury estates. As planned, the project was divided into discrete districts, each with schools, commercial areas, municipal and cultural centers, and transportation infrastructure, including

broad, planted parkways and trails weaving along the coast, punctuated by park nodes and plazas. Interior curvilinear roads conformed to the topography, designed to protect existing steep, fragile terrain.

There was a brief ownership change between 1921 and 1925, when entrepreneur E. G. Lewis acquired the controlling interest in the Palos Verdes Estates property, adding planner Charles Cheney to the team. Vanderlip, who had retained control over the remaining 13,000 acres to the south, rescued the property when Lewis went bankrupt, returning integrated Olmsted planning to this community and to Palos Verdes Estates. However, he and his heirs developed the southern part of the peninsula into the communities of Rolling Hills and Rolling Hills Estates, with distinctly different design advice provided by landscape architect A. E. Hanson.

Within Palos Verdes Estates, five distinct districts were set up, each with its own standards of design and protective covenants, drawn up by Olmsted Brothers and Cheney. To retain continuity among buildings and landscapes, Mediterranean, Italianate, Spanish Revival, or Mexican-influenced architectural styles were deemed acceptable, while central plazas in each community reinforced individuated design character. Several notable buildings and landscapes have been protected and are listed in the National Register of Historic Places, such as Villa Francesca (1985), Myron Hunt's Palos Verdes Public Library with its accompanying Farnham Martin's Park by Olmsted Jr. (1995), the Mirlo Gate Lodge Tower (2019), and Lloyd Wright's Wayfarers Chapel (2005).

Opposite: The Olmsted Brothers' plan for the initial development of Palos Verdes reveals how the roads were planned along the terrain's existing natural contours. There was a heavy emphasis on green spaces for schools, parks, and golf, to attract families. **Upper right:** Neptune Fountain, in Malaga Cove at the entrance to the Palos Verdes development, emphasizes the planners' desire to reflect an Italianate-Mediterranean style.

Above: Lush plantings line the main roads through the Palos Verdes development, giving it true "garden suburb" appeal.
Below: Malaga Cove (n.d.). **Opposite:** One of the first houses in the new residential development.

PALOS VERDES PARKWAY, LOS ANGELES

Despite the initial impetus to establish substantial public transportation linkages for this multi-community development, streetcar and rail systems were not economically viable and Palos Verdes became an automobile suburb. Beginning in 1914 and further developed after 1924, the Olmsted Brothers firm had considered several wide travel routes through the southwest district to connect northward: the Hollywood Palos Verdes Parkway, Sepulveda Parkway, a short parkway to Redondo Beach, and Angeles Mesa Drive (now Crenshaw Boulevard). The Hollywood Palos Verdes Parkway was envisioned as 225 feet wide, made up of a main roadway separated from side roads by tree- and shrub-planted islands for walkways. Such a parkway, widening at intervals to accommodate small parklets, was intended to stimulate attractive residential neighborhoods along its periphery. While the idea was received with enthusiasm, the cost to acquire the land and to build out this vision was not easily forthcoming, especially after the 1929 crash. Thus, verdant parkway routes northward from Palos Verdes never came to fruition beyond the elegant sketches in the plan files.

A contemporary aerial view of Palos Verdes Estates shows its enviable position along dramatic coastal bluffs.

COLORADO

Boulder Park System   43

Denver Park and Parkway System   45

Denver Mountain Parks System   47

BOULDER PARK SYSTEM

The first acquisition of land for parks in Boulder came in 1875 with the purchase of a two-acre parcel in Boulder Canyon, followed in 1898 by the eighty-acre acquisition of former agricultural lands to serve as Chautauqua Park. With its agricultural-based economy, unpaved streets, and mining-related mills that had taken hold along Boulder Creek, there was a need for this university town to make the city more "healthful and beautiful" for its 10,000 residents.

In 1907, to address the situation, the Boulder Civic Improvement Association invited Frederick Law Olmsted Jr. of the Olmsted Brothers firm to visit Boulder. He came in May of the following year with his fee covered by public subscriptions. His considerations were made available to the public in March 1910, with the publication of his report, "The Improvement of Boulder Colorado."

Olmsted's recommendations for Boulder focused on the city's streets, waterways, parks and open spaces, and public buildings. Olmsted urged community leaders to protect the vast tracts of land surrounding the city, stressing the importance of maintaining the natural condition of the forest, plains, and rocky outcrops, and also suggesting that roads, trails, campgrounds, and picnic areas be laid out over a period of years. The work was prescient over both the short and long term, helping to preserve the creek, and providing critical recommendations that would guide land acquisition for parks and open spaces for decades to come.

The vision for Boulder Creek was expansive. Targeting the banks and washes, his plan was significant for its sensitivity to preserving and protecting the floodplain, combating erosion, and for extensive tree plantings that would not only provide shade and achieve the intended picturesque character, but would also frame views to the greater mountainscape setting.

In addition to the well-known 1910 report (which has twice been republished, keeping its ideas alive), the Olmsted Brothers firm carried out two other detailed studies between 1911–1914. This work focused on streets, gutters, and sidewalks, with the goal of eradicating from city streets anything Olmsted found unhealthy and unattractive. It is worth noting that recommendations were made based on detailed traffic counts—a pioneering approach for the time that still informs road building today. During this time, Olmsted advocated for the city's infrastructural improvements in sewers, utilities, and flood control.

Following Olmsted's engagement, the firm's vision continued to be advanced from 1933–1935 by the Civilian Conservation Corps (CCC) work improving area forests, stabilizing slopes, building more than twenty-five miles of trails, and constructing shelters, guardrails, and fences. The CCC also constructed the Green Mountain Lodge, Sunrise Amphitheater, and a structure at Panorama Park. Making good on Olmsted's recommendation that every home should be within about a half mile of a park or playground, in 1967 the City of Boulder approved a tax measure for land acquisition and has since added more than 400 distinct parcels. Today, Boulder's Open Space and Mountain Parks preserves total more than 45,000 acres and 145 miles of trails surrounding the city—bringing to fruition Frederick Law Olmsted Jr.'s vision for the scenic city at the foothills of the Rocky Mountains.

Above: The Sunrise Amphitheater, on the summit of Flagstaff Mountain, was built by the Civilian Conservation Corps (CCC) in 1933 and 1934 of local stone from Boulder, Colorado. **Below left and right:** Chautauqua Park is a designated National Historic Landmark.

The twelve-acre Civic Center Park leads to the State Capitol, the City and County Building, and the Denver Art Museum.

DENVER PARK AND PARKWAY SYSTEM

Begun in the late 1860s, this diverse network encompasses 4000 acres of parks and over thirty miles of urban parkways. Made possible by irrigation via the twenty-seven-mile-long City Ditch completed in 1867, Denver was transformed into a green oasis with street trees, public parks, and a network of parkways and boulevards that frame the city and connect its neighborhoods.

Though not the first master plan for the City of Denver, the City Beautiful design developed in 1907 by Charles Mulford Robinson and George E. Kessler was the earliest implemented plan. With an emphasis on vistas of the surrounding mountains and civic structures, they overlaid parkways upon the existing street grid while preserving and enhancing open space through the construction of new parks. Over the years, landscape architects including Reinhard Schuetze, S. R. DeBoer, and the Olmsted Brothers firm helped realize and develop the plan.

From 1904 to 1912, Mayor Robert Speer was crucial in creating a civic identity for Denver by convincing landowners, businessmen, and citizens that parks and parkways would enhance property values and strengthen the city. The Olmsted firm's design and implementation of parkways that followed the city's topography and natural water courses was their greatest legacy contribution. This includes the planning and design for

Speer Boulevard, today one of Denver's main parkways, circa 1915.

the East 7th Avenue Parkway's lower section (1912); Williams Street Parkway (1909–1914), with its double row of American elms; Downing Street Parkway (1913); East 4th Avenue Parkway (1913); and Denver's premiere parkway, the East 17th Avenue Parkway's lower parkway from Colorado Boulevard to Dahlia Street (1913). It should also be noted that other parkways that reflect the Olmsted design intent, but whose authorship is uncertain, include the East 6th Avenue Parkway (1909–1912) and the Forest Street Parkway (1913).

In addition to parkways, parks, ranging in size from three to 300 acres, represent the Picturesque and Beaux Arts styles while providing formal gardens, recreational fields, and access to a diversity of water features. Unlike the parkways, the Olmsted Brothers firm's contribution can only be evidenced at Washington Park, where they graded a forested hill that was later planted by S. R. DeBoer.

Representing a palimpsest of the work of celebrated landscape architects, and composed of fifteen parks and sixteen parkways, the Denver Park and Parkway System was among the earliest comprehensive systems listed in the National Register of Historic Places when it was designated in 1986.

Red Rocks Trail at Red Rocks Park.

The Lariat Trail Scenic Mountain Drive officially opened in 1913.

DENVER MOUNTAIN PARKS SYSTEM

Located across four counties and spanning 14,000 acres, this system of parks and scenic drives within sixty-two miles of Denver comprises all of Colorado's ecological zones. Between 1901 and 1912, the Board of Commissioners developed a plan to extend the City Beautiful movement into the surrounding mountains and passed a levy for land acquisition. In 1912 the Olmsted Brothers firm, under the direction of Frederick Law Olmsted Jr., provided recommendations that included the procurement of large parcels of land to protect scenery, facilitate the construction of an interconnecting system of roadways, and allow the development of myriad facilities for active and passive uses. Two years later, Olmsted provided a second report that detailed the acquisition of parcels ranging from a half acre to several thousand, totaling 41,310 acres of rugged, forested land.

The first and largest parcel, measuring 2413 acres and located twenty miles from downtown, Genesee Park, was acquired in 1912. A year later, the Lariat Trail Scenic Mountain Drive, twenty feet wide and just over four miles, was completed.

Initially proposed by Olmsted and carried out by S. R. DeBoer, this would be the system's inaugural scenic drive.

By 1918 the system consisted of ten distinct parcels totaling five square miles and including shelters, picnic areas, and pump houses often constructed of local stone and timbers in what was known as a "rustic" style. Ten years later, the system had expanded to more remote locations and included golf courses, comfort stations, and the purchase of the 640-acre Red Rocks Park. Critical to the system's success was the implementation of design requirements for the construction of wide, scenic roads. These were built with gentle grades that accommodated automobiles, allowing them to reach newly opened parks. Between 1936 and 1941, the Civilian Conservation Corps constructed roads, trails structures, and the Red Rock Amphitheater. The final parkland acquisition was made in 1939, while the enabling tax levy expired in 1956. The Denver Mountain Parks System was listed in the National Register of Historic Places in 1990 and in 2015 Red Rocks Park and the Mount Morrison CCC camp were granted National Historic Landmark status.

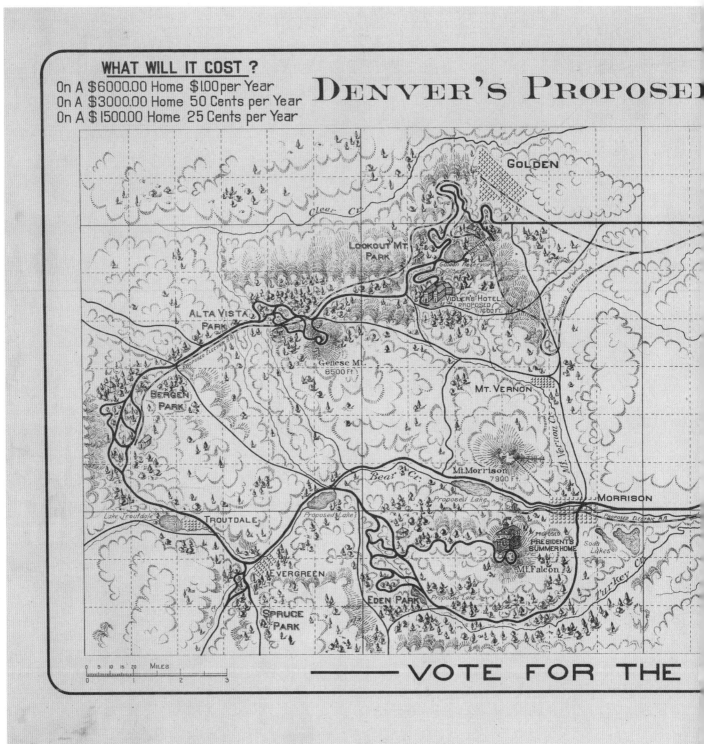

WHAT WILL IT COST ?

On A $6000.00 Home $1.00 per Year
On A $3000.00 Home 50 Cents per Year
On A $1500.00 Home 25 Cents per Year

DENVER'S PROPOSE

GOLDEN

Clear Cr.

LOOKOUT MT. PARK

Golden Reservoir

VIDLER'S HOTEL PROPOSED 7600 FT.

ALTA VISTA PARK

Genese Mt 8500 Ft.

MT. VERNON

BERGEN PARK

Mt.Morrison 7900 Ft.

Proposed Lake

MORRISON

PROPOSED PRESIDENTS SUMMER HOME

Soda Lakes

Lake Troutdale

TROUTDALE

Proposed Lake

Proposed Lake

Mt.Falcon

EVERGREEN

EDEN PARK

Proposed Lake

SPRUCE PARK

MILES

VOTE FOR THE

Flyer encouraging residents to fund the acquisition of large parcels of nearby lands for preservation, 1912.

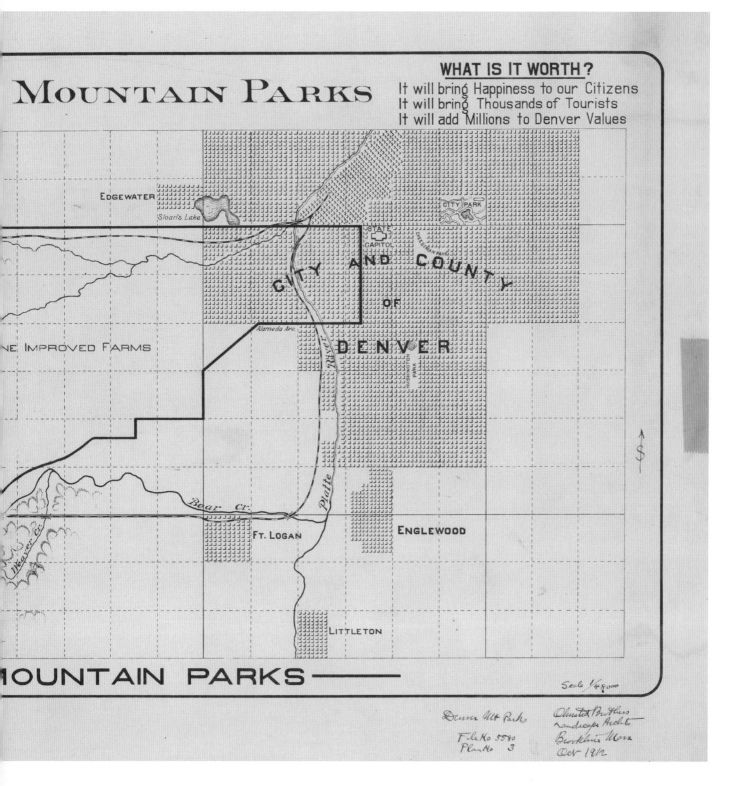

Mountain Parks

EDGEWATER

Sloan's Lake

CITY PARK

CHEESMAN PARK

STATE CAPITOL

CITY AND COUNTY

OF

DENVER

Alameda Ave.

WASHINGTON PARK

NE IMPROVED FARMS

Platte River

Bear Cr.

FT. LOGAN

ENGLEWOOD

Beaver Cr.

LITTLETON

MOUNTAIN PARKS ——

Scale 1/48000

Denver Mt. Parks
File No 5580
Plan No 3

Olmsted Brothers
Landscape Archts
Brookline Mass
Oct 1912

CONNECTICUT

Beardsley Park, Bridgeport   51

Hartford Parks System   52

Goodwin Park, Hartford   53

Keney Park, Hartford   54

Pope Park, Hartford   55

Bushnell Park and Connecticut State Capitol
Grounds, Hartford   56

Walnut Hill Park, New Britain   58

Waveny Park, New Canaan   59

Hillside Cemetery, Torrington   60

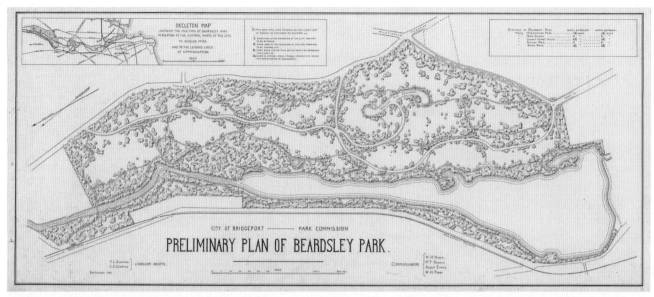

Preliminary plan for Bridgeport's Beardsley Park, 1884.

BEARDSLEY PARK, BRIDGEPORT

By 1881, James W. Beardsley, a wealthy cattle trader, had given 100 acres along the Pequonnock River in the northeast section of Bridgeport, to be forever a public park for the respite and recreation of citizens of this industrial city. Frederick Law Olmsted Sr. and his son and partner, John Charles Olmsted, assessing the distinctive scenic advantages of large trees, hilltop views, boulder outcroppings, and sloping meadows, suggested further land donations. An adjoining field would provide level ground for games; various other strips along the edges were needed for necessary park buildings, playgrounds, or boundary plantings that would provide greater rural seclusion. The 1884 Olmsted report, written by John Charles Olmsted, laid out their suggested improvements—thinning the woods to open glades for parklike character, while encouraging native shrub growth for decorative understory; enhancing hillside areas for distant views while utilizing the natural boulders to create a vine-covered, bastion-like carriage concourse. Cognizant of those without carriages, he suggested a railroad station on the west side of the river for public access. The first building in the park, the Casino, was designed in the Queen Anne style and built at this time. Other statuary and structures followed, which survive today, including a bronze figure of James Beardsley, the park's namesake (1899), two gable-roofed brick barns (circa 1900), the Seltzer Memorial Bridge (1918), and the Island Bridge (1921).

Oliver C. Bullard, a skilled landscape manager who had implemented Olmsted plans for New York parks and the US Capitol Grounds, was hired in 1885 to supervise park work—to shape the spaces for public use while retaining some of the natural wildness. Bullard died in 1890. His well-qualified daughter, Elizabeth Bullard, was recommended by the Olmsteds as his replacement but was ultimately passed over as unsuitable because as a woman, she would cause "political strife." Although by 1903 more land had been added to the park, continued shaping of the park according to the now expanded 1904 Olmsted plan stalled or was poorly implemented, the connecting drives unimproved. Against advisement, a zoo was added in 1920, augmented by retired animals from the circuses of fellow Bridgeport citizen, P. T. Barnum.

By the 1990s, the park, owned by the City of Bridgeport, included the fifty-six-acre zoo and measured 181 acres overall. The city sold the zoo in 1993 and Beardsley Park and Beardsley Zoological Gardens became separate entities. In 1999 the two were listed in the National Register of Historic Places.

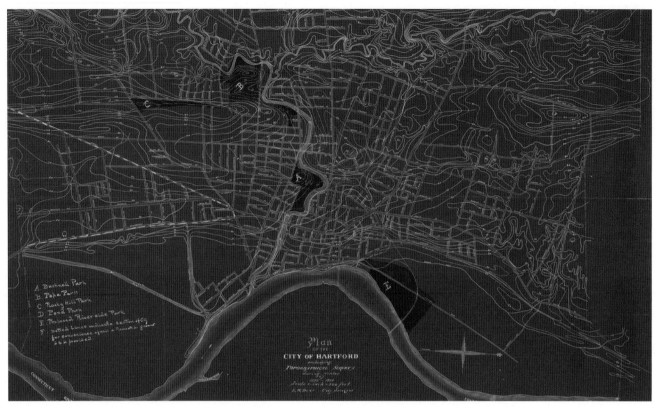

Plan for the city's network of parks, 1893.

HARTFORD PARKS SYSTEM

Developed primarily in the late nineteenth and early twentieth centuries, this 1185-acre municipal park system was among the earliest in the nation. Distributed throughout the city and its outskirts, its thirty-one parks range from squares and greens under one acre to large parks and reservations measuring hundreds of acres.

In 1870, seventeen years after Hartford's civic leaders created the country's first municipal park, Bushnell Park, Hartford native Frederick Law Olmsted Sr. drafted a plan for a network of parks linked by landscaped parkways on both sides of the Park River. His idea was adopted by Reverend Francis Goodwin, with new parks created in 1894 and 1895, namely, Keney, Goodwin, Pope, and Riverside Parks. The Olmsted firm proceeded to shape these spaces to be verdant oases with recreational facilities to serve the growing metropolitan area. Olmsted's intended parkways were never implemented. Other notable parks, acquired around this time and often ascribed to the Olmsted firm, were instead laid out by Hartford Park Superintendent Theodore Wirth. In Elizabeth Park, the former Pond Estate acquired in 1897, Wirth emphasized horticultural decoration, designing the first municipal rose garden, whereas for Colt Park, the former Armsmear Estate, given to Hartford in 1905, he retained many decorative eccentricities of the former owner.

Olmsted Brothers continued to be major consultants for Hartford's parks into the 1960s, working on nearly eighteen commissions for parks, the Connecticut State House Grounds, and various park-related monuments. Although difficult economic times after World War II took their toll on park maintenance, renewed preservation interest in this notable park legacy continues to recapture the intended Olmsted design character.

Goodwin Park and its man-made, four-acre pond.

GOODWIN PARK, HARTFORD

The site chosen by John Charles Olmsted and Charles Eliot in 1895 for the southernmost of Hartford's parks was originally swampy woods with a commercial ice pond, across from the picturesque rural Cedar Hill Cemetery, designed by Jacob Weidenmann. Initially called South Park, this 200-acre rolling landscape, partly in Wethersfield, was renamed Goodwin Park in 1900 to honor the Hartford Park Commissioner Reverend Francis Goodwin.

Without intersecting roads like other Hartford parks, this site offered the opportunity to design for breadth of scenery of woodlands, water, and meadow. Its most significant features were the ninety-acre Great Meadow, a gently sloping descending lawn originally left unmown; and an irregularly shaped four-acre pond to the east enclosed by a mounded boundary and densely planted with trees and shrubs to screen the park from the developing neighborhood. A carriage drive on higher ground encircled the meadow, curving in and out of the former woods, with an overlook concourse at the Maple Street entrance. Recreational facilities, a playground, and an outdoor gymnasium (now a basketball court, tennis courts, and swimming pool), were located within the boundary plantings so as not to impinge upon the pastoral scenery. In 1906 a nine-hole golf course was laid out upon the meadow, followed by another nine holes in 1911.The meadow served as an airfield during the 1920s and in World War II. In 1927 an additional thirty-seven acres were added to the southeast corner of the park, introducing a second pond and extending the golf course by another nine holes to meet intensifying citywide demand.

Even with these changes, the park retains much of its original Olmsted Brothers' design, providing the closely built surrounding communities with green recreational opportunities. Paved vehicular drives and two walking trails wind through the trees, connecting the various park features to the surrounding street grid. In 2018 a restaurant was placed on the overlook at the Maple Avenue entrance.

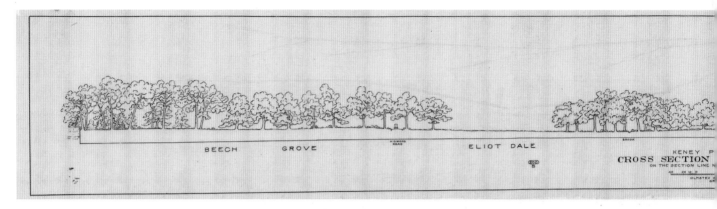

BEECH GROVE   ELIOT DALE   KENEY P
CROSS SECTION

Top: Cross section showing plantings for Keney Park, including a holly wood and a beech grove, 1898. **Right and far right:** Keney Park's original terrain bore little resemblance to the landscaped meadows and woodlands the park retains to this day.

KENEY PARK, HARTFORD

In 1893 Henry Keney bequeathed 533 acres of land for use as a park. The Keney Trustees gradually increased the park to 693 acres, before transferring ownership to the City of Hartford in 1924. This extensive acreage, stretching for miles along Hartford's northern edge and divided into three irregular units by the intersection of two major roads, contained remarkable swaths of sylvan and pastoral landscape. Beginning the park design in 1896, Charles Eliot sought to retain this bucolic beauty, separating the space into four zones according to natural conditions, while also providing for park amenities, a concept expanded upon by the Olmsted firm after Eliot's unexpected death in 1897. Enhancing the intended landscape effects of wildness and rurality involved the addition of quantities of plant material and considerable grading, in particular to create large, planted border mounds to screen out the surrounding city. A sinuous eight-mile carriage road network connected the diverse park zones, offering carefully orchestrated "passages of scenery" into the West Open meadow, the Overlook Hill, Turtle Pond, the varied Ten Mile Woodland, or the East Open, each with its own verdant character. The overall park is accessed via three entrances, marked by gates (two of which were designed by architect Benjamin Morris). The third, the Greenfield Street gates, granite pillars topped with urns designed by superintendent George Parker, is a memorial to Henry Keney.

Intense usage from the surrounding neighborhoods, combined with wavering municipal budgets and labor forces, brought inevitable changes to the intended landscape character. After 1927, 110 acres became an eighteen-hole golf course of increasing popularity. A small zoo, Sherwood Forest, was introduced in 1963 but closed in 1976. Recreational facilities included basketball and tennis courts, a cricket pitch, a swimming pool, and playgrounds. Decades later Interstate 95 impacted park viewsheds in the East Open. The park's condition declined, engendering numerous threatening proposals for non-park uses of its land. Various citizen groups arose to counteract these threats—in particular, the 1988 emergence of the Friends of Keney Park, who determinedly developed effective advocacy and good stewardship practices with coordinated volunteer efforts to recapture Keney Park's intended beauty. The West Open is part of the Upper Albany Historic District, listed in the National Register of Historic Places in 1986.

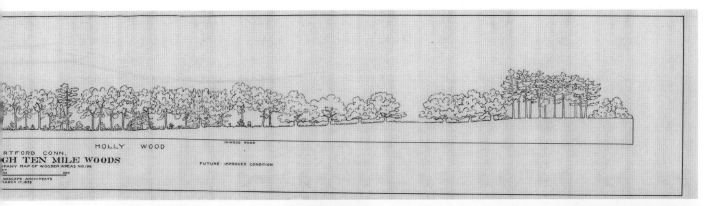

HOLLY WOOD

RTFORD CONN.
GH TEN MILE WOODS
PANY MAP OF WOODED AREAS NO.196

INWOOD ROAD

FUTURE IMPROVED CONDITION

NDSCAPE ARCHITECTS
MARCH 17.1935

Above and right: Two views of Pope Park, circa 1899.

POPE PARK, HARTFORD

In 1894 manufacturing magnate Albert Pope donated seventy-three acres of land abutting his factories to the City of Hartford as parkland. Two subsequent land acquisitions increased the park's size to ninety acres. The Olmsted Brothers, particularly John Charles Olmsted, assisted by Percival Gallagher, completed a design in 1903. Situated along Park River, the park comprises three segments divided by Park Street: Hollowmead, Bankside Grove, and Pope Park North. The firm transformed Hollowmead's sloping terrain into a series of meadows. The largest clearing, featuring a man-made pond, was encircled by sparsely planted trees that allowed views into the park from bordering row houses, while two smaller meadows overlooking the river were given more seclusion. High Mall, a formal overlook with a fountain, sunken garden, and pergola, afforded views of the countryside, while the densely planted Hillside Grove provided meandering walks along the river. North of Park Street, the shaded Bankside Grove served as a pedestrian connection between Hollowmead and Capitol

Avenue, a major thoroughfare. Pope Park North, a four-acre lot adjacent to Park Terrace, was designated a recreational space, complete with tennis courts and a playground.

Although traces of Olmsted Brothers' original design are still evident in the Hollowmead's open lawns and densely planted hillsides, many of the plan's central elements, including the High Mall's gardens, have been replaced by recreational amenities, while Park River was moved and buried in the 1970s. The park's condition declined as neighborhood economics changed. Friends of Pope Park formed in 2000 to focus attention on improvements and maintenance and rehabilitating much of the original design intent so that the park can continue to serve its community. Planning by notable landscape architects has improved circulation by removing Park Drive, improving pathways, and making connections to the Park River Greenway. This has created new gardens and attended to the water retention areas.

Above: The Corning Fountain model, and **(right)** the final as it stands on the capitol grounds today.

BUSHNELL PARK AND CONNECTICUT STATE CAPITOL GROUNDS, HARTFORD

Motivated by his desire to bring the "freshness of nature" into the unhealthy living conditions of the working poor in the central city, in 1853 Reverend Horace Bushnell persuaded the Hartford City Council to spend municipal funds to acquire land and lay out a park. It took until 1861 for this effort to become reality. At the recommendation of Frederick Law Olmsted Sr., Jacob Weidenmann, a Swiss-born landscape gardener, was chosen to shape this land into a suitable public space. He contoured the uneven ground, which was edged by the Park River and divided by Trinity Street, into a picturesque landscape of undulating lawns, tree and shrub groupings, and curving paths. He incorporated a carriage drive, crisscrossing the river on rustic bridges, ending in a concourse with a terrace to the west. With Hartford established as the state capital after the Civil War, a new capitol building, designed by Richard Upjohn, opened in 1878 on the former site of Trinity College. Since this property

abutted Bushnell Park, it gave the impression of the park as an extension of the capitol grounds.

After Weidenmann's death in 1893, John Charles Olmsted was brought in to advise on park matters, many related to the capitol grounds, such as improvements to Trinity Street and other drives, terrace alignment, plantings to screen out the railroad, and locating various monuments, such as the 1899 Corning Fountain. After John Charles's death, between 1925 and early 1932 Edward Clark Whiting and James Frederick Dawson of the Olmsted Brothers firm, originally consulted to locate a memorial to Alfred Burr, founder of the *Hartford Times*, became enmeshed in complicated planning not only for redoing park features, but in rearranging surrounding roads and bridges for greater accessibility to the park and the capitol. With changing traffic needs, problems of river flooding, interfering railroad lines, and Depression economics, a location for a Burr

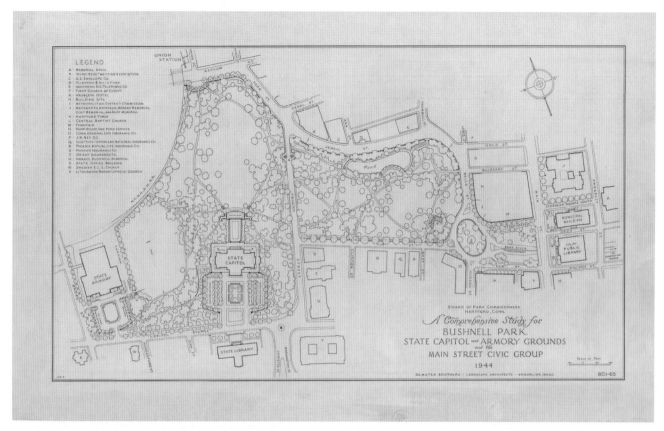

A study for Bushnell Park and the Capitol and Armory Grounds, 1944.

Memorial was not settled until decades later in the 1960s and 1970s, and then relocated elsewhere.

Continued flooding in the park, exacerbated by the Great New England Hurricane of 1938, spurred efforts to put the Park River in a conduit. Extensive planning by Olmsted Brothers staff (Whiting and William B. Marquis) from 1939 to 1947 addressed regrading to construct the pond, rearrange plantings, and redesign abutting streets. They also developed new entrance plazas and terraces, relocated sculptural elements and memorials, and improved the harmonious connection from the park to the capitol. Bushnell Park and the Connecticut State Capitol today have retained much of this work. The two sites were listed in the National Register of Historic Places in 1970. The Capitol building was made a National Historic Landmark that same year.

Meandering pathways at Walnut Hill Park are an extant feature of Olmsted and Vaux's original design.

Stairs to the hilltop Art Deco obelisk.

WALNUT HILL PARK, NEW BRITAIN

The Walnut Park Company established this park with the purchase of a barren hilltop in 1854. Following the construction of a reservoir atop the hill in 1858, landscape gardener B. Munn laid out the park's first circulation system. In 1870 New Britain's park commission hired the landscape architecture firm Olmsted, Vaux, and Company to design the park, shortly before purchasing the site from the Walnut Hill Company, along with fifty-six acres for its expansion. The firm's design resulted in a richly vegetated landscape comprising Walnut Hill and a meadow, called the Common. The firm's plan for a monument near the reservoir was realized in 1928 with the installment of Harold Van Buren Magonigle's World War I Memorial. In 1929 James Burke, the city's gardener, planted a rose garden that was later demolished. The Friends of Walnut Hill Park Rose Garden planted a new garden on the grounds of the reservoir, which had previously been infilled.

The ninety-eight-acre park still reflects Olmsted, Vaux, and Company's original design. Circulation routes laid out by Olmsted connect the park's entrances to the Common and Walnut Hill. Encircled by an elliptical drive, the meadow holds several recreational fields, in keeping with Olmsted's plan. Sharing the lawn are tennis courts, a playground, a band shell, and a memorial garden. Roads ascend the hillside to reach an oval lawn framed by two colonnades on its minor axis. Encircled by rose bushes, the lawn is quartered by paved pedestrian paths that meet at a single-tier fountain. The memorial, which is located to the north on a perpendicular axis, comprises a ninety-foot-high Art Deco obelisk. The lawn's formal entrance, a stone terrace featuring a flagpole and a memorial to female veterans, is to the south. Behind the monument, steps built by Magonigle, and shaded by trees planted by landscape architect Arthur Brinckerhoff, descend the hill, reaching a brick-paved plaza. The plaza's walls are embedded with plaques describing the park's history. The New Britain Museum of Art (1903) overlooks the park from the north, purposefully sited as such for the park to serve as its "front lawn." Walnut Hill Park was listed in the National Register of Historic Places in 1982.

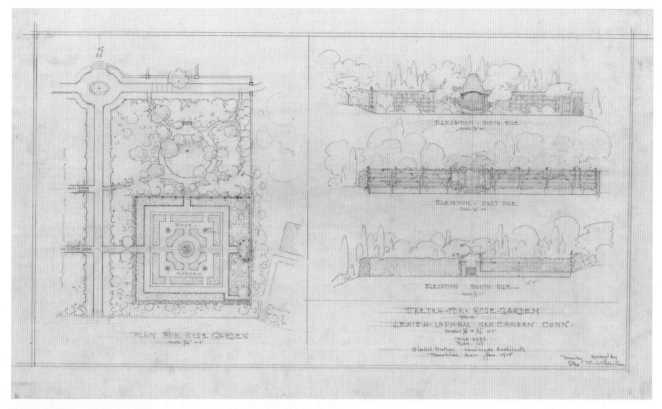

Sketches for the rose garden, 1915.

WAVENY PARK, NEW CANAAN

In 1895 Thomas Hall consolidated several eighteenth-century tracts into Prospect Farm, his 280-acre estate. Architect Frank Shea designed the structures and circulation system. In 1904 Texaco cofounder Lewis Lapham purchased the property, renaming it Waveny Farm, and gradually expanded the grounds to 450 acres. Lapham hired architect William Tubby to build a Tudor Revival summer home and the Olmsted Brothers firm to redesign the grounds into a gentleman's farm. The project, led by John Charles Olmsted and Percival Gallagher, integrated formal landscape elements—including a forecourt, polo fields, and gardens—with the property's fields and woodlands. The firm created a terraced axial walk that extended east from the house to an ice pond. Framed by evergreens, the walk commenced at a parterre garden before opening onto a circular fountain with a sculpture by Abastenia Saint Léger Eberle. The firm's horticulturalist, A. Chandler Manning, arranged garden rooms,

including a rose garden and bowling green, around the walk. Shea's circulation system was simplified to allow uninterrupted views of the southern agricultural fields. North of the house, trees screened utility buildings and provided shade.

In the 1960s Ruth Lapham Lloyd gifted the property to the town of New Canaan, setting aside forty-six acres for a high school. The town established Waveny Park, preserving the estate's two entrances. Curvilinear roads wind through open fields and woodlands to reach the house. A powerhouse was converted into a theater, and a carriage house into an art center. The fields have been replaced by recreational spaces that include soccer and baseball fields, as well as tennis courts and a swimming pool. More than three miles of walking trails traverse the grounds. In the 2010s the Waveny Park Conservancy began converting a former cornfield into a wildflower meadow. The park was listed in the National Register of Historic Places in 2019.

Above and below: Hillside Cemetery has retained its Picturesque character.

HILLSIDE CEMETERY, TORRINGTON

The Olmsted firm's professional involvement with the original sixty-five acres to create Hillside Cemetery began in 1907 and continued for the next sixty years under a succession of partners—James Dawson, Percival Gallagher, Edward Clark Whiting, and finally Joseph Hudak. The cemetery was to serve both the prominent owners and the workers in this factory community and was intended to be developed in sections as the need arose.

Gallagher's initial assessment of the property praised its natural scenic values atop a wooded hill, with good vistas over neighboring land. He advised that clearing and grading be guided by a "discriminating eye" to preserve and protect the land's distinguishing characteristics—that monuments be designed with dignified proportions and tasteful details to avoid monotony and over-ornamentation, with plantings intermingled among them, and that rock outcroppings be reserved for scenic purposes.

Surrounded by straight boundary roads, many laid out by the firm, the cemetery's main drive entered at the northwest corner through a stone gate, leading to a small English Gothic chapel designed in 1913 by Max Westhoff for the Alvord family. Within the cemetery, drives and paths curved gracefully around knolls and through dells, defining varied areas for gravesites, from large family plots to smaller individual lots.

Sale of plots was successful over the decades, requiring rearrangement of some of the earlier lotting, and with all changes respectful of the site's characteristics and the Olmsted design intent. As late as 1959, the Hillside Cemetery Association was contemplating the purchase of more acreage to be developed in harmony with the earlier work, although at that time, demand was greatest for plots containing two to four graves.

Today, the cemetery displays a verdant tranquility as a place for respectful contemplation, a tribute to the Olmsted vision to retain and enhance the site's natural scenery while shaping this area as a memorial park.

DISTRICT OF COLUMBIA

United States Capitol Grounds   63
White House Grounds (President's Park)   64
Rock Creek Park   65
McMillan Plan   67
Thomas Jefferson Memorial   68

Lincoln Memorial Grounds   70
Washington Monument   71
Theodore Roosevelt Island National
   Memorial   72
National Cathedral Grounds   74

The parklike plan for the grounds surrounding the Capitol gracefully junctions with the twenty-one city streets converging there.

Details and embellishments in the landscape direct views and mark the space as an important location.

The Summerhouse, a beloved folly on the Capitol Grounds.

UNITED STATES CAPITOL GROUNDS

Following the expansion of the US Capitol in the mid-nineteenth century, the task of redefining its surroundings, constrained for such a grand and symbolic building, fell to Frederick Law Olmsted Sr., who would work on the project from 1874 to 1892, often in concert with English architect Thomas Wisedell (1846–1884).

Unlike Olmsted's parks and residential landscapes, the Capitol Grounds place landscape in the service of architecture rather than architecture in the service of landscape. Most important are the transitions orchestrated between the monumental edifice and its parklike setting. The periphery, elevated above street level by a retaining wall, is densely planted with trees and shrubs, with select openings to channel the twenty-one radiating streets which converge there.

On the flatter terrain of the East Front, Olmsted centered a straight ceremonial drive, flanked by a quincunx planting of majestic tulip poplars, separating the entrance from symmetrical path-edged ovals of lawn and trees. Each tree allée ended at the forecourt plaza with decorative fountains and lightoliers. Manipulating the vistas from which the building could be viewed, Olmsted terminated the ovals at the plaza with Wisedell's bluestone benches, facing the Capitol's grand staircases, above which the impressive building loomed. From northeast and southeast edges, two trellis structures were placed for fuller diagonal building views and dappled shade. Paths, accompanied by shrub plantings, arced throughout the grounds to give an enlarged sense of space and further control vistas.

To settle the building above its sloping western terrain, mitigating the height of the new dome while enhancing the dramatic views from the National Mall, Olmsted developed an expansive marble terrace with two descending staircases, echoing an idea that architect Charles Bullfinch had suggested decades earlier. Carefully graded curving drives and paths provided access from the west, while two straight, diagonal, tree-bowered paths continued the lines of Pennsylvania and Maryland Avenues. Tucked into a slope at the juncture of paths, Olmsted situated a uniquely textured hexagonal structure, designed by Wisedell. Partially open to the sky, the structure has three arches and a fourth wall with a window framing a grotto. Serving as a summerhouse, it was furnished with canopied benches, a drinking fountain, and a carillon. The building was densely enshrouded by fragrant plantings and was intended to provide cool respite. The carefully sequenced components of Olmsted's designs for the East Front were considerably altered by the new underground Capitol Visitor Center, which opened in 2008. In 1960 the US Capitol was made a National Historic Landmark.

Lafayette Park, a prominent feature of the grounds to the north of the White House.

WHITE HOUSE GROUNDS (PRESIDENT'S PARK)

The White House, the centerpiece of L'Enfant's President's Park, is the official residence and workplace of the President of the United States. The mansion, designed by James Hoban in 1792, was meant to have a vista of the Potomac River, now hidden by nineteenth-century infill projects. The grounds have changed repeatedly over time, altered by virtually every US president. In his 1928 review of the White House Grounds, Frederick Law Olmsted Jr. had been disappointed by their lack of distinction and useful beauty for such a residence. In his 1934–1935 plan, he modified the configuration in keeping with historical character, increasing privacy and accessibility while improving planting compositions to achieve formal yet dignified simplicity. The current general configuration greatly reflects considerations derived from this plan, sustained by his recommended management plan.

The parklike setting, with carefully orchestrated groups of shade trees, understory plantings, and open spaces, enhances the residential character of the site, yet strengthens its southern axial views. Facing Pennsylvania Avenue, the symbolic North Lawn serves as the ceremonial entry to the mansion. The more secluded upper South Lawn includes the East or First Lady's Garden (designed by Rachel Lambert Mellon) and the West or Rose Garden (designed by Mellon with Perry Wheeler), the President's or Oval Office Patio, and a private swimming pool and putting green. The lower South Lawn is a buffer from the public Ellipse grounds and is used for occasional activities such as the annual Easter Egg Roll. Due to security concerns, the grounds, surrounded by tall metal fencing, are closed to the public except for special events.

Boulder Bridge, a park landmark (n.d.).

ROCK CREEK PARK

The fate of the picturesque Rock Creek Valley, stretching over 3100 acres through northwest Washington from the Potomac River into Maryland, had long been debated. By the late nineteenth century, the lower valley at the river was severely degraded by dumping, following the idea of filling the declivity for more surface land. An alternate concept, the "open valley" solution, advocated for rehabilitation of the greater landscape's unique scenic character for a park and parkway. The idea gained traction, and by 1890 the park was officially authorized, making it the third national park to be designated by the federal government in the United States. Also at this time, a National Zoological Park was being planned on 166 of its forested acres by Frederick Law Olmsted Sr. and John Charles Olmsted. It was to be both park and national institution for scientific study.

This parkland acquisition was in keeping with the landscape tenets set forth by Frederick Law Olmsted Jr. for the McMillan Commission's reinvigoration of Washington, DC. He considered this picturesque, topographically intricate, and historically significant valley in need of careful preservation, and its protection through park and parkway planning continued to accommodate the growing abutting residential districts. As the energetic landscape member of the Fine Arts Commission, Olmsted Jr., together with his Olmsted Brothers' colleague Edward Clark Whiting, produced a comprehensive report in 1918. They assessed the existing growth patterns of forest, woodlands, and grasslands; evaluated future land acquisitions; and considered road and parkway layouts and park crossings—all with suitable but restrained management recommendations.

Above: A photo of Rock Creek in its natural state, from the original album documenting the job (n.d.). **Right:** The parkway was meant to preserve the character of the highly scenic valley through which it curves.

Their long-term goal was to preserve the unity and harmony, "precious" scenery, and intermingled pastoral and wilderness areas of the Rock Creek Valley, while making the valley accessible for public enjoyment and an asset to the nation's capital. Their report has guided Rock Creek Park's management for decades, as diverse circulation modalities and recreational and cultural amenities have been added, including a planetarium. Planning by Olmsted Brothers also extended beyond the DC line for the valley park's continuation into Maryland. Today measuring 1754 acres, Rock Creek Park was listed in the National Register of Historic Places in 1991 as part of the Rock Creek Park Historic District.

The McMillan Plan organized the National Mall into the grand space we recognize today.

McMILLAN PLAN

By the late nineteenth century, Washington, DC, was far from the elegantly ordered city that Pierre L'Enfant had envisioned in 1791, when at the behest of President George Washington he had undertaken to plan a suitably imposing capital for this new American nation. In particular, the capital's core, the National Mall—intended to be a grand symbolic east–west greenspace, with the domed Capitol anchoring the eastern end, its westward sweep lined by harmoniously arranged institutions—was instead a disunified collection of buildings. In the 1874 words of Frederick Law Olmsted Sr. when he came to design the Capitol Grounds, the effect was "broken, confused, and unsatisfactory," without its intended harmonious motive to signify the grandeur and power of a great nation. After the demonstrated success of planning as evidenced by the 1893

World's Columbian Exposition, with its emerging City Beautiful concepts, various Washington groups pressed for improvement in the capital's appearance.

The chair of the Committee for the District of Columbia, Senator James McMillan of Michigan, assembled experts ostensibly to improve the city's park system, but, in fact, to reinvigorate and amplify L'Enfant's plan, recapturing the scenic promise, the harmonious grandeur and symbolic stature appropriate for a powerful nation. His experts were those distinguished planners who had developed the Chicago World's Fair: architects Daniel Burnham and Charles McKim, sculptor Augustus Saint-Gaudens, and landscape architect Frederick Law Olmsted Jr. (substituting for his ailing father), with Charles Moore as secretary. After extensive research and travel, this remarkable collaboration set forth ambitious proposals in a 1902 published report, which featured beautifully rendered plans and perspective drawings to redefine the physical environment for the nation's capital, reasserting coherent aesthetic ideals. To recapture the intended artistry of the National Mall as the monumental core, they recommended removal of inappropriate buildings such as the railroad terminal, exerting design control over all construction within and along the mall's cruciform shape. Their further recommendations—to increase citywide parkland and restructure the intended hierarchy of parkways and streets—reflected Olmsted's influence in this report.

At that time, there was no extant authority to enforce such pervasive aesthetic control. It would take until 1910 for a permanent US Commission of Fine Arts to be appointed to advise upon the character of monuments, buildings, and their settings. The National Capital Park Commission, with vested oversight powers to ensure development according to comprehensive and coordinated plans for the nation's capital and its environs, would not be established until 1924 (renamed the National Capital Park and Planning Commission in 1926).

THOMAS JEFFERSON MEMORIAL

Situated on the shores of the Tidal Basin, the Jefferson Memorial occupies a prominent position as the southern anchor of the District of Columbia's meridian line, on axis with the White House and complementing the cross-axis of the Lincoln Memorial and Capitol. As originally conceived, the Jefferson Memorial was on a site complicated by conflicting traffic routes and drainage issues. It was also controversial because of scale issues, causing the removal of cherry trees and other aesthetic concerns within the McMillan Plan.

Between 1939 and 1943, Frederick Law Olmsted Jr. and Henry V. Hubbard worked to subtly reduce the monumentality of John Russell Pope's edifice to fit it within its complicated waterside location. This Neoclassical memorial consisted of a portico, a circular colonnade surrounded by marble steps, and a shallow, open-air dome, encircling the grand statue of Thomas Jefferson by Rudulph Evans. The Beaux Arts landscape designed by Olmsted and Hubbard set the structure on a plinth of three circumscribed earthen terraces of equal width, with walls descending to meet a round drive previously lined at its base with elms. Axial views of and from the monument are framed with four significant groupings of hollies, pines, and evergreen shrubs. The paved north plaza affords expansive views across the Tidal Basin, while the parklike south side contains a central lawn and perimeter shade trees complemented by the preexisting cherry trees of the Tidal Basin. Later alterations due to highway expansion, the reconfigured circular drive and north plaza, and the addition of perimeter security barriers have foreshortened the intended pastoral landscape south of the memorial. On April 13, 1943, the 200th anniversary of Thomas Jefferson's birth, President Roosevelt dedicated the Jefferson Memorial as a "shrine to freedom." The memorial was listed in the National Register of Historic Places in 1966.

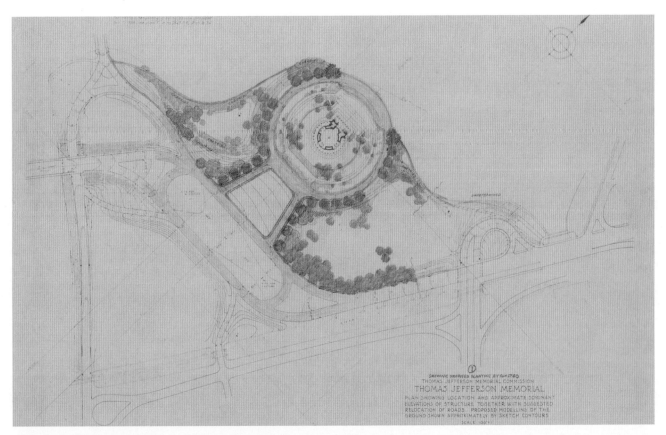

A plan for proposed planting around the memorial shows Olmsted working to partially reroute surrounding roads and to shield visitors' views of them.

The Jefferson Memorial, flanked by suggestively pastoral greenery that also blends the monument's scale into the surrounding landscape.

The Lincoln Memorial's grandeur and famous reflection are bestowed in part by the setting, on a rise slightly above the National Mall.

The Lincoln Memorial Reflecting Pool anchors the Lincoln Memorial to the Washington Monument.

LINCOLN MEMORIAL GROUNDS

Originating in the 1902 McMillan Plan, the Lincoln Memorial anchors the west end of the National Mall on axis with the Washington Monument and US Capitol. The grounds extended the mall by 2500 feet and include reclaimed swampy Potomac River flats and established monumental vistas. Henry Bacon and Frederick Law Olmsted Jr. are credited with interpreting McMillan's concept.

The setting comprises the Lincoln Memorial, with its memorial circle and reflecting pool, the Watergate steps, and the Elm Walks. The Neoclassical Lincoln Memorial National Monument was designed by Bacon and constructed between 1913 and 1922, and houses Daniel Chester French's monumental marble statue of President Abraham Lincoln. James Greenleaf, who replaced Olmsted Jr. on the US Commission of Fine Arts in 1918, developed the planting plan surrounding the memorial. The reflecting pool, opened in 1924, mirrors the sky, the Washington Monument, and the Lincoln Memorial itself, extending the memorial's formal design and contemplative character. The pool, which runs 2029 linear feet, is flanked by double allées of Dutch elms which were planted in the 1930s.

Allées of Dutch elms along the reflecting pool build anticipation of arriving at the memorial itself.

The Lincoln Memorial Grounds have played a central role in American civil rights and free speech, as the site of Marian Anderson's Easter Sunday concert in 1939 and Dr. Martin Luther King Jr.'s "I Have a Dream" speech in 1963. The site was listed in the National Register of Historic Places in 1981.

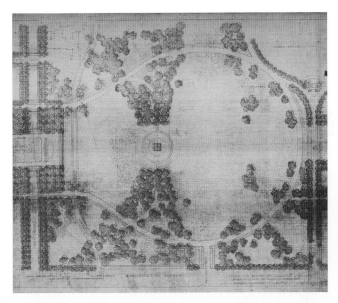

A planting study for the Washington Monument from 1931 reveals how Olmsted Jr. and Henry Hubbard framed views from various points along the surrounding elliptical walks.

The monument's towering height allows it to be seen from many points in the surrounding National Mall, even if those points are wooded or otherwise densely planted.

WASHINGTON MONUMENT

Established in L'Enfant's plan as a place of significance, the monument was intended to align with the visual axes of the president's house (White House) and US Capitol Building. In the 1840s the Washington National Monument Society selected Robert Mills's 600-foot masonry obelisk to honor George Washington. The monolith's weight necessitated its relocation east of center, upon a prominent knoll. The cornerstone was laid in 1848, but its completion was delayed until 1888.

The monument's seventy-two-acre grounds changed frequently throughout the nineteenth and twentieth centuries. In 1851 Andrew Jackson Downing envisioned an "Evergreen Garden" and "Monument Park" as part of his vision for the National Mall. The McMillan Commission's 1902 plan tried to rectify the misaligned axis by subtle adjustments, including formal parterre gardens and water features around the monument, but the requisite regrading needed for these was considered too risky.

To celebrate Washington's Bicentennial in 1932, Frederick Law Olmsted Jr. and partner Henry V. Hubbard developed a distinctive tree-massing plan, restricting traffic and framing vistas out of which the Washington Monument would appear to rise. The National Capital Park and Planning Commission tabled this idea ostensibly until traffic issues and a formal tree planting for the length of the National Mall were resolved. Instead, they chose intersecting ellipses, still encircled by roadway.

Over the years, other schemes were suggested. Following the terrorist attacks in September 2001, the Olin Partnership employed curving granite walls designed to a comfortable seat height that would also restrict vehicles. The firm also carefully regraded sweeping concrete pedestrian paths that brought visitors to the granite plaza at the monument's base, and renewed canopy and flowering tree plantings. The Washington Monument was listed in the National Register of Historic Places in 1966.

The Olmsted Brothers firm's original plan for an island full of rambling foot trails and bridle paths through densely replanted native vegetation.

THEODORE ROOSEVELT ISLAND NATIONAL MEMORIAL

Dedicated to the legacy of America's twenty-sixth president, the Theodore Roosevelt Island National Memorial is a ninety-one-acre wooded island, originally named Analostan Island, located in a flood-prone section of the Potomac River within view of the end of the National Mall. An earlier attempt to recognize Roosevelt after his death in 1919—with a grand memorial by John Russell Pope at the National Mall's cross-axis at the Tidal Basin, later to be occupied by the Jefferson Memorial—did not find consensus in its day, due to architectural and engineering controversies.

From the outset, the McMillan Commission had recommended acquisition of Analostan Island, to protect it from inappropriate development and to use its wilderness for recreational respite, in contrast to the formality intended for the National Mall. A natural geological feature, as opposed to the highly planned city of Washington, DC, the island had a colorful history: a fishing ground for the Necostin peoples; a land grant to Lord Baltimore by King Charles I. At one point owned by a Caribbean Sea captain and later by the Mason family from Virginia (who built a brick mansion and cultivated extensive gardens), with its 1913 purchase by Washington Gas Light Company, it was destined for industrial purposes.

In 1931 the Theodore Roosevelt Memorial Association purchased the island, deeding it in 1932 to the federal government, but with control over the creation of a memorial to the American political leader and renowned conservationist. The Olmsted Brothers firm was engaged, with Frederick Law Olmsted Jr. and Henry V. Hubbard charged with developing an approach for this memorial park. Hubbard described their work as a "sanctuary," primarily pedestrian, and expressive of

Densely planted as an homage to Roosevelt's love of America's wild places, the island combines striking hardwood trees with a formal memorial site.

Roosevelt's values. Olmsted's desire was to restore the overgrown woodlands, removing non-native vegetation. This was achieved with Civilian Conservation Corps labor, who under Olmsted's direction from 1934–1937 also planted 20,000 native hardwood trees and shrubs, returning the site to a richly diverse "climax forest." A network of foot trails and bridle paths wound through the woodland, with attention to vistas. On a ridge at the southern end, in view of the National Mall, a simple commemorative structure was anticipated in an overlook plaza placed near a boat landing.

Lack of funding from the late 1930s through the late 1940s hampered the planning and implementation of the Olmsted plan. Though the association tried to sustain its goal of completion by the Roosevelt centenary in 1958, traffic congestion interfered with fulfillment of this vision. Instead, by 1964,

after heated negotiations, a bridge was placed across the southern end of the island, destroying the visual connection to the National Mall. In 1967 architect Eric Gugler sited the memorial at the island's northern end. He designed a grovelike terraced landscape with plantings of boxwood and willow oaks creating a contemplative space around the formal memorial. A seventeen-foot bronze statue of the former president designed by sculptor Paul Manship is prominently featured as the memorial's centerpiece, while four twenty-one-foot granite stelae are inscribed with quotations expressing Roosevelt's philosophy on manhood, youth, nature, and the nation.

This wildlife sanctuary serves as a living memorial to Theodore Roosevelt's leadership in land and resource conservation. Managed by the National Park Service, it was listed in the National Register of Historic Places in 1966 and dedicated in 1967.

Two views of the National Cathedral's Bishop's Garden.

NATIONAL CATHEDRAL GROUNDS

In 1895, when John Charles Olmsted was working on the master plan of streets for the Washington D.C. District Commissioners, he wrote to Bishop Henry Yates Satterlee regarding the possible location of the National Cathedral and where the entrance would best be placed on the proposed streets. In 1898 Satterlee chose a site bordered by Wisconsin (west) and Massachusetts (south) Avenues, overlooking the Federal City. Landscape architect Frederick Law Olmsted Jr., assisted by Percival Gallagher, carried out the fieldwork and developed a master plan for the fifty-nine-acre site. Olmsted was also involved in the plan's execution from 1907 to 1928. His plan included internal roadways, locations and grading for institutional buildings, an outdoor theater, a series of open spaces and gardens, and a pilgrim's path through the existing five-acre woodland. In 1916, while the firm was refining the overall plan, they went so far as to prepare a series of seasonal shadow studies to assess whether future building additions would cast shadows on or across the windows of the Boys Choir School (Saint Albans).

Florence Brown Bratenahl, the wife of the first Dean of the Cathedral, worked alongside Olmsted Jr. to implement the plan, especially the planting of the Bishop's Garden, a private garden "out back" of the bishop's house. Hans Koehler prepared the planting plans for the garden. Completed in 1928, this garden included plants of historical interest, and employed biblical references and native plants.

The National Cathedral's gardens are cared for by the All Hallows Guild, founded in 1916—during the Olmsted firm's engagement. To honor Olmsted's work, a remnant stand of the original oak beech forest on Alban Hill (south of the original amphitheater) was named Olmsted Woods. Accessible via stone path, this contemplative area also features native plants and wildflowers. The guild works in concert with the cathedral's horticultural staff to preserve and beautify the historical grounds. Washington National Cathedral was listed in the National Register of Historic Places in 1974.

DELAWARE

BRANDYWINE PARK

While long appreciated as a natural resource for the city, protection for the scenic banks of Brandywine Creek was slow to take hold. In 1883, with development pressure facing the city's remaining undeveloped land, the Wilmington Board of Park Commissioners was established, and the Olmsted firm was hired to evaluate the city's potential public lands. They affirmed the site's potential as a park, and the park commission followed the firm's recommendations, acquiring 115 acres beginning in 1886. Continued acquisitions in the 1900s expanded the park to over 178 acres, and the Brandywine Zoo was established in 1905. Development of the park continued throughout this period, with the addition of monuments, gardens, and other features. Later in the century, an overpass for Interstate 95 was constructed through the park, its road deck and arched supports framing views along the river and the park's major circulation routes.

Samuel Canby, the first president of the park commission, consulted with Frederick Law Olmsted Sr. as he developed the park's original scheme, and his plan reflects the latter's design principles. Park drives and pedestrian ways follow the contours of the creek. A historical mill race, reflective of the city's industrial heritage, runs along the south bank, paralleled by a walking trail. Its calm waters provide visual contrast to the rocky shoals of the creek itself. Framing the creek are wooded hillsides, where native vegetation has been preserved. Playfields and other active recreational spaces occupy the uplands on the northern edge of the park, their open greens in contrast with the residences and other buildings that form a well-defined street wall around the park. Brandywine Park was listed in the National Register of Historic Places in 1976.

KENTMERE PARKWAY, WILMINGTON

Proposed as part of the Olmsted firm's 1885 report to the Wilmington Board of Park Commissioners, Kentmere Parkway was designed to link Rockford and Brandywine Parks. Commissioner William Bancroft acquired the right of way for the corridor in 1889 and sent a proposed scheme to the Olmsted firm for comment. The Olmsteds refined the design, crafting a proposal with a more curvilinear route for the four-block corridor. Implementation proceeded in the 1890s, though it deviated somewhat from the Olmsted plan.

Extending southeast from Rockford Park, the parkway frames a narrowing canopied green that wraps through a collection of historical residences. The southern terminus of the parkway gathers together Lovering Avenue, aligned to its primary axis, and South Park Drive, which follows a sloping draw into Brandywine Park. While the parkway's western drive forms a clearly defined street edge, the eastern drive curves more generously. The result is a buffer between sidewalk and street that swells to accommodate larger trees and provides a generous cushion between pedestrians and vehicular traffic. As the parkway widens and turns into Rockford Park, its circulation becomes increasingly complex, with pathways crossing the expanded green. The vehicular routes likewise become more intricate as the parkway resolves conflicts between two street grids offset slightly from one another.

Top and above: Drives in Brandywine Park wind through rocky, wooded hillsides where much native vegetation has been preserved.

FLORIDA

Memorial Park, Jacksonville   79   Bok Tower Gardens, Lake Wales   81
Mountain Lake, Lake Wales   80   Pinewood Estate, Lake Wales   82

Above: An Italianate balustrade marks the transition between the park and a river with a variable water table. **Right and lower right:** Charles Adrian Pillars's sculpture *Spiritualized Life*, 1924, has become a Jacksonville landmark feature near the Olmsted firm's balustrades.

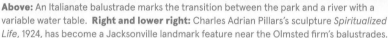

MEMORIAL PARK, JACKSONVILLE

This open space along the sandy banks of the Saint Johns River had been traditionally used for picnicking and occasional baptisms by Black church congregations. In 1919, in response to a Jacksonville Rotary Club drive to create a memorial to fallen soldiers of World War I, the city purchased the land, and planning began for Florida's only statewide memorial to those who had died in the war.

Aspiring to create a worthy civic gesture, Ninah M. H. Cummer, the founder of the Jacksonville Garden Club and whose own waterfront property (now the site of the Cummer Museum) was located nearby, commissioned the Olmsted Brothers firm to plan a park on this city-purchased land. The riverfront site was challenging; it had a high water table and difficult planting conditions. The Olmsted firm's simple design of 1922 consists of a central lawn surrounded by an oval walk, enclosed by a dense tree planting, with promenades along the water's edge. The focal point of the park is a bronze sculpture by C. Adrian Pillars, allegorically depicting "the winged figure of Youth," rising above struggling figures representing the "swirl of material forces." This is surrounded by an elevated water basin embedded with dedicatory bronze tablets. Like the Italian Garden designed by Ellen Shipman in 1931 for Mrs. Cummer, this commission included many Italianate details surrounding the sculpture's setting, including brick paving patterns, tree bosquets, balustrades, walls, and jardinieres. The Memorial Park was listed in the National Register of Historic Places in 2017.

The Mountain Lake neighborhood retains much of its original character, in terms of both architecture and planting.

MOUNTAIN LAKE, LAKE WALES

Recognizing the investment potential of the rolling land he had inherited in central Florida, real estate speculator Frederick S. Ruth increased his holdings around Iron Mountain and Buck Lake to nearly 3000 acres between 1914 and 1918. Having grown up in the Olmsted-designed suburb of Roland Park in Baltimore, Ruth understood the value of good design for a successful development. Naming his property Mountain Lake, he hired Olmsted Brothers, specifically Frederick Law Olmsted Jr., to plan an exclusive resort community for attractive winter residences, with significant recreational amenities surrounded by the investment potential of citrus groves.

Construction began in 1916 based on the Olmsted plan of that year, which included a central golf course designed by Seth Raynor, a substantial clubhouse, and residential properties of various sizes around the lake and beyond, connected by curving roads and paths. Charles R. Wait, an architect working with the Olmsted firm, designed many of the buildings, predominantly in the Spanish-influenced Mediterranean style. The landscapes surrounding many of the homes—designed by Florida-based landscape architect William Lyman Phillips, who had trained with the Brookline firm—were planned using a tropical plant palette, enhanced by appropriate decorative elements with particular attention to interior and exterior vistas. The clientele was, and continue to be, the elite of business, political, and social leaders from widespread locales. Most of the properties were developed from 1918 through the early 1930s. In 1952 an Olmsted firm study of the community revised the original plan, enabling the development of former citrus groves into residential properties. The development was listed in the National Register of Historic Places as a historic district in 1993.

Above left: Planting study for the base of Bok Tower, 1928. **Above right:** The 205-foot carillon tower is the park's landmark structure to human visitors, but the diversity of plants also makes it a landmark for wildlife.

BOK TOWER GARDENS, LAKE WALES

Edward Bok, author, publisher, and philanthropist, realizing the unique qualities of the land comprising the "Iron Mountain"—at 295 feet, the highest elevation in Florida—convinced the Mountain Lake developer, Frederick Ruth, to sell him this acreage. Bok then commissioned Frederick Law Olmsted Jr. to shape the land as a sanctuary for birds and humans, a place for spiritual rejuvenation and contemplation. Together with William Lyman Phillips, Olmsted transformed the sandy slopes into a reserve with meandering paths winding around bodies of water, with lush subtropical vegetation or meadow expanses for diverse habitats. A natural halt for native and migratory birds, Olmsted and Phillips retained the existing pine stands and added thousands of large live oaks, sabal palms, magnolias, gardenias, azaleas,

and sword and Boston ferns to create the desired naturalistic hammock scenery, providing food and shelter for the more than 100 bird species living within the sanctuary. For the mountain top, Bok commissioned Milton B. Medary to design a picturesque 205-foot carillon tower. Constructed of translucent pink Georgia marble and Florida coquina stone, the "Singing Tower" is reflected in the skillfully placed moat that surrounds its base.

In gratitude for the opportunities that America had afforded him as a Dutch immigrant, Bok gave his sanctuary to the public in a dedication ceremony delivered by President Calvin Coolidge in February 1929. The Bok Tower Gardens were listed in the National Register of Historic Places in 1972 and designated a National Historic Landmark in 1993.

Moorish accents and lush plantings are used throughout the Pinewood Estate.

PINEWOOD ESTATE, LAKE WALES

Originally called *"El Retiro"* (the retreat), this estate was built as a winter home for Bethlehem steel magnate Charles Buck. With the Olmsted Brothers working on the nearby sanctuary around the Singing Tower (the current Bok Tower Gardens), Buck approached the firm to design a retreat reminiscent of his childhood in Latin America. Beginning in 1929, working closely with Buck, architect Charles Wait positioned a Mediterranean-style home to take advantage of views and shade. In laying out the grounds, landscape architect William Lyman Phillips combined Moorish influences of walled gardens, axial views, and water features with more picturesque English horticultural emphases, the latter reflecting Buck's personal interest in gardens. Referencing the native longleaf pine, once prevalent in the area, Phillips made extensive use of various pines to shape the formal and informal areas.

Beginning in 1947, following Buck's death, the estate passed among several owners with diminishing attention to the landscape, until it was purchased by Nellie Lee Holt Bok in 1970 and renamed Pinewood Estate.

In the 1990s landscape architect Rudy Favretti began to recapture the essence of the estate's original Olmsted-Phillips design and plantings, now part of Bok Tower Gardens. The estate contains a cluster of courtyards and porches that effectively merges indoor and outdoor rooms and reinforces a sense of sanctuary. At the back of the house, a densely shaded patio with a small Spanish-tiled fountain looks out onto manicured hedges and lush plantings of palms and olives. Announced by large clay jars once used for storing olive oil, a linear path leads directly to a half-hidden stone grotto that surrounds a small pool. Elsewhere, a brick-walled, rectangular, terraced lawn opens onto a jet spray fountain via a distinct circular portal called a moon gate. Along with the shade from tall live oaks and pines, the water features provide respite in the hot climate. The home, positioned near the middle of the more than seven-acre grounds, is bordered to the west by an open, rolling lawn edged by perimeter plantings of native trees and shrubs. The Pinewood Estate was listed in the National Register of Historic Places in 1985.

GEORGIA

Druid Hills, Atlanta   84

Grant Park, Atlanta   88

Piedmont Park, Atlanta   90

Bradley Olmsted Garden, Columbus   92

The parks' curvilinear paths remain popular with current residents.

DRUID HILLS, ATLANTA

On his property of approximately four square miles, Joel Hurt, who created Atlanta's first streetcar suburb, Inman Park, hired Frederick Law Olmsted Sr. to develop a master plan for a picturesque residential community, named after a park in Baltimore, Maryland. Olmsted Sr. worked with John Charles Olmsted on the 1893 plan, which featured a divided, curvilinear parkway called Ponce de Leon Avenue that served as the community's central spine. The parkway was interlaced with six linked public parks that progressed along a broad, grassy median, transforming the traditional village green into a linear form.

Olmsted Brothers updated the plan in 1905, and construction of the 1500-acre development commenced that year. Parkland was concentrated in the valleys formed by Peavine Creek, with denser tree planting in pockets throughout the neighborhood and along the streets. The spacious residential lots stipulated deep setbacks from the street, with stately mansions designed in various revival styles along Ponce de Leon Avenue by many of Atlanta's notable architects. The development opened in 1908; financial difficulties forced Hurt to sell his interests to a syndicate led by Asa Griggs Candler, founder of The Coca-Cola Company, that same year. In 1915 Candler relocated the main campus of Emory University to 631 acres within the community, and in 1924 a country club and golf course were built in the southeast corner of the neighborhood. Residential construction continued through 1936. In 1979 the 1300-acre Druid Hills Historic District was listed in the National Register of Historic Places.

Each house receives an enviable amount of shade and verdure.

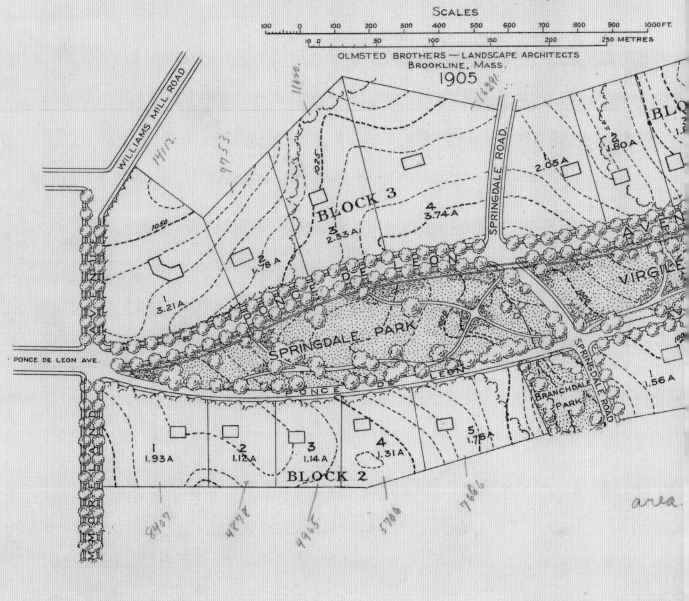

A partial plan for the development reveals the proximity of each residential lot to green space.

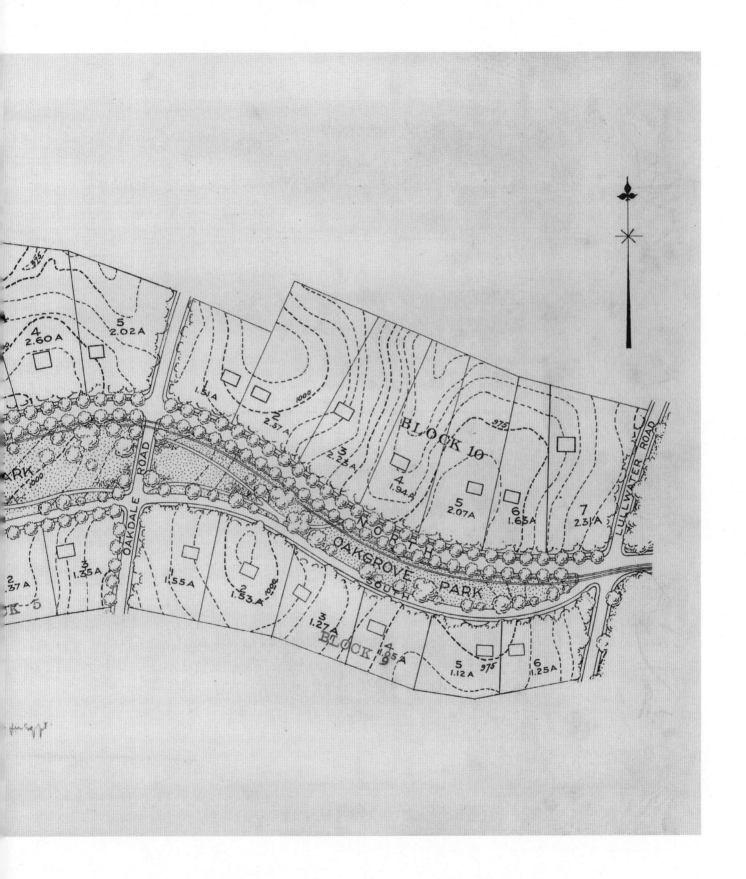

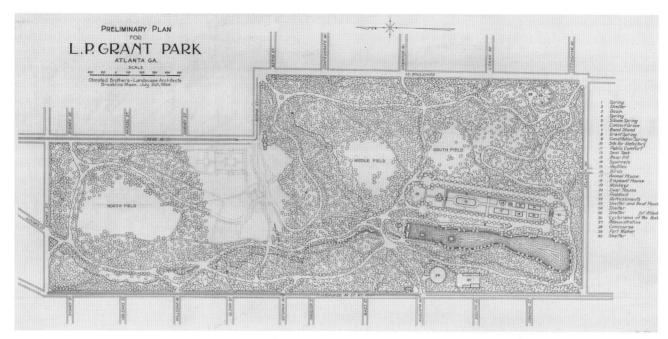

The 1904 preliminary plan for Grant Park.

GRANT PARK, ATLANTA

Atlanta's oldest park, Grant Park, was established in 1883, when successful engineer and businessman Colonel Lemuel P. Grant gifted 100 acres of parkland to the city. The city expanded its limits to the southeast to include Grant Park and the surrounding neighborhood, purchasing forty-four additional acres in 1890 to allow room for the new Grant Park Zoo. John Charles Olmsted of the Olmsted Brothers firm was contracted to draw up plans for the park in 1903. During his site visit, Olmsted sketched and photographed the parkland and its context, noting the high quality of the homes in the area but also the monotony of oak trees covering the parkland. In reaction, Olmsted proposed a naturalistic planting scheme, which carved out glades by

thinning the existing stand of trees and replacing it with diverse understory plantings. Olmsted also suggested the park expand Lake Abana to manage storm water and develop a pedestrian system of sinuous walks separate from the park drives, perhaps the lasting legacies of the Olmsted Brothers plan.

In 1996 a master plan for the park was commissioned, and a citizen group, Grant Park Conservancy, was formed. Recent efforts have focused on the pedestrian experience of the park as well as stream rehabilitation, including planting along steep banks. The park is included in the eponymous historic district, listed in the National Register of Historic Places in 1979.

Top and above: Elegant stonework is an enduring part of Grant Park's appeal.

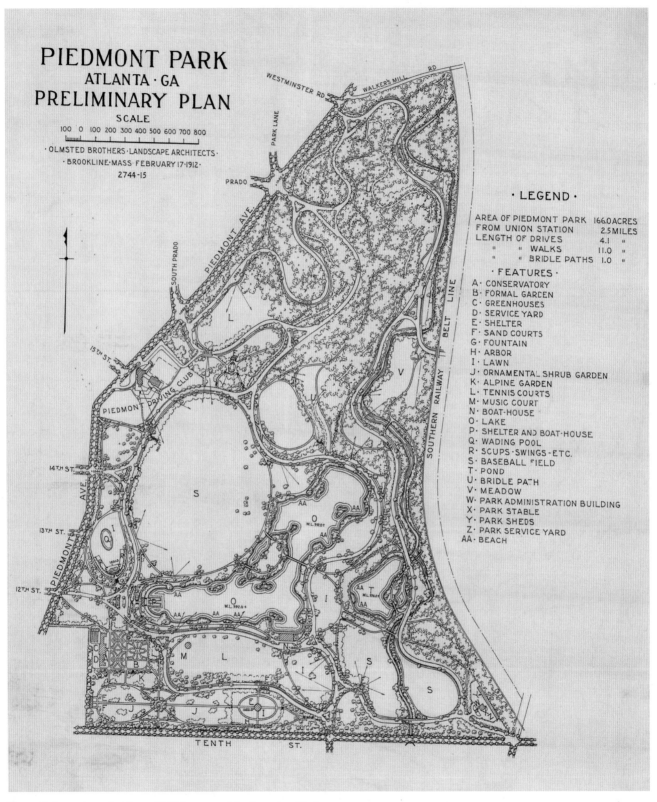

PIEDMONT PARK
ATLANTA · GA
PRELIMINARY PLAN
SCALE

100 0 100 200 300 400 500 600 700 800

· OLMSTED BROTHERS · LANDSCAPE ARCHITECTS ·
· BROOKLINE · MASS · FEBRUARY 17 · 1912 ·
2744-15

· LEGEND ·

AREA OF PIEDMONT PARK 166.0 ACRES
FROM UNION STATION 2.5 MILES
LENGTH OF DRIVES 4.1 "
  " " WALKS 11.0 "
  " " BRIDLE PATHS 1.0 "

· FEATURES ·

A · CONSERVATORY
B · FORMAL GARDEN
C · GREENHOUSES
D · SERVICE YARD
E · SHELTER
F · SAND COURTS
G · FOUNTAIN
H · ARBOR
I · LAWN
J · ORNAMENTAL SHRUB GARDEN
K · ALPINE GARDEN
L · TENNIS COURTS
M · MUSIC COURT
N · BOAT-HOUSE
O · LAKE
P · SHELTER AND BOAT-HOUSE
Q · WADING POOL
R · SCUPS · SWINGS · ETC.
S · BASEBALL FIELD
T · POND
U · BRIDLE PATH
V · MEADOW
W · PARK ADMINISTRATION BUILDING
X · PARK STABLE
Y · PARK SHEDS
Z · PARK SERVICE YARD
AA · BEACH

The preliminary plan makes the park's Picturesque-style elements evident.

Lake Clara Meer in Piedmont Park provides more than eleven acres of welcome calm in the middle of the bustling city.

PIEDMONT PARK, ATLANTA

Located in northern Atlanta on the site of the 1895 Cotton States and International Exposition, Piedmont Park encompasses 189 acres of parkland. The purchase of this land in 1904 extended the city limits to incorporate both the park's acreage and several developing neighborhoods. Between 1909 and 1912, the Olmsted Brothers offered a park design that greatly reflected the Picturesque style and design principles of Frederick Law Olmsted Sr.: it featured broad, grassy lawns and playing fields, a shaded woodland with over fifteen miles of sinuous walks, drives, and bridle paths, the nearly twelve-acre Lake Clara Meer, and various formal gardens and recreation areas. Some, though not all, of the Olmsted Brothers design for Piedmont Park was realized. The park flourished nonetheless, given its proximity to popular residential enclaves. Over time, other significant attractions were added, including a bathhouse for swimmers, the Park Drive Bridge, and the Isamu Noguchi–designed playground, Playscapes. Following two decades of decline, in 1982 the City of Atlanta adopted a master plan to rehabilitate the park and a public-private partnership, the Piedmont Park Conservancy, was formed the following year. Piedmont Park was listed in the National Register of Historic Places in 1976.

Photographs of the original site **(opposite page)** and the garden today **(above)** show how diligently the firm worked to retain the landscape's natural features, such as ravines and native vegetation, still extant today.

BRADLEY OLMSTED GARDEN, COLUMBUS

Originally known as Sunset Terrace, the Country Place Era estate just east of downtown Columbus was designed for the noted industrialist and philanthropist William C. Bradley by the Olmsted Brothers firm between 1920 and 1937. In 1947 the estate was subdivided and thirteen acres were donated to the City of Columbus. The gift included the Mediterranean Revival style home (1912) and several of the garden's signature landscape features.

Bradley grew up on a cotton plantation and had a keen interest in the garden's natural and physical features. He collaborated extensively on the design and construction with William Marquis of the Olmsted Brothers firm. Of particular interest to Bradley was the use of native flora, with plant materials coming from P. J. Berckmans Company (a large Augusta nursery at which Marquis was previously employed), and from a former Alabama plantation just twelve miles away, which provided

many of the site's oaks, laurels, and red cedars. Nonliving native materials that were brought to site included rustic steps from a nearby plantation and boulders that came from the Chattahoochee River and were used in the waterfall.

This residential commission is considered the largest and most important of thirteen residential projects carried out by the firm in Georgia. Today, the garden's extant Olmsted-era features include many of the mature plantings and the original

natural spring ravine as well as a grotto and pool house. Current horticultural practices maintain the original design intent of planting native flowering shrubs and trees. The property was the only Olmsted Brothers commission included in the seminal publication, *Garden History of Georgia, 1733–1933*, published by Atlanta's Peachtree Garden Club. The garden is a component of the Wynn's Hill-Overlook-Oak Circle Historic District, which was listed in the National Register of Historic Places in 2005.

IDAHO

A planting scheme that allows the Neo-Gothic architecture of the Administration Building to stand out proudly gives the campus gravitas.

UNIVERSITY OF IDAHO, MOSCOW

Following a fire and the reconstruction of the Administration Building in spring of 1907, University of Idaho president James McLean invited the Olmsted Brothers to provide a plan to guide the campus's growth. John C. Olmsted visited that summer and filed a narrative report the following year. A sketch accompanying the report illustrated the broad contours of the proposal, which called for the acquisition of property between the town, with its railroad depot, and the reconfiguration of the roadways leading toward the campus. A pair of diagonal avenues were to converge on the central tower of the new Administration Building and to then stop short, ending with open views to the tower across a rectilinear green—now known as Admin Lawn—and be flanked by new academic buildings. New dormitories for men and women would be placed to the north and south. To complement the new academic structures, Olmsted recommended a conservative use of lower trees, so that the buildings might not be overwhelmed.

The plan went largely unrealized due to lack of funding, though a curving road leading to the Administration Building was removed, allowing for the open lawn to be knit together. However, the firm remained a resource for the university, which again reached out in 1913 for advice on the design of athletic facilities to the west of the Administration Building, and on the layout of new circulation for the Admin Lawn. Again, John C. Olmsted proposed diminishing roadways, and suggested a gentle curve to the at-the-time rigid path approaching from the northeast, now known as "Hello Walk." This path, while generally following the primary trajectory identified by Olmsted, has now grown to be covered by an allée of trees, thus obscuring the approach to the Administration Building as he had envisioned it. Today, the university ensures that the Olmsted legacy remains active as subject matter in their landscape architecture programs.

ILLINOIS

South Park System, Chicago   97   Riverside Community, Riverside   99

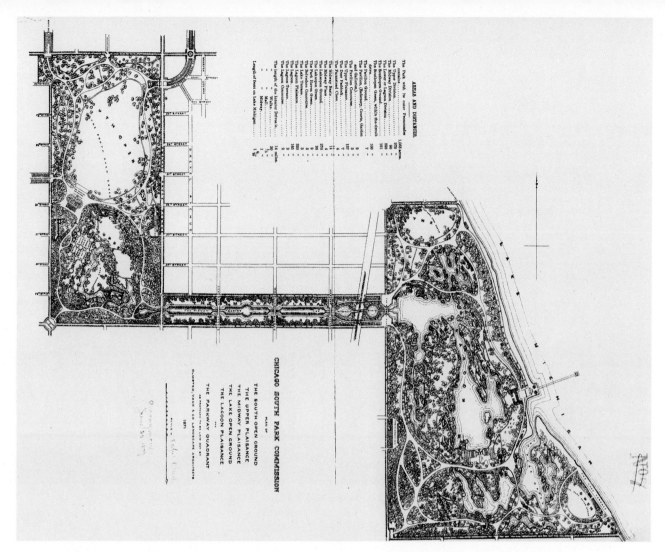

Chicago South Park Comission Plan, 1871, Olmsted, Vaux, and Co.

SOUTH PARK SYSTEM, CHICAGO

Chicago's South Park Commission was established in 1869 to oversee the development of boulevards and parks south of the Chicago River. One year later, Frederick Law Olmsted Sr. and Calvert Vaux were hired to design the 1055-acre system. The designers transformed the swampland along Lake Michigan, to become Jackson Park, into a large lagoon for sheltered boating, while providing a beach and long pier for lakeside activities. The interior flatland, the future Washington Park, was to become a large meadow with a pavilion, a carriage concourse, and surrounding tree groves for picnicking. A connecting strip, the mile-long Midway Plaisance, was to contain a canal for boating, with broad allées for promenades. Various major parkways were also proposed. In the dire economic times following the 1871 fire, H. W. S. Cleveland was hired to implement some of the Olmsted-Vaux plans, beginning with Washington Park. He oversaw construction of drives, greenswards, picnic grounds, and a ramble, adding elaborate floral displays. But by the late 1880s, Jackson Park remained an unimproved marshy area until the site was selected for the 1893 World's Columbian Exposition.

Olmsted and Henry Codman, working with Daniel Burnham, developed grand plans for the architecturally splendid exposition grounds, while also providing respite from its formality via the luxuriantly planted Wooded Island across the lagoon. The Midway served as the amusement section, while

Clockwise from top left: Young swimmers circa 1904 in the pool at McKinley Park. Canoeing on one of several waterways in the park system. The Midway Plaisance's allée of trees still lines the southern edge of the University of Chicago campus. Washington Park's open meadow continues to serve a variety of uses and groups.

throughout the rest of Jackson Park, general improvements resembled the original Olmsted-Vaux design.

In 1895, following the exposition, John Charles Olmsted redesigned Jackson Park, taking advantage of the wide-ranging lakeside views while offering areas for sports, boat-houses, and family gatherings, all intersected by meandering drives and walks. The Midway's central canal was replaced by sunken grass panels, while Washington Park continued to provide for more expansive pastoral experiences. Over the years, the intended parkways—Drexel, Garfield, and Grand Boulevards (the third now Martin Luther King Jr. Drive)—were also constructed. Concern about the growing worker population crowded into tenement neighborhoods in the South Side prompted formation of a Special Park Commission, tasked with the construction of small playground parks for recreation, education, and social reform. On oddly shaped small

lots, the Olmsted Brothers firm planned spaces for active uses. Field houses, designed by Edward Bennett of the Burnham Company, provided public bathing facilities, indoor gymnasia, auditoriums, libraries, and classrooms for "Americanization" lessons. Quickly constructed between 1902 and 1910, this system was praised by President Theodore Roosevelt as ". . . one of the most notable civic achievements in any American city." Twenty of these spaces continue to afford neighborhood-based recreational opportunities and other amenities today. A significant number of these parks and boulevards are listed in the National Register of Historic Places including Armour Square Park (2003), Cornell Square (2005), Davis Square (2005), Drexel Boulevard (2018), Fuller Park (2002), Garfield Boulevard (2018), Hamilton Park (1995), Jackson Park (1972), Midway Plaisance (1972), Palmer Park (2007), Sherman Park (1990), Trumbull Park (1995), and Washington Park (2004).

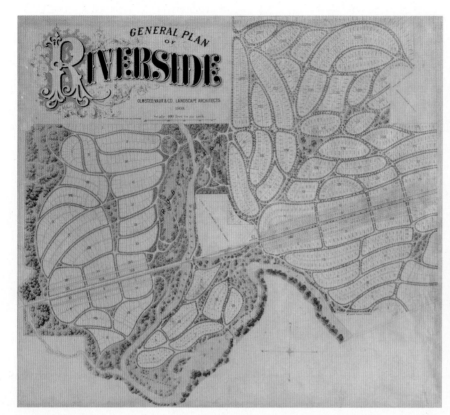

Above left: The general plan for the generous estates of the Riverside community, 1869. **Above right:** The water tower next to the Riverside train station has become a landmark.

RIVERSIDE COMMUNITY, RIVERSIDE

In 1869 Frederick Law Olmsted Sr. and Calvert Vaux presented a plan to a group of investors, led by Emery E. Childs, to develop 1600 acres six miles west of Chicago into a model commuter town, or "bedroom suburb," offering the advantages of town life in a rural setting. Initially flat farmland, the site was enriched by gentle elevation changes and lavish plantings throughout, with a park along the Des Plaines River. The town center hosted a railroad station (the first stop on a new commuter line from Chicago), hotel, commercial buildings, and community amenities. The ornate 1871 water tower by William Le Baron Jenney at the town center has become an icon for the community. Curvilinear streets delineated elongated residential blocks, carved into large lots for suburban "villas." Each house was to be set back at least thirty feet from the street, and each homeowner was required to plant several trees, orchestrating a transition between private gardens and public spaces. While respecting family privacy, Olmsted's landscape design facilitated the interaction of neighbors by providing informal parks and playgrounds, as well as areas for strolling, boating, skating, and other recreational activities. Although the landscaped parkway connection to the city was not realized, the internal parkway system remains today as an early example of this new roadway and greenway hybrid. Designated a National Historic Landmark in 1969, Riverside is home to some 8900 residents.

INDIANA

Indiana University, Bloomington   101   Oldfields, Indianapolis   102

Meandering paths, historical clocks, and Neo-Gothic architecture combine to give Indiana University a quintessential American college campus feel.

The Rose Well House, 1908, still provides drinking water to students crossing campus.

INDIANA UNIVERSITY, BLOOMINGTON

The "State Seminary" in Bloomington, Indiana, was created in 1820 and in 1838 officially became Indiana College. The campus burned down in 1883 and a new twenty-acre site, Dunn Woods, was purchased. Rebuilding commenced in 1884 and continued through 1908.

The Olmsted Brothers firm was first consulted in 1929 to develop a master plan for the 166-acre campus. Existing conditions included large groves of trees in the four quads and many walkways. The preliminary grading plan retained much of the woods and designated those areas for future growth and improved access. In 1935 and 1936 the firm produced many grading studies, planting plans, and an assessment for the locations and materials for campus circulation. Because Indiana University is a state university, it was able to obtain federal Works Progress Administration (WPA) funding for campus improvements during the Great Depression. Much of the construction work was completed by WPA workers, following the plans prepared by the Olmsted Brothers. The design and location of new walkways was especially challenging because, as is noted in correspondence, students create their own pathways. These paths did not appear logical on a plan, but they functioned as the most direct routes depending on origin and destination, and it was deemed better to formally pave those efficient and well-used pathways. This approach resulted in the many crisscrossing paths that course through the greens and quads of the older section of campus.

The campus has since grown to encompass 1933 acres. The large, wooded areas around the President's House, the curvilinear cul-de-sac access road that serves it, and much of the original academic quads have been retained. Post-1940s campus expansions were built on land north of the 1929 campus, thus preserving and protecting the original twenty-acre core, known as "Old Crescent," which was listed in the National Register of Historic Places in 1980.

Above and next page: Formal landscape elements including fountains, bridges, and gates are hallmarks of the Oldfields property.

OLDFIELDS, INDIANAPOLIS

The French château–style residence at this twenty-six-acre American Country Place–Era estate was built in 1912 for Hugh Landon by his brother-in-law, architect Lewis Davis. Its oldest feature is a walled, sunken garden of symmetrical planting beds centered on a circular fountain pool.

Impressed after a 1920 visit to the Thomas Lamont garden on North Haven Island, Maine, designed by a partner in the Olmsted Brothers firm, Percival Gallagher, Landon hired Gallagher to develop a comprehensive plan for Oldfields. Taking advantage of the property's unique landscape assets, Gallagher reorganized the existing spatial design, bringing coherence while distinguishing dedicated spaces for different uses. Deploying an arsenal of formal and informal design styles, he provided for flexibility and diversity of use, while also creating the appearance of a larger landscape by taking full advantage of "borrowed" views.

Oldfields has several primary visual-spatial components, each with its own character while also contributing to the whole. These include a choreographed entry sequence with an ornate iron gate (designed by architect Fermor S. Cannon); the grand allée on axis with the house, flanking a rectangular lawn with pedestrian-scale woodland border gardens, a circular fountain, and a replica of

The Three Graces statue as its visual terminus; the ravine garden, organized along curvilinear stone paths and a meandering water course, with an explosion of flowering plant materials from herbaceous to small trees and shrubs; a redesigned formal garden maintained on the southern axis of the house while revising the shape of planting beds and introducing new art and furnishings; and finally, a hillside ramble along the property's sloping wooded western edge, above the water canal, providing visual and physical connectivity to myriad landscape spaces.

Supplementing these major landscape features were an orchard, cutting garden and greenhouse area, a service area with gardener's and chauffeur's cottages, and pasturelands.

After Landon's wife, Jesse, died in 1930, Landon sold Oldfields to J. K. Lilly Jr. and his wife Ruth in 1933. When J. K. Lilly Jr.'s estate was settled in 1966, his children donated Oldfields to the Art Association of Indianapolis (now Indianapolis Museum of Art). Preservation efforts have since been undertaken to restore and rehabilitate the landscape's historic character within the context of the museum grounds.

Oldfields was listed in the National Register of Historic Places in 2000 and designated a National Historic Landmark in 2003.

KENTUCKY

Bernheim Arboretum, Clermont   105

Kentucky State Capitol Grounds, Frankfort   106

Ashland Park, Lexington   107

Parks and Parkways System, Louisville   109

University of Louisville   111

A variety of deciduous trees makes a stunning autumn display along Lake Nevin, near the arboretum entrance.

BERNHEIM ARBORETUM, CLERMONT

In 1929 Kentucky bourbon-distilling magnate Isaac Bernheim purchased more than 13,000 acres of barren land, formerly used in ore mining, for the development of an arboretum with a natural history museum and art gallery. In 1935 the Olmsted Brothers firm, overseen by James Dawson, created a design plan that realized Bernheim's vision for a reforested landscape that would connect people with nature. The plan called for adding three small bodies of water (Holly and Cedar Ponds and Mac's Lake) and an entrance road that stretched from State Highway 245 to the arboretum's forty-eight-foot-tall fire tower. The land was transformed into a series of open lawns and meadows bordered by collections of trees, including crab apple, holly, and maple. In 1949 Lake Nevin, a thirty-two-acre water feature, was placed near the arboretum entrance. The arboretum opened to the public in 1950. In the 1960s the landscape architecture firm Miller, Wihry, and Brooks designed the gardens surrounding the Garden Pavilion, as well as the Quiet Garden. A research

and visitors' center were built on the grounds in 2004 and 2005, respectively. By the early twenty-first century, the site's total acreage had been expanded to 16,137.

The landscape is divided between a 600-acre arboretum and over 15,000 acres of beech maple forests, known collectively today as the Bernheim Arboretum and Research Forest. The arboretum holds more than 8000 varieties of trees, shrubs, and perennials. Networks of paved trails connect to the arboretum's main attractions, including the Olmsted Ponds (formerly Holly and Cedar Ponds), Lake Nevin, a grassland prairie, Bluegrass savanna, cypress-tupelo swamp, and Bernheim's gravesite. Over thirty-five miles of hiking trails weave across the landscape's varied topography of ridges and slopes through forests, grasslands, and watersheds. Installed on the grounds are various permanent and temporary sculptures, including Thomas Dambo's "Forest Giants in a Giant Forest," and George Grey Barnard's "Let There Be Light."

Above and right: The Olmsted firm recommended a broad classical staircase as an approach to this seat of government.

🏛

KENTUCKY STATE CAPITOL GROUNDS, FRANKFORT

Sited on a thirty-four-acre hill along the Kentucky River, with expansive panoramic views in every direction, Kentucky's state capitol building in Frankfort was designed by Ohio architect Frank Mills Andrews. The grounds were designed by the Olmsted Brothers firm, one of eleven capitols the firm worked on. As with such designs laid out by the Olmsteds in Olympia, Washington, and Montgomery, Alabama, this capitol was dramatically situated on a promontory, in this case overlooking Fort Hill. Sited west of the Kentucky River, the Neoclassical building, oriented on a north–south axis, is set onto a plinth rising above a series of broad, paved terraces. The building setting is nestled within a generous expanse of sloping parkland, with trees along the perimeter.

The Olmsted firm's involvement began in 1905, the year the project broke ground, with plans generated between 1908 and 1910, when the project was completed. John C. Olmsted visited the site in May 1908 for a few days, and after a thorough examination, recommended that additional land be acquired to best develop the appropriate setting for the monumental building, widening Main Street (Capital Avenue) to upward of 160 feet, with a median for a more dignified approach. He also proposed planting Norway maples and enlarging the plaza at the base of the hill, and suggested that the stone-paved terraces be reconfigured from those proposed by the architect to better screen the structure's basement

level and to provide an area for generous foundation plantings. Finally, Olmsted recommended that the pedestrian walk leading to the principal entrance be at least fifty feet wide, possibly with two brick walkways on both sides, separated by turf and plantings of hydrangeas. Capital Avenue bifurcated at the plaza, circumventing the base of the hill symmetrically and then in asymmetrical drives following the contours through the rear. The plantings around the building were extensive and featured many varieties of shrubs that would fill in, but not obscure, the building. Native trees like the Kentucky coffee tree were included in the plant list.

The project received over $1,000,000 in federal funds, as reparations for damages incurred during the Civil War and past-due compensation for services rendered during the Spanish-American War.

Later additions to the grounds included parking lots and a 1961 floral clock southwest of the building. In 2008 the scenic parkland at the northwest corner of the grounds was converted into a space to memorialize the state's history.

A 1984 master plan and study led to the re-establishment of the original Olmsted design, including a circular entry drive and brick terraces surrounding the building. The Kentucky State Capitol was listed in the National Register of Historic Places in 1973.

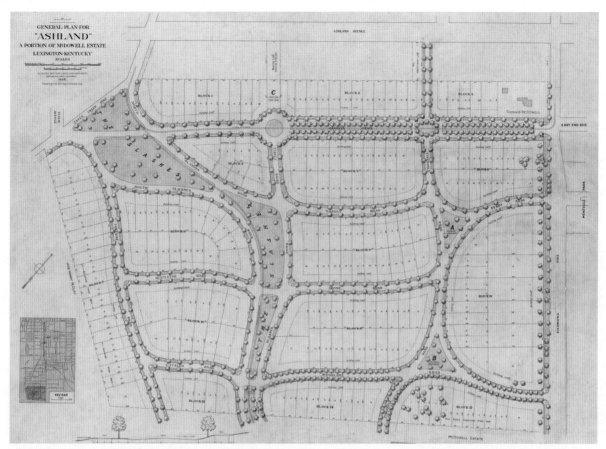

Tree-lined streets and a broad serpentine park that follows the natural topography were used to define Ashland Park in this 1908 plan.

ASHLAND PARK, LEXINGTON

Following the death of his father in 1899, Henry Clay McDowell Jr., great-grandson and namesake of the Kentucky senator, hired the Olmsted Brothers firm to plan a residential subdivision to be constructed on portions of the plantation he inherited. John C. Olmsted visited the estate beginning in 1904 and delivered a proposal in 1908, calling for a network of curvilinear streets, generous parkways, and triangular greens at major intersections. In 1919 the first lots of the development were listed for sale, and construction continued for the next decade. Though not overseen by the Olmsted firm, later phases of construction complemented their approach by offering triangles of green and curving lanes at major crossroads.

Two major green spines anchored the design. The first, Hanover Avenue, was a formal boulevard, with a broad verge punctuated by traffic circles through which streetcar tracks ran. The Slashes, meanwhile, was intended as a curving parkway (its name was an homage to McDowell Jr., known as the "mill boy of the slashes" for his supposedly humble roots—despite a fairly well-to-do upbringing—and was recommended by the client). The final result was considerably more modest, however: perhaps an unintentionally fitting tribute to McDowell Jr.'s mythos of provincial origins. Several blocks of the parkway were reconfigured for lots, and a considerably reduced parkway was constructed, the owners anticipating that a more economical and less grand approach to development might lead to better sales. The Ashland Park Historic District was listed in the National Register of Historic Places in 1986.

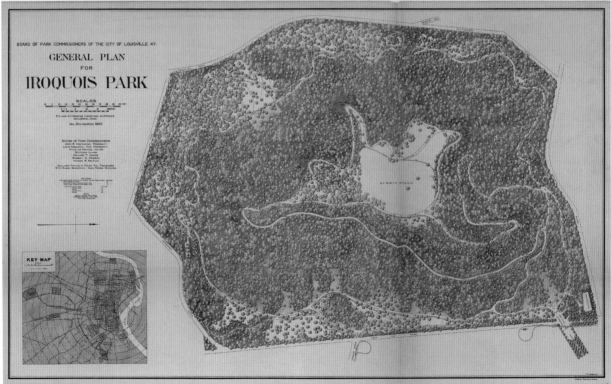

Above: General plan for Iroquois Park, 1897. **Top:** General plan for Cherokee Park.

Iroquois park views.

PARKS AND PARKWAYS SYSTEM, LOUISVILLE

In 1891 Frederick Law Olmsted Sr. addressed the Salmagundi Club, a small group of Louisville civic leaders, to further their interest in establishing a park system. The resulting commission created a network of parks and boulevards, one of five such systems in the country, representing the last design of this type in the elder Olmsted's career—and, along with Rochester, New York, the only system that was designed by all three Olmsteds over the succeeding decades.

Anchoring this system were three flagship parks along the city's perimeter. To the south was the 785-acre Iroquois Park, envisioned as a scenic reservation on heavily wooded steep terrain with a forty-five-acre summit (and with Mount Royal in Montreal, one of only two mountain parks in cities designed by Olmsted); to the east, the 409-acre Cherokee Park, with its rich and varied scenery following the contours of gently rolling slopes and pasturelands; and to the west, the 180-acre Shawnee Park, on a low-lying plain of river bottomland, with natural tiers sloping down to the Ohio River.

In addition to these large parks, over the years, fifteen smaller neighborhood parks (including Algonquin, Bingham (formerly Clifton), Central, Elliott, Shelby, Stansbury, Tyler, Victory, Wayside, and Willow Parks), and squares (Baxter and Boone) were designed to offer a variety of active and passive uses. Of particular note is the sixty-one-acre Chickasaw Park, designed by the Olmsted Brothers firm in 1923 and fully implemented in the 1930s. Unlike the other Olmsted-designed parks

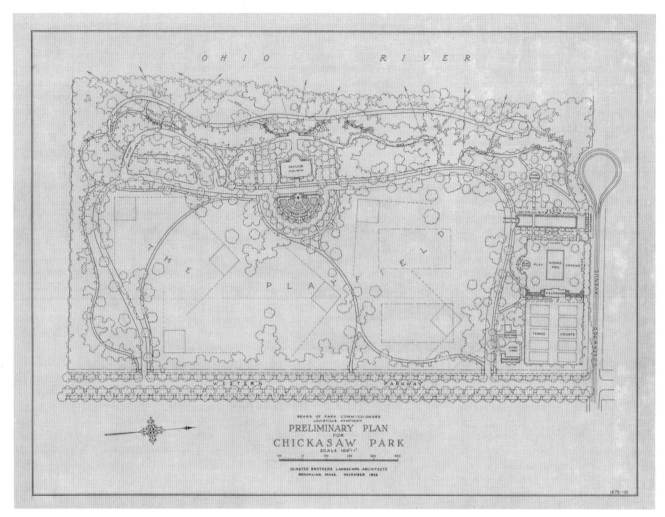

Chickasaw Park was planned specifically for the needs of the city's Black residents.

in the city, which were closed to the Black community until the parks were desegregated in 1954, Chickasaw was designed specifically to meet their needs.

Weaving together this system are nearly fifteen miles of parkways realized over a thirty-year period, including Algonquin, Cherokee, Eastern, Northwestern, Southern, and Southwestern Parkways—all with their own unique character, width, and spatial organization providing connectivity for pedestrians, cyclists, and vehicles.

In addition to designing the city's park system, the Olmsteds truly shaped the city, planning and designing residential subdivisions (among them Alta Vista, Braeview, Cherokee

Gardens), estates, cemeteries, institutions (University of Louisville, Southern Baptist Theological Seminary, and others), and religious grounds (Saint Frances in the Fields Church), country clubs (Louisville Country Club), arboreta (Bernheim Arboretum), and gardens.

The firm remained involved in the city into the 1970s, when Olmsted Associates advised on tornado damage in Cherokee Park. The Olmsted Park System of Louisville was listed in the National Register of Historic Places in 1982. In 1989 the Louisville Olmsted Parks Conservancy was formed as a nonprofit partner of Louisville and Metro Parks to preserve and restore this legacy.

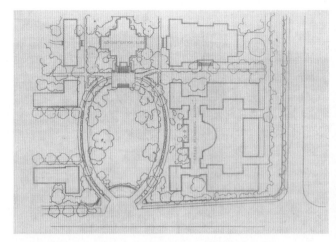

The Jeffersonian Administration Building's landscape plan, 1930, called for a large oval lawn, as opposed to more usual campus quadrangles.

UNIVERSITY OF LOUISVILLE

In 1922, Arthur Ford, president of the University of Louisville, contacted the Olmsted Brothers firm for assistance in planning a piece of property the school had recently acquired. The firm responded, sending James Frederick Dawson to inspect the site, but the university was in no hurry to proceed. Two years later, another piece of property was acquired, the former "House of Refuge," a children's home and industrial school. Desiring to adapt this ground for the university, Ford again approached the Olmsted firm. Edward Clark Whiting guided the work on the firm's behalf, recommending that various drives and walks be rerouted, and plantings adjusted accordingly, to create a more cohesive campus. Funding for a new fine arts museum was offered by a local benefactor shortly thereafter, and Ford asked for assistance in siting the new structure. This afforded Whiting the opportunity to recommend a more comprehensive plan for the campus, which he suggested be conducted in partnership with an architect—ideally one used to partnering with the Olmsted firm.

A 1930 drawing by Olmsted Brothers for the memorial gates entrance to the oval lawn, as seen from street level.

While consulting with the Olmsted firm, Ford also engaged local architects, who offered their own proposals for the campus plan in addition to designing new campus buildings. Whiting's various concepts for the campus proposed a series of quadrangles, typically anchored by a library. The Louisville architects suggested an elaborate cross-shaped lawn, anchored by a Jeffersonian rotunda. The end result was something of a compromise, with a modest oval green fronting the Administration Building (now Grawemeyer Hall) designed by Arthur Loomis

and constructed in 1926. While the oval form appears among the 1925 working drawings of Whiting, its conceptual origin is unclear. What is apparent, however, is that the Belknap Gates at the head of the oval were constructed against Whiting's recommendation. He suggested a single entry, with the drive diverging once inside the campus's fence. Although this recommendation was not followed, the firm continued to consult for the university, providing some planting recommendations around the gates and the Administration Building's steps in 1931.

LOUISIANA

Audubon Park, New Orleans   114   Louisiana State University, Baton Rouge   116

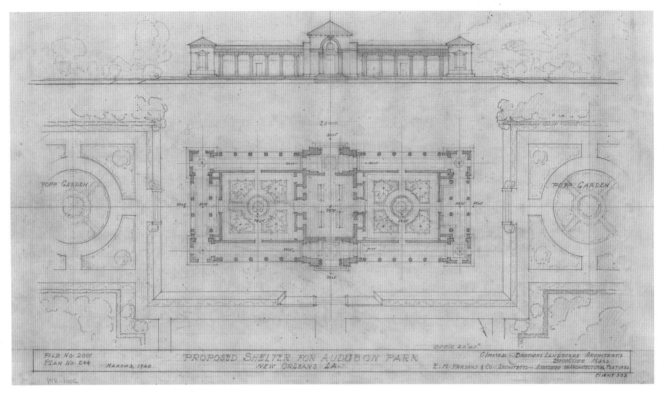

Sketch for a classical shelter, on parchment, 1920.

AUDUBON PARK, NEW ORLEANS

A former failed sugar plantation located six miles upriver from the old city center, whose original owner fled back to France before the Civil War, this 350-acre site became successive encampments for both Confederate and Union soldiers. This water-logged land was acquired in 1871 for a park, to be known as Upper City Park, but languished for lack of development funds. Real estate speculation in this area brought the World's Industrial and Cotton Centennial Exposition to the southwestern section of the parkland in 1884. Of that failed venture, only a Victorian-style conservatory, Horticultural Hall, with its gardenesque flower beds and plantation oak allées, remained. Although a

park commission was formed in 1887 and the park was renamed for John James Audubon who had studied birds in the area, there was not enough civic momentum to shape the park for public use.

This problematic rectangular acreage stretched from Saint Charles Street in the northeast to the batture along the Mississippi River shoreline, separated into sections by Magazine Street and the railroad running along the levee. In the 1890s, Tulane University, Loyola College, and several residential ventures began development across Saint Charles Street from the park, motivating the formation of an Audubon Park Improvement Association with the ability to collect funds. Efforts by businessmen J. Ward

Gurley and Lewis Johnson to engage professional planning advice brought John Charles Olmsted to inspect the grounds in 1897. He was enchanted by the "magnificent live oaks" for their scenic advantages, the mildness of climate, and richness of soil. Although the contract was financially meager, planning for Audubon Park would become his first major independent park project since the retirement of the senior Olmsted and would begin a relationship with the Olmsted firm that would continue into the 1940s.

The general plan developed by John Olmsted reflected an ingenious resolution of the site's detriments. To drain its swampy conditions, he created a water course meandering throughout the park, unifying the parts north and south of Magazine Street, similar to the Fens in Boston (under construction at that time). He used the fill from excavation to alter the flat contours into an undulating pastoral meadow, which quickly became an eighteen-hole golf course. He also used the majestic scale of grouped live oaks to provide a sense of topographic variation, while outfitting the stream banks and curving pathways with textured plantings, and adding numerous shelters for needed shade. A presentation portfolio rendered by Arthur Shurcliff from the firm illustrated these transformations in "before" and "after" perspectives.

To achieve these changes was a constant struggle between adequate funding and efforts to keep out inappropriate structures and uses in conflict with the park's purpose: to provide natural scenery for public respite and enjoyment. Construction was slow, beginning after 1916, after storms had destroyed Horticultural Hall. Generous citizens donated funds for fountains and playgrounds, but powerful golf interests confined the intended water course only to the western side of the park. After John Olmsted's death, other alterations occurred, some with Olmsted firm advice. By the late 1920s, ballfields, tennis courts, and an enormous swimming pool—the natatorium (no longer extant)—had been inserted. An area containing a few caged animals expanded into a full zoological garden with an aquarium, thanks to guidance from Frederick Law Olmsted Jr., augmented by WPA money in the 1930s.

After World War II, maintenance money was limited, and there was much deterioration to the landscape. Major efforts to recapture a zoo according to modern humane standards brought about revival for Audubon Park. Today, although there is pride in the park's Olmsted heritage, it is the restored zoo and golf interests which dominate the park administration.

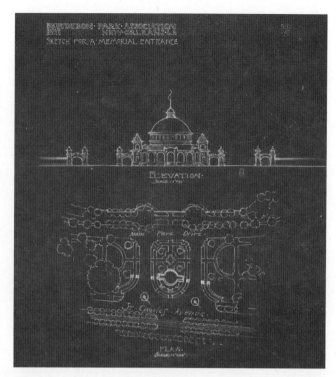

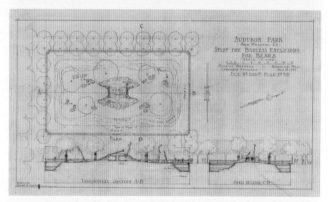

Top: sketch for a Victorian-style memorial entrance, in blue (n.d.), and a classical shelter, parchment, 1920. **Center:** "Study for Barless Enclosure for Bears," 1935. **Bottom:** Allées of live oaks still feature prominently as part of Audubon Park today.

Heritage trees and an open quadrangle still very much form the character of the central LSU campus.

LOUISIANA STATE UNIVERSITY, BATON ROUGE

The current campus of Louisiana State University was established in 1918, situated on a 650-acre plateau south of downtown Baton Rouge overlooking the Mississippi River. The campus plan was designed by Frederick Law Olmsted Jr. of the Olmsted Brothers firm in 1921, when the landscape architects were asked to study the visual and spatial relationships between the existing campus and 2000 recently acquired acres of agricultural tracts. After their major contributions to Audubon Park decades earlier, the firm and their work was known to J. K. Newman, whose father Isidore, a New Orleans banker, had long been involved

with both the state and the university. The younger Newman brought in Olmsted Jr. and underwrote the work.

The Olmsted Brothers plan was originally intended to accommodate 3000 students. It established a cruciform-shaped quadrangle as the center of campus. The plan that took form in the fall of 1921 included three quadrangle-like open spaces that ran along the natural bluff and were reinforced by a fourth (for arts and sciences) laid out along the axis of entry. This quadrangle scheme—converging at a central open space and preserving and protecting characteristic site features (an existing grove of

Drawing of the Olmsted proposal for campus, 1921.

magnolias, ancient mounds)—is the foundation of the Olmsted Brothers plan. The northern part of the campus was intended to be more scenic in character, taking its cues from the existing ravine and topographic variation. This area also included a grassy amphitheatre, which was not developed as harmoniously with nature as the Olmsted sketches had intended; rather than evoking a Greek theatre, in the end the space was less fluid and more architectural.

Following their work in 1921, the Olmsted firm did not further develop these campus master plans but was engaged to redesign the farm building complex (including the "Swine Palace") at the southern edge of campus. This would be the firm's last involvement with the campus design.

The realization of the campus plan was taken over by architect Theodore Link, who continued to build out the Olmsted firm's plan while designing the core campus buildings in an Italian Renaissance style. After his sudden death in 1923, Link was replaced by New Orleans architects Wogan and Bernard. Today, reviewing what was built then, many of the building shapes, their orientations, and the use of quadrangles can be "read" as the Olmsted firm had advised. Link's approach, however, was more internally focused, and he abandoned many of the visual and axial framing devices that would have been reinforced by an armature of canopy trees.

During the 1930s the campus received significant funding and began a pattern of expansion that continues today with over 250 buildings, an arboretum, and several military memorials. The historic core of the campus was listed in the National Register of Historic Places in 1988, with no mention of Olmsted.

MAINE

Acadia National Park, Mount Desert 119
Maine State Capitol Grounds, Augusta 121
University of Maine, Orono 122

Portland Parks, Eastern and Western
Promenades 123

Mount Desert Island, tumbling directly into the sea, is one of America's best beloved green spaces.

ACADIA NATIONAL PARK, MOUNT DESERT

Situated less than a mile off the coast of Maine, the once-isolated Mount Desert Island became a popular summer retreat in the late nineteenth century. Preserving portions of the island as a public park was first proposed by landscape architect Charles Eliot. After Eliot's death, his father, Harvard President Charles W. Eliot, sought the help of conservationist and local resident George Dorr in securing land donations. Recognized by the federal government as the Sieur de Monts National Monument in 1916, the land was redesignated as Lafayette National Park in 1919, becoming the first national park east of the Mississippi River. In 1929 the park was renamed Acadia National Park. Dorr was named the park's first superintendent and oversaw many early improvements, including carriage roads designed by landscape gardener Beatrix Farrand and John D. Rockefeller Jr., the financial patron for the park. A system of scenic drives was designed by Olmsted Brothers. The Blackwoods and Seawall Campgrounds were developed by the Civilian Conservation Corps (CCC) during the Great Depression. A 1947 fire devastated 10,000 acres of parkland, with subsequent restoration largely underwritten by the Rockefeller family.

The park encompasses some 49,000 acres across Mount Desert Island, Schoodic Peninsula, and numerous other coastal islands.

Trail systems implemented largely by Dorr and the CCC trace 125 miles of granite coastline, running through forests, wetlands, and over a series of twenty-six peaks. Farrand's carriage roads wind through fifty-seven miles of dense woodland on the eastern half of Desert Island, offering panoramic views of both the mountains and the Atlantic Ocean. Additionally, she advised on planting for various rustic structures throughout the park. Recognizing that automobiles were a necessary mode of transport, between 1929 and 1939 Frederick Law Olmsted Jr. and Henry V. Hubbard of the Olmsted Brothers firm adroitly inserted a sequence of vehicular roads into the rocky coastal terrain, providing access to varied scenic feature areas, such as freshwater glacial lakes and Cadillac Mountain. Praised for their skilled engineering in road alignment and grading and in the craftsmanship of rustic walls and bridges, Olmsted and Hubbard designed access ways such as the Otter Cliff and Stanley Brook Roads to maximize views and sightlines, while preserving attractive topography and vegetation. Contributing features of the park were listed in the National Register of Historic Places from 1988 to 2007.

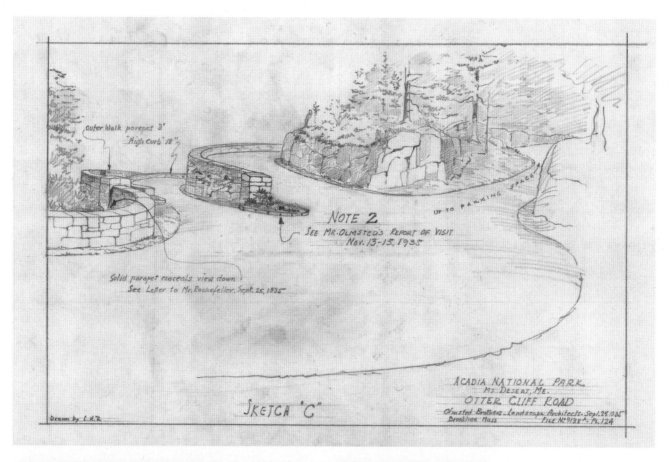

Outer Walk parapet 3'
"High curb" 18"

Solid parapet conceals view down
See Letter to Mr. Rockefeller, Sept. 25, 1935

NOTE 2.
SEE MR. OLMSTED'S REPORT OF VISIT
Nov. 13-15, 1935

UP TO PARKING SPACE

SKETCH "C"

ACADIA NATIONAL PARK
Mt. Desert, Me.
OTTER CLIFF ROAD
Olmsted Brothers - Landscape Architects- Sept. 25, 1935
Brookline Mass   File No. 9138ᴬ- Pl. 124

Drawn by L.H.Z.

Above: A 1935 sketch by the Olmsted firm shows the attention paid to directing sightlines and views along Otter Cliff Road—the design became reality and endures today. **Left:** Rustic bridges and infrastructure help the many Olmsted-planned scenic roadways to blend unobtrusively into the surrounding landscape.

Loose allées of trees still line the park walks behind the Maine capitol.

Drawing for Maine State Park, 1920.

MAINE STATE CAPITOL GROUNDS, AUGUSTA

The original Maine State House and Capitol Grounds were designed by Charles Bulfinch and built between 1829 and 1832. Bulfinch's landscape plan showed three terraced ovals surrounding the building, with trees delineating the edges of the terraces. A major redesign and enlargement in 1909 and 1910 led to significant expansion of the building footprint and subsequent removal of the terraces on each side of the building; the front portico and terraces facing Capitol Park remain intact.

In 1920, the same year that Maine celebrated the 100th anniversary of its separation from Massachusetts, Governor Carl Milliken moved into the newly remodeled Governor's Mansion adjacent to the State House. He commissioned the Olmsted Brothers firm, represented by Carl Rust Parker, to prepare plans for improving and uniting the complex of the Governor's Mansion (known as the Blaine House), State House, and Capitol Park to the east. The firm proposed planting improvements around the mansion and the State House, leaving the Bulfinch terraces intact but with improved alignment to State Street. For the park, the plans retained historical features and tree allées, while providing strong visual connections between the capitol, the Soldier's Memorial, and the Kennebec River, within a park setting that also offered recreational opportunities. Completed in the early 1920s, these plans were partially implemented.

Blaine House's front balustrades and front steps were realized according to Olmsted Brothers plans.

Major landscape rehabilitation of the grounds of the capitol complex began in the 1990s and included improved drainage, reconstruction of the extensive granite retaining wall that encircles the State House on three sides, and restoration of the iron fence on top of the wall, based on original castings. The Capitol Complex Historic District was listed in the National Register of Historic Places in 2001.

Fidelity to the original Olmsted Brothers plan for an allée of trees to line the main quadrangle has been maintained from inception to the present day.

UNIVERSITY OF MAINE, ORONO

The Morrill Act of 1862 provided for grants of land to states to finance the establishment of colleges specializing in "agriculture and the mechanic arts." In 1867, Olmsted and Vaux provided an initial campus plan for a "village" approach to a land-grant college for Maine, one of the first states to take advantage of the act. Frederick Law Olmsted Sr., who wrote the report for what became the Maine State College of Agriculture and Mechanic Arts, planned for self-sufficient students to live in clustered residential cottages surrounded by academic buildings, a military parade ground, agricultural fields, orchards, and an arboretum. The trustees retained some of this plan, including the basic orientation along the Stillwater River. As the academic offerings expanded over the following decades to include engineering, forestry, and more liberal arts—and, as women were admitted, beginning in 1872—the campus evolved with revised green spaces in 1893 and a plan by architects Little and Russell in 1923.

The Olmsted Brothers firm was selected in 1932 to address future campus growth. Led by Carl Rust Parker and Henry

Hubbard, the firm's plan called for a rectangular green space lined by elms along a north–south axis. This was divided by a central auditorium into the campus mall and south mall, each flanked by symmetrical buildings and various walkways. The plan included a naturalistic lake in the arboretum, relocated athletic fields, and other improvements. While the malls were implemented, the formal building alignment was not, and a 1948 plan revision eliminated the lake.

Today's 600-acre campus reflects elements of both the earlier and later Olmsted plans. The original riverside parade ground and arboretum remain open for recreation, river access, and to aid with flood control. The malls by the Olmsted Brothers firm (now planted with oaks) and some of the campus buildings are the most significant remaining aspects of their two plans. Renamed the University of Maine at Orono in 1897, the campus was listed in the National Register of Historic Places in 1978, augmented in 2010.

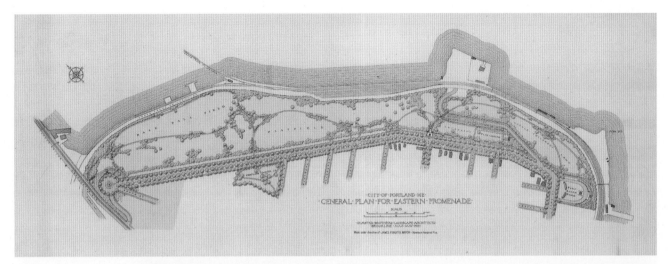

The Eastern Promenade takes advantage of views out over the sound **(above)**, while the Western Promenade commands views over the Fore River **(right)**.

PORTLAND PARKS, EASTERN AND WESTERN PROMENADES

Although land for the Eastern and Western Promenades was purchased as early as 1823, these tracts remained essentially undeveloped until 1878 when William Goodwin, the City of Portland's civil engineer, began improvements to capture their remarkable views of Casco Bay Islands to the east or the White Mountains to the west. His designs, carried out over the next decade, were to provide attractive places with distant prospects for "neighborly good fellowship" and exercise. At the seventy-three-acre Eastern Promenade, Goodwin laid out new roads between existing elms, adding gracious lawn areas down the slope with paths, a gazebo and monuments, and access to the water, with a beach for swimming. To grace the Western Promenade, abutting a growing neighborhood of substantial homes and the General Hospital, Goodwin widened the approaching streets into tree-lined esplanades with sidewalks and a terrace with a gazebo for looking out to the mountains and Fore River.

Sharing Goodwin's vision, Mayor James Phinney Baxter went to Boston in about 1893, to inspect the Olmsted, Olmsted, and Eliot work to transform the unsightly Fens and Muddy River into parkland, thereby attracting abutting residential

Above: The Western Promenade is a popular gathering area above the hubbub. **Right:** For a gorgeous scene out over the sound, the Eastern Promenade delivers.

development. He contacted the firm in 1894 to conduct similar improvements in Portland. Of particular concern was making the stagnant mud flats of tidal Back Cove attractive and healthful, and connecting to or acquiring Deering Oaks, an area with a multilayered history, to enhance integrated parklands for Portland (both properties were then in the separate town of Deering).

John Charles Olmsted's 1896 recommendations were to acquire this land and make sanitary improvements in the cove for a water park for pleasure boats, with a surrounding circuit drive, parkland, and subsequent developable land. Many of these ideas were partially achieved decades later. Regarding broader guidance, Olmsted, accompanied by Henry Hubbard, expanded his planning evaluations citywide, recommending more parkland to secure Eastern Promenade's outlook with seating and planting along curving paths, some level areas for playfields, and accessible trolley service. At Western Promenade, likewise, more land was needed to enable road regrading down the escarpment, for shaping a concourse and developing a hillside ramble. Deering Oaks, having been gifted to and purchased by Portland, had been improved by Goodwin with a lake with swan boats, a zoo, and architectural amenities, many of which John Olmsted criticized as wasteful investments. Instead, he envisioned tree-lined connections to this woodland park, enhanced within by walks, drives, and a shelter.

Olmsted's recommendations and improvements for Portland's parklands were only partially implemented, but these design principles still guide the city's current open space management. The Promenades were listed in the National Register of Historic Places in 1989.

MARYLAND

Parks and Parkways System, Baltimore | 127

Roland Park, Baltimore | 129

Sudbrook Park, Baltimore County | 130

Guilford Park, Baltimore | 131

Homeland Park, Baltimore | 132

Johns Hopkins University, Baltimore | 133

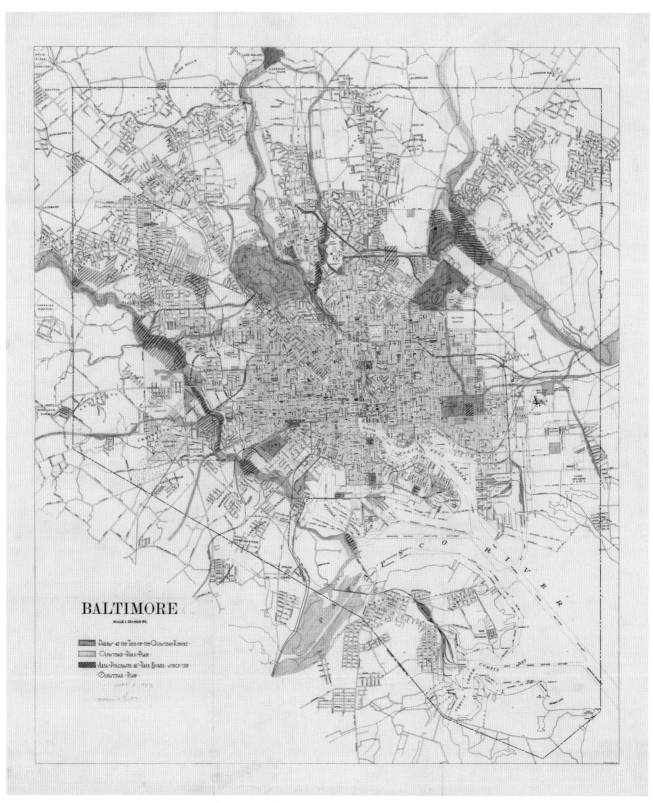

BALTIMORE

SCALE 1 IN.=8000 FT.

Parks at the Time of the Olmstead Report

Olmstead Park Plan

Area Purchased by Park Board since the Olmstead Plan

JUNE 2, 1924

A 1924 plan shows how continuing efforts to expand Baltimore's parks expanded on the original 1904 Olmsted plan.

A superimposed drawing for the Lafayette sculpture at Mount Vernon Square, circa 1902.

PARKS AND PARKWAYS SYSTEM, BALTIMORE

Baltimore was visionary when it acquired an English-style country estate in 1860 and hired Howard Daniels, landscape gardener, to oversee its transformation into a pastoral public park. The city was also visionary in designating a fraction of a trolley fare to pay for this endeavor. In 1876 Frederick Law Olmsted Sr. was engaged to create small parks to surround the Washington Monument in Mount Vernon Square while he was working on the US Capitol Grounds.

These were among the preexisting park spaces when, in 1902, the Municipal Art Society and the Park Board commissioned the Olmsted Brothers firm to create a plan for a citywide park system. Since Frederick Law Olmsted Jr. was working in Washington, DC, at the time, like his father before him, he responded to Baltimore's request. Heavily influenced by the

principles of the City Beautiful movement, civic leaders believed that a park system providing Baltimoreans with more access to natural, recreational space, would improve both their mental and physical health while directing urban growth away from the city center and toward the northwest suburbs, which had been annexed in 1888. Published in 1904, the resulting plan (titled "Report Upon the Development of Public Grounds for Baltimore") envisioned an interconnected system of "parked" (planted) boulevards linking preexisting parks to new recreational areas being acquired to encircle the city. These green corridors were intended not only to guide city growth, connecting to various public spaces along the route, but also to protect the stream valley environments with large park reservations to manage flooding, reminiscent of the work Charles Eliot

Row houses along 33rd Street face onto ample park space.

Many of the parks in Baltimore have a distinct character; Patterson Park has the pagoda, designed in 1890 by Charles H. Latrobe and fully restored in 2002.

had done with Boston's Metropolitan Park System. The report further recommended wise street layout to enable attractive residential patterning, thus stimulating developments such as Guilford and Homeland.

Among the significant results of the Olmsted Brothers firm's plan were the creation of parkways, often accompanying the stream corridors (Wyman, Jones Falls, Gwynns Falls), along with new parks (Wyman, Swann, and Latrobe) and improvements to existing parks (Druid Hill, Clifton, and Patterson). Implementation of the 1904 plan was largely overseen by Frederick Law Olmsted Jr. with his colleagues P. R. Jones and Percival Gallagher. Despite the enthusiasm of city leaders and the public, the park system was slow to develop, delayed by a devasting 1904 fire that destroyed much of downtown Baltimore. Budget cuts and rapid urban growth presented further

challenges to the original plan, not all of which came to fruition, also hampered by lack of a coordinating regional agency. In a follow-up report by Olmsted Brothers in 1926, the firm's Henry V. Hubbard addressed these lapses, calling for the creation of more parkways and stream valley reserves, using lands gained in a 1918 annexation. Although many of the recommendations were unrealized because of a lack of funding, the addition of Leakin Park to Gwynns Falls Park was one direct outcome.

A number of the parks are listed in the National Register of Historic Places, including Carroll (1970), Clifton (2007), Druid Hill (1973), and Patterson (2002). Mount Vernon Place is included in the Mount Vernon Historic District (1971). In 1986 the Friends of Maryland's Olmsted Parks and Landscapes was founded to advance the Olmsted legacy through advocacy, education, and preservation.

Broad, leafy, curving streets and properties of architectural distinction and artistry characterize Roland Park.

ROLAND PARK, BALTIMORE

This three-square-mile suburb northwest of Baltimore, comprising more than 800 acres on mixed terrain, developed between 1890 and 1920 and was one of the most successful and widely imitated of the so-called "streetcar suburbs." It was the city's first residential subdivision to incorporate deed restrictions that conveyed with the property. Such "restrictive covenants," originally intended to ensure a high quality of design and standard of construction, unfortunately also became a tool for social and ethnic exclusions.

In 1891, Edward Bouton, the general manager of real estate developer Roland Park Company, engaged Kansas City landscape architect and planner George Kessler to lay out Plat 1, a relatively flat site. In 1901 the development expanded to Plat 2, which held more topographically complex acreage, and where Frederick Law Olmsted Jr. shaped the challenging hillsides into a scenic landscape of hills, valleys, forest, and open space. The resulting community was characterized by good sanitation, electric lighting, carefully planted curvilinear streets, and a network of connective pathways between house lots and small parklets. Over time a total of six plans were developed, mostly for families of wealth, with eclectic architectural groupings referencing both historical styles and the Arts and Crafts movement. Architect Charles Platt designed all of the houses and landscape features on the street known as Goodwood Gardens. Bouton facilitated the construction of an elevated railway link to the city, as well as University Parkway, which connected the suburb to major city roads. Bouton is also credited with developing the first planned shopping center in the country, built in the English Tudor style, as a community amenity. Now home to more than 11,000 residents, Roland Park was listed in the National Register of Historic Places in 1974.

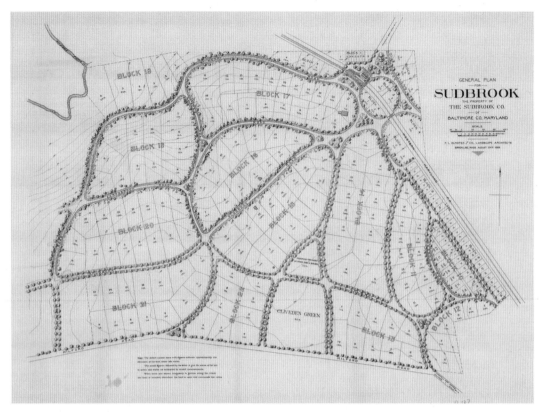

Sudbrook Park's original plan called for each property to consist of a lot of at least one acre.

SUDBROOK PARK, BALTIMORE COUNTY

In 1889 Frederick Law Olmsted Sr. presented plans to developers for a summer resort community west of the Baltimore city limits. Sudbrook Park was built on 204 acres of James Howard McHenry's estate. Among the small residential communities designed by the senior Olmsted, it prefigured an evolution in the popular form of the American suburb. To ensure a pastoral setting and prevent cutting through the neighborhood, curvilinear streets with accompanying sidewalks were carefully laid out on rolling topography. Deed restrictions required each single-family home to be placed on a lot of at least one acre, with houses set back forty feet or more from the street and ten or more feet from neighboring property lines. This reinforced the open, rural atmosphere of the neighborhood.

Triangular green spaces located at several intersections were also included in the original plan to serve as informal community gathering places. In keeping with the character of a resort community, the original development included a hotel, swimming pool, stables, and a nine-hole golf course; these amenities were eventually replaced by additional homes. The Western Maryland Railway Station at the community's eastern edge afforded easy commuter access to the city, and Sudbrook Park soon became a prominent and desirable suburban neighborhood. Home to more than 2000 residents, while present-day Sudbrook Park is surrounded by additional residential enclaves, much of Olmsted Sr.'s original design intent for the community remains intact. Sudbrook Park was listed in the National Register of Historic Places in 1973.

Property—both communal and private—continues to be lovingly maintained in the Guilford Historic District.

GUILFORD PARK, BALTIMORE

In 1911 the Roland Park Company purchased land once belonging to the Guilford Estate to develop this suburban neighborhood just north of what was then the Baltimore city line. The 210-acre site contained rolling hills on its western portion and sections of oak forest throughout. Frederick Law Olmsted Jr., of the Olmsted Brothers firm, directed the planning and design of the residential community, with the first lots sold in 1913. Development was substantially complete by 1950. Four primary roadways take curving routes from north to south, crossed by many narrower, secondary roads, thus discouraging through traffic and leaving ample space for sidewalks, expanses of lawn, and generous setbacks.

Faced with extant development across York Road, the eastern edge of the plan included multiple residences combined within large buildings that were clustered to form "places."

Three public parks were built within the community: Little Park (now Guilford Gateway Park) along Saint Paul Street; Stratford Green (now Sherwood Gardens) near the neighborhood center; and Sunken Park, which included an outdoor performance space with a raised ground surface for a stage and evergreens to serve as theater wings. As an additional amenity, semiprivate parks occupied the interiors of several blocks, intended for use by the residents of adjoining lots. In addition to the carefully devised site plan, Guilford included progressive amenities and infrastructure, such as underground conduits for telephone and electric cables, streetlights, and separate stormwater and sanitary sewers. The Guilford Historic District was listed in the National Register of Historic Places in 2001 and is home to more than 4500 residents.

Homeland Park retains ample canopy trees, sidewalks, and setbacks to create generous yards—enviable details for a neighborhood since enveloped by the surrounding city.

HOMELAND PARK, BALTIMORE

Located in northern Baltimore, this suburb was built on 391 acres of hilly, partially forested terrain, which was once a farm and country estate owned by the Perine family. In 1924 the Edward Bouton–led Roland Park Company, following the successes of the Roland Park and Guilford suburbs, purchased the land and began constructing a new residential community. While he was heavily involved in the design process, Bouton again enlisted the Olmsted Brothers firm to plan the suburb, which is bounded on the south by Homeland Avenue, on the north by Melrose Avenue, on the west by North Charles Street, and on the east by York Road and Bellona Avenue.

The Olmsted Brothers plan was sensitive to the existing landscape. A chain of stream-fed ponds dug during the Perine era were retained and enhanced, becoming a defining feature of the community along Springlake Way, while the ellipse-shaped roadways along Saint Albans Way echoed the looping carriage drives that once faced the Perine mansion. Balancing the needs of access and circulation with those of privacy, the Olmsted Brothers plan also included a distinct street hierarchy, with broad arterial boulevards serving as gateways and running through the neighborhood, where they connected to smaller secondary streets and courts, the latter insulating residents from the city's noise and traffic. The streets were lined with sidewalks and large canopy trees, with the houses set back uniformly to create ample front lawns. Parcels were also set aside for community uses, such as parks, schools, and churches. In addition to careful street planning, the Homeland Park community also benefitted from modern amenities, which included underground conduits for telephone and electric cables, streetlights, and separated stormwater and sanitary sewers. The Greater Homeland Historic District was listed in the National Register of Historic Places in 2001.

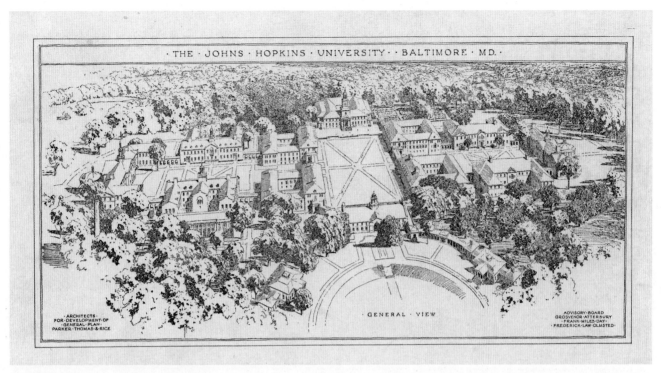

The architecture and landscape were conceived to work in harmony, as seen in this drawing submitted by Parker, Thomas, and Rice and Frederick Law Olmsted Jr. (n.d.).

JOHNS HOPKINS UNIVERSITY, BALTIMORE

This 140-acre campus in north Baltimore was established on the site of the Homewood Estate, originally the residence of Charles Carroll Jr., the son of Founding Father Charles Carroll. The university had been located in the city's Mount Vernon neighborhood since its inception in 1876 but by 1894, required room for expansion. University board member William Wyman, then-owner of Homewood, partnered with his cousin William Keyser to reassemble the divided estate, which was then given to the university. In 1904 the firm Parker and Thomas was selected to design the new campus, the final plan coming to fruition in 1914. Warren Manning submitted early planting plans for the campus landscape, and the Olmsted Brothers firm crafted myriad plans for the campus between 1905 and 1917, establishing the design of the two original quadrangles and the grading around academic buildings. The 1904 report by the Olmsted Brothers

firm on the city's parks and parkways proposed a division of the Homewood Estate into parkland and campus, and the university did indeed cede land to the city for the creation of Wyman Park and the Wyman Park Dell.

The core of the campus was laid out in a "T" comprising two adjacent, perpendicular quadrangles, each an open expanse of lawn crossed sparingly by walking paths and framed by Federalist-style buildings. Keyser Quadrangle (constituting the shorter, east–west axis) is bordered on the west by Gilman Hall, the university's first academic building, completed in 1915. Large canopy trees line the quadrangle and frame views of the stately building. A brick-paved plaza connects the Keyser Quadrangle to Wyman Quadrangle (forming the longer, north–south axis) to the south, which runs parallel to North Charles Street along the site's eastern border. A circular drive marks the primary entrance

Top and above: The quadrangle planning and design espoused by the Olmsted firm is evident today.

to the campus from North Charles Street, passing in front of the former Carroll residence, Homewood House (now a museum and National Historic Landmark). Subsequent growth has accrued around this original core, including a cluster of academic buildings directly to the north (and a large athletic complex beyond, bordering University Parkway); Decker Quadrangle to the west; Freshman Quadrangle to the northeast; and Decker Gardens to the northwest (established circa 1915 and originally known as the Botanical Gardens, used to cultivate plants for research). From 2000 to 2002, the campus underwent a major renovation, which converted many paved roads to brick walkways and rehabilitated the original entrance circle, among other modifications.

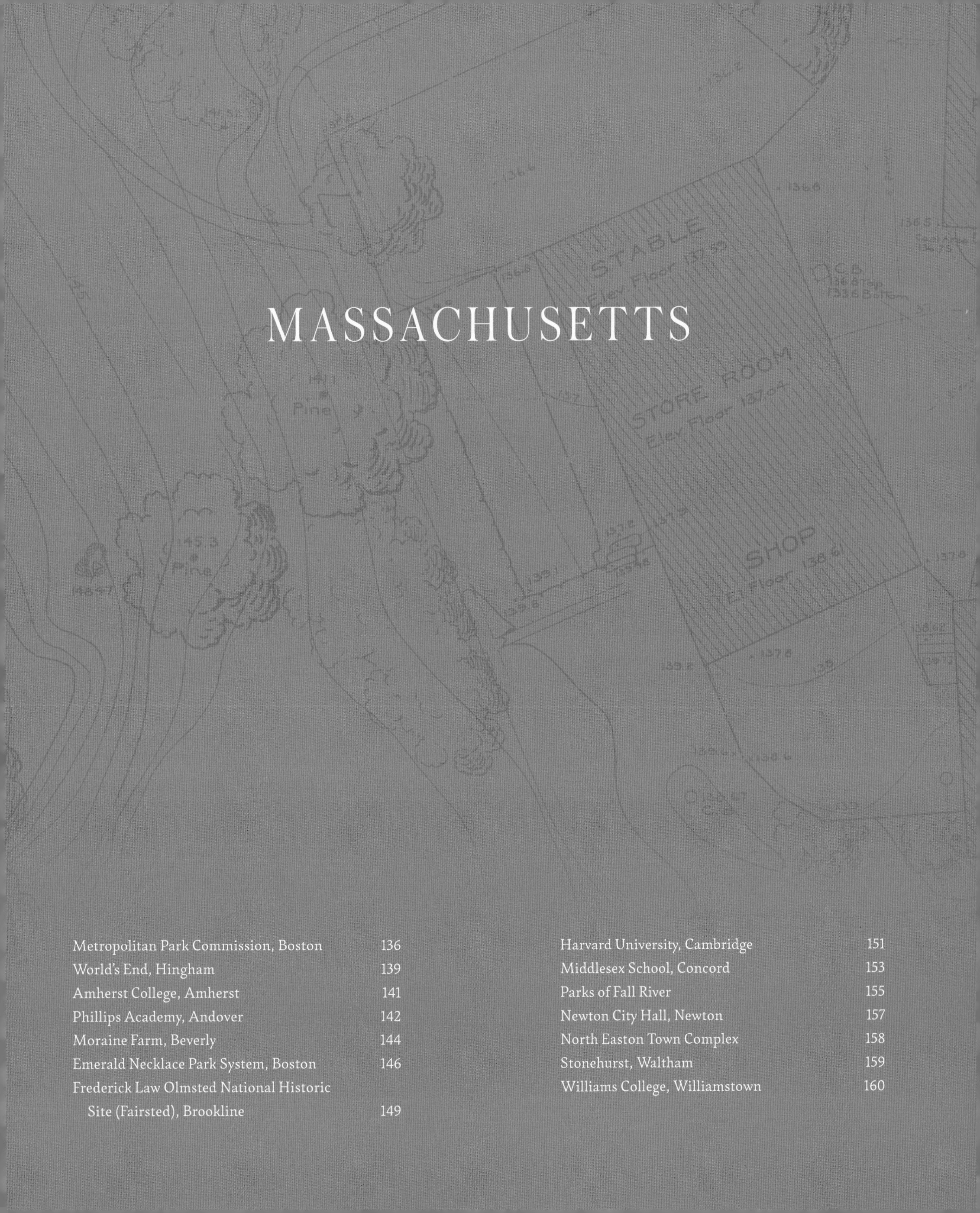

MASSACHUSETTS

Metropolitan Park Commission, Boston — 136

World's End, Hingham — 139

Amherst College, Amherst — 141

Phillips Academy, Andover — 142

Moraine Farm, Beverly — 144

Emerald Necklace Park System, Boston — 146

Frederick Law Olmsted National Historic
    Site (Fairsted), Brookline — 149

Harvard University, Cambridge — 151

Middlesex School, Concord — 153

Parks of Fall River — 155

Newton City Hall, Newton — 157

North Easton Town Complex — 158

Stonehurst, Waltham — 159

Williams College, Williamstown — 160

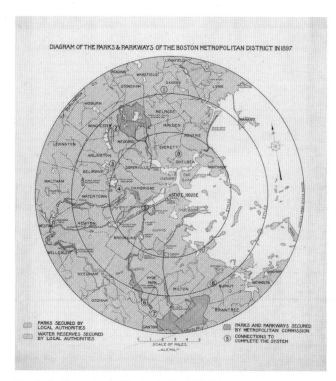

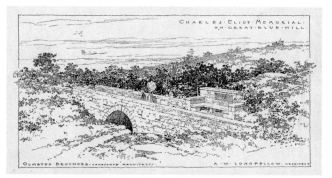

Clockwise from above: Diagram by the MPC as it works to secure and connect parkland across greater Boston, 1897. Drawing for the Charles Eliot Memorial Bridge by Arthur Shurcliff; Eliot was a landscape architect who founded The Trustees, in the Blue Hills Reservation. The Charles River Esplanade provides recreational opportunities for pedestrians and boaters alike.

METROPOLITAN PARK COMMISSION, BOSTON

Dismayed that rampant development of the late nineteenth century was threatening characteristic geomorphic landscape features in the Boston metropolitan area, many of which extended over several municipal boundaries, landscape architect Charles Eliot and journalist Sylvester Baxter explored ways to permanently protect these places for public enjoyment, as great artworks are protected in a museum.

Their considerations led to the creation of the country's first regional agency to acquire and manage land, regardless of jurisdiction, to be developed as publicly accessible, minimally disturbed parkland reservations and to be protected for their unique qualities and scenic beauty. Within a ten-mile radius of Boston, thousands of acres of large and small properties were purchased or gifted, determined by Eliot's five categories: ocean-front, inner bay shores and islands, tidal estuaries, outer rim forest, and small squares and parks in the city's densely populated areas. It was of utmost importance to Eliot that the geography of the region should inform the selection of park sites. Today, the system encompasses nearly 20,000 acres of public reservations, connected by parkways in a comprehensive network.

The impetus for the establishment of the system was an 1890 article by Eliot published in *Garden and Forest*, in which he discussed the importance of preserving landscape assets to be held in public trust, such as the Waverly Oaks in Waltham. The next year, he suggested protecting landscapes of more historic value, which were often private in nature, such as great estates, an idea

Clockwise from top left: The Esplanade in an early incarnation (n.d.). The Charles River Esplanade provides recreational opportunities for pedestrians and boaters alike. Revere Beach, roughly five miles north of downtown Boston. Small sailboats are a popular sight in coves along the Charles River.

which led to the 1891 founding of The Trustees of Reservations (The Trustees), to hold such properties in the public interest. By 1893 persistent efforts by Baxter and Eliot had enabled legislation establishing the Boston Metropolitan Park Commission (MPC) to oversee this system of diverse landscapes.

Beaver Brook Reservation, a typical mill stream flowing between Belmont and Waltham, was the first acquired, partly by gift and partly by purchase, in order to protect the Waverly Oaks, ancient white oaks grown to immense size on the rich alluvial soil. Other early MPC acquisitions were the reservations around the Blue Hills, the Hemlock Gorge, Middlesex Fells, and Stony Brook. By 1900, connecting parkways and coastal reservations had been added to protect Revere and Nantasket Beaches, shorelines in Quincy and Lynn, and riversides along the Charles, Mystic, and Neponset Rivers.

In 1919, the MPC became the Metropolitan District Commission when it merged with the metropolitan water and sewer district. Significant properties continued to be added, such as the Boston Harbor Islands, and other metropolitan responsibilities. Eventually, this regional agency became inefficient and unwieldy to manage. The metropolitan parks and ancillary services split from the water and sewer services and are now under the jurisdiction of the Massachusetts Department of Conservation and Recreation. The whole system, as well as many individual reservations and parkways, are listed in the National Register of Historic Places.

Above: Waverly white oaks, whose existence spurred the creation of the Beaver Brook Reservation to protect them (n.d.). **Center left and right:** Before and after interventions at the tree–clogging notch near the southeastern escarpment of the Fells. **Bottom left:** The mill race at Hemlock Gorge. **Bottom right:** Fall view of the Blue Hills Reservation.

The Trustees of Reservations have restored natural habitats and preserved Olmsted-designed carriage routes as walking paths on World's End.

WORLD'S END, HINGHAM

This 251-acre peninsula is located fifteen miles south of Boston in Hingham and features panoramic views of the Boston skyline and Boston Harbor. Included in the Boston Harbor Islands National Recreation Area, World's End was an island before it was dammed and infilled by farmers in the 1880s.

Owned by Boston businessman John Brewer during the late nineteenth century, World's End was initially a site with active farming. In 1890 Brewer hired Frederick Law Olmsted Sr. to design a subdivision on the land. The planned community was never built, but Olmsted's design for the 163-house residential district was partially realized in the creation of tree-lined carriage roads that are currently maintained as walking paths.

World's End has faced redevelopment several times since Brewer and Olmsted abandoned their residential community plan. In 1945 the site was a finalist for the headquarters of the United Nations. Twenty years later, it was considered for the site of a nuclear power plant. Fearful of losing access to land, residents of Hingham facilitated the property's purchase by The Trustees of Reservations in 1967. Since then, The Trustees have maintained this popular park (including the Olmsted-designed circulation system) and restored natural habitats with the goal of promoting biodiversity. World's End now offers diverse ecological features, including a rocky shoreline, four drumlin hills, saltwater marshes, meadows, and woodlands, in addition to the spectacular views it provides—in particular, north to the Boston skyline.

Above: Amherst, showing the sloping hillside prominently (n.d.). Below: Students still gather on the quad.

AMHERST COLLEGE, AMHERST

A private liberal arts university, Amherst College was founded in 1821 and built on land owned by poet Emily Dickinson's grandfather, Samuel Fowler Dickinson. Established as a men's college, Amherst admitted women beginning in 1975.

The original campus was situated on a prominent hill bounded by Pleasant Street (west) and College Drive (north), with a railway and fields to the south and east, respectively. There are panoramic views out over the surrounding landscape. The grade across the hills involves a 100-foot drop to the west and a thirty- to forty-foot drop north to College Street. The campus in 1870 consisted of three buildings built in the 1820s: Johnson Chapel flanked by North and South College Buildings, situated on the hill fronting Pleasant Street and looking west to the town over an expansive green. On a perpendicular axis to College Street was Walker Hall, with many steps down the hill and a circular drive (Noah Webster Circle) at the base.

Campus development involved multiple generations of the Olmsted firm under its various names: Olmsted and Vaux; F. L. Olmsted and Company; Olmsted, Olmsted, and Eliot; and concluded with the Olmsted Brothers. In 1870 Frederick Law Olmsted Sr. wrote that none of the suggested sites were suitable for a proposed church because the building would exist by itself in the landscape, and buildings need to be placed among other buildings. He further explained that the college should not locate buildings focused outward to the town, as the existing structures were, but should take advantage of the two hills to create an intervening internal campus. In 1883 Olmsted reiterated his opinion about locating buildings, this time regarding a new gymnasium, to take best advantage of the grades and other buildings, noting, ". . . this requires serious studying."

The relationship between the school and Olmsted firms continued into the 1890s, first with John Charles Olmsted aided by Herbert J. Kellaway evaluating the progress of grading plans. During a collaboration between J. C. Olmsted and the architecture firm McKim, Mead, and White on the location and grades for a new science building (Fayerweather Hall), the need for an overall campus plan resurfaced. In 1903 Charles S. Norton (class of 1893) contacted Frederick Law Olmsted Jr. to explore creating a commission to develop a general plan. By 1906 the trustees of the college had created the Commission for Improvements to Amherst College and appointed architects Charles Follen McKim, his partner William Rutherford Mead (an Amherst graduate), Daniel H. Burnham, sculptor Augustus Saint-Gaudens, and Olmsted Jr, all of whom had been involved in the Chicago 1893 Exposition planning.

The Commission was directed to prepare a general plan to site new buildings and laboratories, more effectively use the hillside conditions, and to make recommendations for beautifying the grounds. The 1906 report, penned by Mead and Olmsted Jr., reiterates Olmsted Sr.'s ideas concerning locations for certain buildings, keeping the oldest section intact and placing new buildings between the Walker Building and College Street wherever the terrain permitted. It also makes recommendations for land acquisition. In 1916, during a second collaboration between Olmsted and Mead on a library location, the university's trustees accepted the building design and location, and agreed to continue to honor the general plan. The plan was overseen by an honorary commission, on which Olmsted Jr., assisted by Edward C. Whiting, served until 1925.

The campus today measures 1000 acres with over 1800 students and, to a great degree, retains the original idea conceived by Olmsted Sr.—a campus with an internal series of nested quads to best take advantage of the site.

The contemporary campus retains many of the earlier planning elements, including geometric quadrangles and a heavy use of deciduous trees to delineate and define space.

PHILLIPS ACADEMY, ANDOVER

Established in 1778 by Samuel Phillips Jr. as a male preparatory school in a historical mill town north of Boston, the academy was joined in 1808 by Andover Theological Seminary to train Calvinist ministers, in 1827 by the short-lived Teachers' Seminary, and in 1828 by Abbot Academy to educate young women (merging into full coeducation by 1973). The "campus" formed by these institutions was bisected by Main Street running north and south and segmented further by numerous east–west streets. Eventually, these schools would become part of a single entity, requiring expansion and rearrangement of the campus footprint.

The Academy Hill area experienced periods of expansion in 1810–1835 and 1900–1935, the second expansion involving land acquisition, new construction, building relocation, and landscape development. Just prior to the 1900s expansion, the academy contacted Frederick Law Olmsted Sr. to develop a master plan in connection with new cottage-like dormitories. As a fifteen-year-old (1837 and 1838), Olmsted Sr. had lived on the campus when studying with Frederick Augustus Barton, a surveyor, civil engineer, and mathematics teacher at the Academy. Although the senior Olmsted was too ill at the time to respond, this request would commence an engagement with

the Olmsted firm that continued for more than five decades, involving projects of diverse sizes and typologies, respectful of historical spatial character while ensuring an aesthetically cohesive campus as an immersive learning environment.

John Charles Olmsted responded to the request, soon joined by Frederick Law Olmsted Jr. and firm assistants Herbert J. Kellaway and George Gibbs, among others, advising on locations for new buildings (including a heating plant, archeology museum, and gymnasium), for roads and paths, and for grading and planting. By 1908, the seminary had moved off campus. In acquiring their buildings, the academy realigned its spatial focus regarding the Great Lawn, which was surrounded by Federalist-style halls (Foxcroft, plus the Charles Bulfinch–designed Pearson and Bartlet). New Georgian-style buildings were added around the edges. Olmsted work during this period, now supervised by Percival Gallagher, involved both sides of Main Street, siting new academic buildings, dormitories, and an infirmary; improvements to the Main Street corridor; and advice about tree care, particularly the great elm walk. For the latter, Hans J. Koehler, the Olmsted firm's chief horticulturist, began a consultation for the campus which continued for years.

A historical photograph of the campus shows how canopy trees greatly embellish the quadrangle's geometry.

After 1919, Edward C. Whiting joined Gallagher in planning, collaborating with architect Charles Platt, who was hired in 1921 to design new buildings. Instead, during the next decade, Platt's work substantially reconfigured the campus with his Beaux Arts–inspired master plan. He strengthened the axial vista across Main Street, adding cross-axes to define the Great Quadrangle, all reinforced by building placement, either new or moved, and by planting patterns of elms, oaks, lindens, and evergreens. A 1923 Olmsted planting plan and a grand model, which the firm fabricated, guided these horticultural embellishments and visual linkages. During the 1930s, in addition to various garden renovations, Olmsted contributions involved designing the Moncrieff Cochran Bird Sanctuary (a wildlife refuge on the outer campus) and designing faculty housing. Final involvements of the Olmsted firm—in 1954 for a student union and in 1964 for new circulation around the West Quadrangle—were not implemented as planned.

Today, the Andover campus of Phillips Academy measures over 700 acres with a student population of more than 1100. The school has taken great care to harmoniously steward its rich architectural and landscape heritage, ensuring that the intended compositions of orchestrated visual and spatial experiences are retained, as it continually adapts to changing demands. The Academy Hill Historic District was listed in the National Register of Historic Places in 1982.

MORAINE FARM, BEVERLY

In 1880 Frederick Law Olmsted Sr. began planning a country estate for John C. Phillips on 200 acres of rolling woods (and exhausted farmland) overlooking Lake Wenham. Urging Phillips to make this property more than either a gentleman's farm or a decorated country mansion, Olmsted Sr. crafted grounds which retained the beauty of the natural conditions to surround a substantial country dwelling, while enhancing the productive potential of the land. In so doing, he created the template for his later recommendations to George Vanderbilt regarding the much more extensive North Carolina grounds at Biltmore.

Through a rural stone wall next to a modest cottage, the entrance drive curves sinuously among shadowy woods, with textured verges of flowering trees and shrubs, unexpectedly enlivened by occasional cross-views along trails and meadows, or brief glimpses through foliage of the agricultural complex. This interplay of light and shade terminates at an oval, open lawn before a substantial rusticated shingle and boulder house, designed by Peabody and Stearns.

Olmsted Sr. reshaped the land on which the house is sited, so that there is no inkling of the scenery beyond. It is upon passing through the house that the lake vistas are revealed. Working with the architects and John C. Olmsted, he designed a gracefully curving, paved terrace thrust out over the steep slope to capture lakeside views, enclosed by a robust sitting wall. Below, he placed meandering paths along the water's edge amid a wild garden of ferns, herbaceous plants, and rhododendrons. From the terrace on the south side of the house, Olmsted Sr. placed a series of "open air apartments," beginning with the long lawn sequestered from the entry road by that impervious green "wall," edged by vertical boulders terminating at a tea house. Steps descending on each side reach a colorful sunken flower garden, replete with a bench in a picturesque grotto and fountain. Radiating paths lead to steps which descend still further to distant trails.

From the house, looping carriage drives lead through diverse landscape experiences to the property's edges. To enhance the natural effect of this moraine, Olmsted Sr. had suggested that Phillips embark upon a program of tree planting—conifers, elms, and basswood to intersperse with the native hickory and birch—creating a forest effect west of the house and surrounding pastures and farmland. For the latter, Olmsted improved drainage to return tired land to productivity.

In the 1920s, part of this property was purchased by the Batchelder family, who increased their holding to 180 acres. They have been remarkable stewards of Olmsted's vision. Generous in providing access to public and professional audiences, their legacy has been to develop a partnership of nonprofit organizations, to own, manage, and maintain the landscape into the future. The Essex County Greenbelt Association holds a conservation restriction; the Cape Ann Waldorf School owns eight acres and runs a school, and The Trustees owns seventy-eight acres and runs a sustainable agricultural project with Tufts University. The Batchelder Family Trust still holds sixty acres. The remaining sixty-six acres, including the house and surrounds, currently owned by Project Adventure, an educational team-building organization, will soon be acquired by The Trustees (who will continue to enable Project Adventure to retain use of the property for its educational mission). Friends of the Olmsted Landscape at Moraine Farm have worked cooperatively with all entities to assist in rehabilitating, sustaining, and interpreting the landscape integrity of this Olmsted icon.

Above: The tea house and its grotto. **Right:** A sitting wall overlooks Wenham Lake.

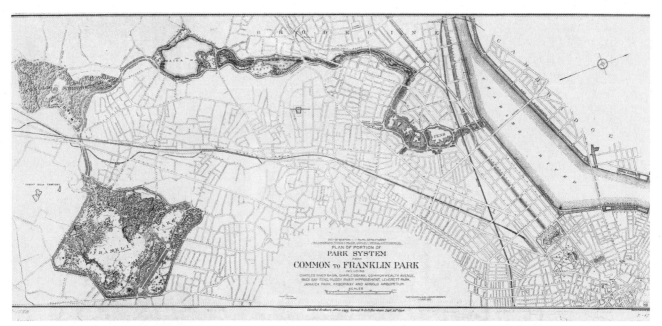

Partial plan of Boston's park system, 1894.

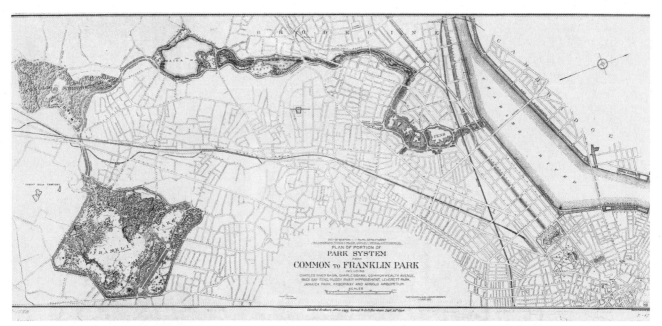

EMERALD NECKLACE PARK SYSTEM, BOSTON

This park system stretches from the Boston Common (in the Back Bay) to Franklin Park (in Dorchester). Designed between 1872 and 1895 by Frederick Law Olmsted Sr. with Charles Eliot, John Charles Olmsted, and Frederick Law Olmsted Jr., it is perhaps the first urban greenway in the world.

The core of the 1100-acre system connected the Colonial-era Boston Common (1634), the Public Garden (1837), and the Commonwealth Avenue Mall (1860s–1880s) to five new parks and an arboretum, designed as components of the "Sanitary Improvement of the Muddy River" (1881). These consisted of the Back Bay Fens (originally a malodorous tidal wetland, channelized, cleansed, and planted into a meandering scenic stream to absorb floodwaters); the Riverway (a more linear waterway with passages of riverine scenery, terminating in parkland around Leverett Pond, now known as Olmsted Park, described by the senior Olmsted as "a chain of . . . freshwater ponds, alternating with attractive natural groups and meads"); Jamaica Pond (a seventy-acre pond formed by an ancient glacier, the largest freshwater body in Boston, noted by Olmsted Sr. as "a natural sheet of water, with quiet graceful shores . . . for the most part shaded

by a fine natural forest growth."); the Arnold Arboretum (120 acres transferred to Harvard College in 1872 for the creation of an arboretum—Olmsted Sr. and Charles Sprague Sargent drafted the 1000-year lease for this naturalistic design that respected the site's existing topography and vegetation while adding the rich range of trees and shrubs suitable for a scientific collection); and West Roxbury Park, now Franklin Park. At 527 acres, West Roxbury was the largest park in the system and had two sections: the Country Park portion, which represented two-thirds of the acreage, and the remaining space, known as Ante Park, with a zoo and otherwise dedicated to active recreation. The parks were linked by parkways (the Arborway, Jamaicaway, Riverway, and Fenway), resulting in a comprehensive system of water, meadows, and woodland, measuring more than five miles in length.

These richly vegetated parks were furnished with numerous built features, many composed of local stone. Architect H. H. Richardson designed several notable examples in the form of bridges (for instance, Boylston Street Bridge in the Fens), structures (Stony Brook Gate House in the Fens) and gates (the South Street entrance at the Arnold). John Charles Olmsted

Clockwise from top right: Benches and a broad walk line Jamaica Pond. New England's stone walls are well represented by Franklin Park's Ellicott Arch. The improved Riverway in 1920, twenty-eight years after its completion. The Riverway's bridge in autumn.

also contributed designs for a number of landscape features, including bridges (Agassiz and Fen), buildings (shelters and overlooks) and walls (the surrounding stone wall and entries of the Arnold Arboretum), as did several other local architects.

The Olmsted firm continued to consult on the parks until the 1920s, including collaborations on the Back Bay Fens between the Olmsted Brothers and their former associate, Arthur Shurcliff, who was by that time practicing independently.

A state-funded Olmsted parks preservation project in the mid-1980s resulted in a major master planning process for Emerald Necklace parks; implementation continues today to recapture and sustain the intended character for these spaces. An area

along the Muddy River which had been culverted and paved for a parking lot in 1959 was returned to parkland in 2016, now named for former Parks Commissioner Justine Liff, who had overseen the process. River dredging and bank restoration according to the master plan continues to return these riverine parks to a healthy ecosystem, sustained by a unique consortium of federal, state, and local funding and collaborative citizen oversight.

The Emerald Necklace was listed in the National Register of Historic Places as the Olmsted Park System in 1971, while the Fens and Franklin Park are Boston landmarks. In 1996 the Emerald Necklace Conservancy was created to protect, restore, maintain, and promote the park system.

Clockwise from top: As of 1903, sheep were still grazing in Franklin Park. Enjoying a promenade in Marine Park, circa 1900. Enjoying the Arnold Arboretum in the 1920s.

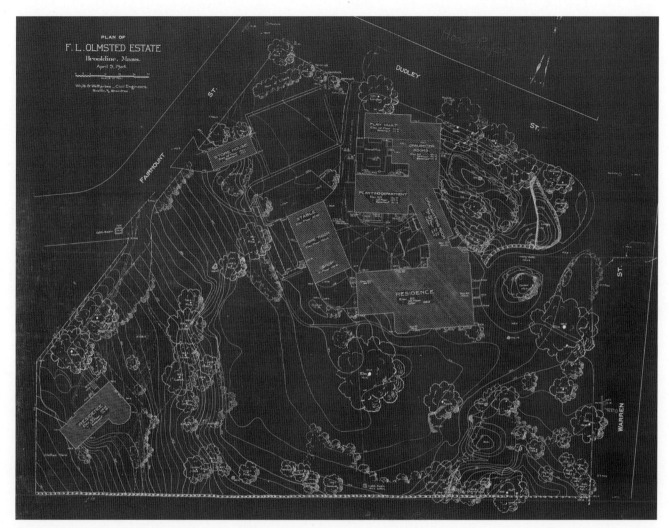

Plan of the F. L. Olmsted Sr. Estate, 1904.

FREDERICK LAW OLMSTED NATIONAL HISTORIC SITE
(FAIRSTED), BROOKLINE

After being awarded the commission to design the Emerald Necklace, Frederick Law Olmsted Sr. moved his home and office to a farmhouse in Brookline in 1883, naming the property Fairsted. Transforming the one-and-three-quarters-acre agrarian property into a Picturesque landscape was a initially a collaboration between Olmsted Sr. and John Charles Olmsted, who oversaw most of the construction. In later years, other firm members worked on the landscape, including Hans J. Koehler, who played an integral role in the horticultural development of the grounds between 1910 and 1930.

Working within a hilly residential neighborhood of country roads, Olmsted Sr. created grounds around his home office to

Above: A curved entrance drive and a glimpse of planned plantings, at left, hint at how Olmsted used his home as an example of the Picturesque style. **Left:** Views of the property in 1900.

exemplify his domestic landscape ideals for a small plot. For privacy, he screened out the nearby streets with massed vegetation along vine-covered, spruce-pole fences, with an arch over the entrance drive which circled around a central hemlock. On the north side of this drive, a sunken hollow, the remains of a former gravel pit, was transformed into a mysterious grotto-like space, reached by stone steps, with textured plantings scrambling among the Roxbury puddingstones of its steep slopes. To the south, abutting a glass-enclosed plant room, he shaped an ample lawn, surrounded by layers of shrubs, with a stately elm for shade. In the southeast corner, a small ramble among evergreens provided another area of interest. The clapboard house was covered with trellises to hold the dense vines intended to encase the structure, subordinating the house to the landscape

and reinforcing the desired ambiance of wildness and the "profusion of nature." Beginning in the 1890s, connecting structures were added to the house to provide necessary office space as the practice grew. An additional barn and workshop were constructed, all entered from the service drive on the western side of the property.

Fairsted was named a National Historic Site and designated a National Historic Landmark in 1963, and was listed in the National Register of Historic Places in 1966. In 1980 the National Park Service acquired the property, including the house and its contents. During the 1990s, under a major landscape rehabilitation program, hundreds of invasives were removed, replaced with herbaceous plants, shrubs, and trees in accordance with plans and photographs dating to the 1930s.

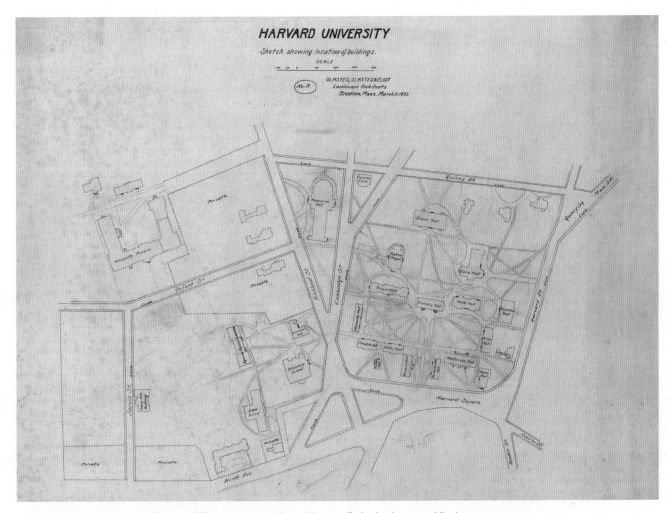

A plan showing buildings and walkways in 1893, the same year Harvard began offering landscape architecture courses.

HARVARD UNIVERSITY, CAMBRIDGE

Harvard University, founded in 1636 in Cambridge, was the first institution of higher learning established by the British colonies. The Harvard campus was at the edge of wilderness when the first buildings were built, but by the early nineteenth century, the school had grown such that the medical school had moved across the Charles River to Boston. By the 1890s, to accommodate the expanding educational curriculum, the university had spread throughout the growing city of Cambridge, again crossing the river into Boston's Allston neighborhood

with several facilities. The university had increased its offerings in various programs for graduate degrees, particularly under the presidency of Charles W. Eliot (1869–1909) whose son was an early apprentice, later a partner, of Frederick Law Olmsted Sr.

Architecture became a graduate school in 1874, while landscape architecture began as an 1893 course, expanded to a full program in 1900, and later became a separate school which included urban planning in 1913. Frederick Law Olmsted Jr., along with former Olmsted firm apprentices including Arthur

Historic buildings and stately trees imbue Harvard Yard with a sense of age and dignity.

Shurcliff and Henry Hubbard, developed the landscape and planning programs.

The historical core of the Harvard campus was, and continues to be, a twenty-five-acre, tree-shaded green surrounded by the university's earliest buildings. As buildings were built beyond this core, the university became involved in ameliorating its urban surrounds and melding its needs with the business and residential concerns of the city beyond. As a landscape architect, early planner, Olmsted partner, and son of Harvard President Charles W. Eliot, Charles Eliot applied his skills and those of the Olmsted firm to addressing these growing concerns. Of particular note were his attempts to gracefully pattern street routes to shape land blocks, providing easy accessibility for university mini-campuses beyond the core. Beyond advising on settings and plantings for new buildings and roads, tasks included locating university residential halls, libraries, museums, laboratories, academic buildings, sports complexes, and many ancillary service structures.

Before his untimely death in 1897, Eliot was also engaged in planning for parkways and parkland along the banks of the Charles River, to both accommodate recreational needs for an increasing population and to provide green space to absorb river floods. Olmsted Jr. and the Olmsted firm continued this planning, integrating dignified approaches from the river to Harvard Square, incorporating Harvard's recreational grounds and stadium, now in Allston, with parkways across the river, and working with a series of architects to locate new residential facilities along the river shores. As the medical school outgrew its downtown locale, in 1903 the Olmsted firm connected their new Longwood Avenue campus with the developing Fens park, part of the iconic Emerald Necklace park system. More than twenty years later, work led by Henry V. Hubbard shaped a new campus for the Harvard Business School on an Allston site across from the Harvard Stadium that they had helped locate decades before.

Harvard Yard was listed in the National Register of Historic Places in 1973, with a boundary increase in 1987; a number of residential colleges and discrete academic buildings have been additionally listed since. As Harvard expands today, there is a wealth of Olmsted-influenced projects to guide this work.

A 1902 sketch for Middlesex (**above**), proposing main buildings looking inward over a circular green, did become reality.

MIDDLESEX SCHOOL, CONCORD

In 1901 Frederick Winsor, together with other Harvard alumni, founded the Middlesex School, a nondenominational residential school to prepare young men for college. (His sister, Mary Pickard Winsor, had in 1886 founded a similar school in Brookline for young women, later known as the Winsor School.) Winsor would head Middlesex for the next thirty-seven years.

Winsor turned to Frederick Law Olmsted Jr., newly appointed head of Harvard's landscape architecture curriculum, to develop the campus, which was situated on 300 rolling acres surrounded by woodlands in a community steeped in history. Located only twenty miles northwest of Brookline, serviced by train, this was a highly accessible project for members of the Olmsted firm.

John C. Olmsted took on the project, spending hours on the land with Winsor, discussing building locations and settings. The main drive off Lowell Road crossed the marsh around the man-made, twenty-six-acre Bateman's Pond and turned uphill to

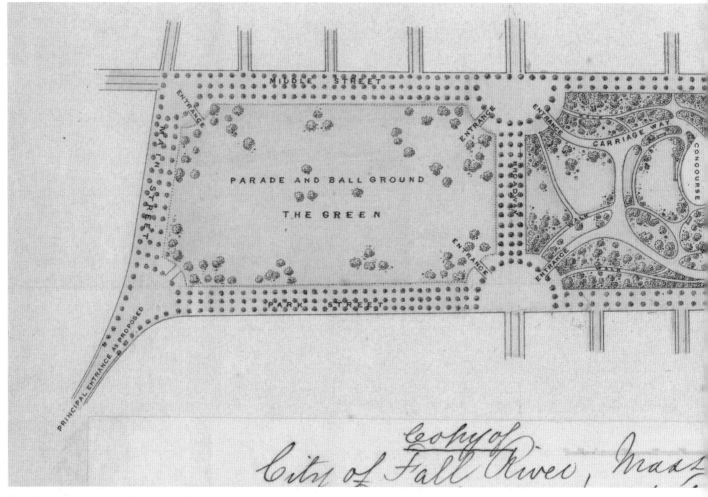

The 1904 plan for narrow South Park, now Kennedy Park.

reach the main campus. At the top of the hill, Olmsted designed a large, circular green around which new dormitories and academic buildings could be arranged. Working with architects Peabody and Stearns, he located buildings and designed drives and walkways, careful to minimize grading to preserve extant large trees, while also developing new plantings, including an allée of twelve-inch elms.

For more than three decades, from 1902 until the 1930s, members of the Olmsted firm (Herbert J. Kellaway and George Gibbs assisting John Charles Olmsted in the early days; Edward Clark Whiting leading after John Charles Olmsted's 1920 death), supervised the development of this campus to become a pastoral enclave in the woods. Among their tasks were siting the gym and athletic fields on additional land (1915); a memorial chapel (1922); a flagpole (1924); and gates and walls (1924 and 1925), which continue to mark the entrance to the school.

Becoming coed in 1974, today the Middlesex School educates about 450 students, almost triple the original size envisioned by Winsor. The mature tree plantings along the curved drives and around the buildings, and the Colonial Revival architecture of the older buildings, are characteristic of a New England landscape. The careful siting of the athletic buildings and fields uphill and newer academic buildings on the slopes downhill have respected the original setting. The great circular lawn remains as originally designed, framing panoramic views out over the campus.

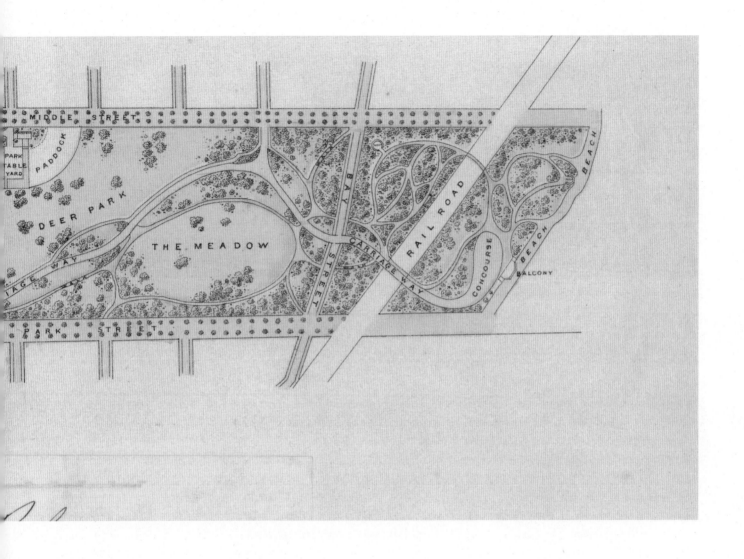

🪑

PARKS OF FALL RIVER

Located on an escarpment above Mount Hope Bay, blessed with ample water resources and easy access to markets, Fall River changed post–Civil War, from scattered mill villages into the largest American textile manufacturing center. The resultant population growth, squalid housing congestion, unhealthy working conditions, and social dislocations, made the need for public open space critical. By 1868, two parcels had been acquired, the fifteen-acre Ruggles woodland and a

fifty-four-acre linear pastureland running from hilltop down the steep slope to the bay. In 1870 Frederick Law Olmsted Sr. and Calvert Vaux were engaged.

South Park, though scenic, was a narrow, steeply sloping strip of land cut across by two major roads and railroad tracks. It presented numerous challenges. The designers turned the top tableland into a greensward, surrounded by tree-lined carriage drives, with a central pavilion for viewing. The middle ground,

A shelter on the western end of Kennedy Park frames views of Mount Hope Bay below.

a rock-encrusted slope, became the Deer Park, with a rustic shelter at the crest, below which a drive and paths meandered among plantings. In the third section, bridging the railroad tracks brought the park drive to a terminating terrace, overlooking the beach. Considerable buffer plantings were deployed to screen abutting mills and tenements.

Erratic economic conditions in the 1870s complicated implementation. Grading of the top section allowed for cricket and baseball games; the 1874 installation of the bandstand enabled concerts, as well as union gatherings. Elaborate centennial observances took place in July 1876. However, until the late 1890s, the unconstructed middle section was still used for pasturage, while the waterside section had become rail yards. Likewise, the Ruggles Woods and a newly acquired hillside space, North Park, remained unimproved.

In 1902 a new Fall River Park Commission consulted with John Charles Olmsted, from the Olmsted Brothers firm, on all its parks. Changing urban priorities now put greater emphasis on recreation and social education. Respecting the 1871 plan's handling of difficult site conditions, John C. Olmsted suggested in 1904 that ad hoc ball fields of the upper section be improved and separated by paved paths, with plantings at the periphery. He planned the middle section with a concert grove; there was a wading-skating pond, a children's playground, and a large,

open shelter at the brow of the hill for boat watching. He curved paths around plantings and rock outcroppings on the sloping pasture.

Two other city parks with designs from the Olmsted Brothers firm were planned for different opportunities, to balance those offered by South Park. Surrounded by a dense neighborhood, Ruggles Park's wooded slopes were terraced to create flat areas for a children's playground, a tennis court, and a ball field with perimeter plantings. North Park, also steeply sloping, was graded for recreational facilities and floral display. South Park, the largest open space, remained the primary venue for citywide events, such as President Roosevelt's 1936 visit.

Howard Lothrop, park superintendent from 1903 until 1946, struggled to steward Olmsted's plans for the parks. The departure of textile manufacturing left Fall River financially precarious, while increased recreational use post–World War II challenged maintenance budgets, leaving spaces degraded. While still retaining much of its Olmsted design heritage, South Park (renamed Kennedy Park in 1963) was in poor condition until the mid-1980s, when it received $1 million in state funding to spur its revitalization.

Kennedy Park is the only park in Massachusetts designed by Olmsted and Vaux and later by Olmsted Brothers. It was listed in the National Register of Historic Places in 1983.

City Hall as seen from across one of the three ponds on the eastern end of the site.

Newton City Hall and a view from across the lake.

NEWTON CITY HALL, NEWTON

Incorporated as a town in 1766 and nicknamed the Garden City in 1874, Newton, Massachusetts, grew from a collection of historical agricultural and mill villages west of Boston. Until 1931, this on-the-rise wealthy suburb had used an attractive multifunction Victorian building in West Newton to serve as its city hall, library, and early jail. After much debate, a ten-acre triangular parcel of uneven boggy land in a residential area, nearly the geographic center of the villages, but not the business center, was purchased, bordered on one side by historic Commonwealth Avenue where the last leg of the Boston Marathon is run. Noted Boston architects Allen and Collens were chosen circa 1930 to design a distinctive city hall and a war memorial, with the Olmsted Brothers firm charged with creating a suitable landscape.

The challenges were many. The surrounding community required a parklike setting; the triangular lot necessitated a building attractive on all facades and the extant Hammond Brook, which fed the bog, had to be controlled. To meet the lot's strictures, the architects created a single T-shaped building for both functions, the broad end, the prominent City Hall, faced east with two wings to accommodate its many municipal functions, while the western-facing pedimented and colonnaded narrow end with its steeple, the War Memorial, was to honor all who had perished in wars from the Revolution onward. It would contain a museum and civic meeting rooms for all the associated commemorative groups. Disregarding the architects' stiff ideas for surrounds, Henry Hubbard, with Carl Rust Parker to supervise, instead created an imaginative, graceful solution to the numerous site issues. He manipulated the grade to elevate the building for both visual and practical engineering reasons. He transformed the unruly brook into three low-lying but linked ponds, in which the Georgian Revival City Hall was reflected, encircled by grassy banks to absorb flooding, meandering paths with benches, and crossed by a stone bridge. Rich tree and shrub plantings set along lawns throughout the site were a reminder of Newton's horticultural heritage, offering shady, textured respite for the neighborhood. To the west, a commemorative flagpole and lawn provided appropriate spaces for Armistice Day celebrations, with thick tree plantings along the abutting streets encasing this municipal triangle in verdure. Winner of the Harleston Parker architectural award in 1936, Newton City Hall and War Memorial were listed in the National Register of Historic Places in 1990.

Above: The Rockery, inspired by Gaelic memorial stone mounds.
Left: Ames Memorial Hall, with a broad stair designed around boulders.

NORTH EASTON TOWN COMPLEX

In the early nineteenth century, Oliver Ames began the manufacture of shovels in North Easton, a small village south of Boston. His business surged when the company, then managed by his brother, Oakes Ames, was appointed to make shovels for the Union army and for the transcontinental railroad (construction of which began in 1863). To recognize the early family entrepreneurs and to give the town a more refined character, in the late 1870s, the next generation of Ames leaders commissioned several public buildings— a town hall, a free library, and a train station— all to be designed by noted architect H. H. Richardson with Frederick Law Olmsted Sr. crafting some of the settings. In 1882 Olmsted Sr. was further commissioned to design a Civil War Memorial at the road junction in front of the Town Hall.

To complement Richardson's architecture for the Oakes Ames Memorial Hall, set atop a rocky hill, Olmsted Sr. designed wide stairs and landings while cloaking the exposed surrounding boulders with wild shrubs and vines. Leading to and complementing the Town Hall, at the triangular island between roads, he designed

a cairn (also known as the Rockery), reflective of the ancient Gaelic memorial stone mounds. He intended the cairn to look like the remnants of an old bastion with an arched passage through it, topped by a flagpole, its boulders draped by vines, its crevices filled with rock plants, to which the community would add stones yearly in commemoration of those lost. Instead, what was built profoundly dismayed Olmsted as a "rude and ungainly jumble of rocks" never clothed with the plants as he had intended.

The grounds of the North Easton Railroad Station were characteristic of other regional stations, where Richardson designed small buildings with overhanging roofs for waiting rooms, graced by Olmsted Sr.'s simple harmonizing landscapes. The station is now the home of the Easton Historical Society and Museum, and the Memorial Hall and cairn give a unique presence to the town's core.

The H. H. Richardson Historic District of North Easton, which includes five structures and their associated landscapes, was designated a National Historic Landmark in 1987.

Glacial boulders sourced on-site were used in construction of both the house and Olmsted Sr.'s terrace.

This turn-of-the-century photograph provides a sense of the scale of the stones used in the terrace.

STONEHURST, WALTHAM

At Stonehurst, a country estate for Boston lawyer Robert Treat Payne Jr. and his wife Lydia, who shared Frederick Law Olmsted Sr.'s deeply held sense of social responsibility, Olmsted Sr. and architect H. H. Richardson were inspired by the unique genius of place to create surroundings for the house respectful of the natural boulder-strewn site.

Since 1880, Olmsted had experimented with the concept of "a forest lodge for the summer . . . bold, rustic and weather-proof . . . set high . . . supported by a terrace boldly projected . . . highly picturesque in its outlines and material." This vision, conceived of but not fully realized at Moraine Farm, found its ultimate expression at Stonehurst in the hands of Richardson, whom Olmsted Sr. considered "the most potential stimulus that has ever come into my artistic life." Richardson achieved the dramatic Picturesque-style experience that Olmsted Sr. wrote of years earlier: "I . . . would have a stranger . . . enter the house without suspicion of the broad and extended views in its . . . overlooks; the

unexpectedness of them . . . being its most striking distinction." Even more striking than the vistas at Stonehurst are the great rockworks of the house and terrace, composed of glacial boulders sourced from the wooded hilltop site and evocative of immense natural and social forces that shape communities.

Olmsted's "open-air apartment" in the form of a curved fieldstone terrace is seamlessly integrated with the surrounding landscape of glacially scoured outcrops, pastoral meadows, and woodlands. Richardson's bold plan and flowing spaces combine with rich textures and handcrafted details celebrating the creativity and skill of the immigrant craftsmen from around the world who provided the artisanship.

In 1974 descendants donated the 113-acre estate to the City of Waltham. The Friends of Stonehurst was founded in 1991 to help support and advocate for the property in concert with the City of Waltham. Stonehurst was listed in the National Register of Historic Places and as a National Historic Landmark in 1975.

Well-placed trees have graced the historical campus's planned green spaces and shaded its walkways for many years.

WILLIAMS COLLEGE, WILLIAMSTOWN

This private liberal arts college, chartered in 1793, is situated on 450 acres of rolling hillside in the Hoosic Valley in northwestern Massachusetts. Originally the Williamstown Free School, it was formed from funds bequeathed by Colonel Ephraim Williams Jr., an extensive landowner and colonial soldier.

Williams College's early planners eschewed a traditional quadrangle plan, instead freely siting the principal buildings upon adjacent, low hilltops. By 1828, numerous campus buildings, including East and West Colleges and Griffin Hall, were set in open yards clustered around Williamstown's Main Street. The first quadrangle was formed with East College, reconstructed after a fire in 1841, South College (now Fayerweather) in 1842, and the Hopkins Observatory, built in 1836.

Beginning in 1902 and for more than six decades, Olmsted Brothers guided the campus formation. Hired initially to advise on the location of the Thompson Memorial Chapel, the firm went on to make large-scale planning recommendations for the entire campus, advising that future development should be more cohesive and planning around discrete quadrangles be interwoven with shared green spaces. Beyond the campus plan, prominent Olmsted firm projects included the gardens of the President's House, the grounds of the Hopkins Observatory, the layout of the college cemetery, improvements to the Taconic Golf Course, and to the former estate of alumnus and trustee George A. Cluett, which was incorporated into the campus acreage. The Cluett summer estate, with its vistas to the Berkshires, had extensive "garden rooms" and plantings designed by Olmsted firm associate partner Edward Clark Whiting in the early 1920s. The property was acquired by Williams College in the 1960s, who sold it in the 1970s to become what is now the Pine Cobble School.

Today, the college grounds reflect much of the Olmsted design intent, defined by quadrangles with diagonal walks, the east–west axis of Main Street, and majestic views of the adjacent mountains.

MICHIGAN

Belle Isle Park, Detroit   162
Barton Hills, Ann Arbor   164

Washtenong Cemetery, Ann Arbor   165

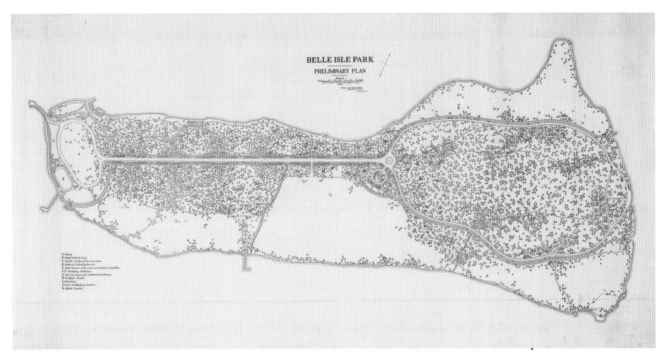

BELLE ISLE PARK
PRELIMINARY PLAN

Olmsted Sr.'s 1883 initial plan for Belle Isle.

BELLE ISLE PARK, DETROIT

Known as Hog Island and situated in the Detroit River, the original 700 acres of what is today 982-acre Belle Isle was purchased from a private owner in 1879 by the City of Detroit for $200,000. With its desirable upriver location, a beneficial distance from the industrial landscape of the city, this swampy land already had a history of informal recreational uses. The existing marshland conditions were subject to frequent soaking or severe flooding and would prove challenging for Frederick Law Olmsted Sr., who deemed the situation "favorable to the breeding and nursing of mosquitos."

In March 1883 Olmsted Sr. prepared a preliminary plan, a simple design that would preserve the park's primary asset: its old-growth forestland. In addition, the plan called for a pedestrian-oriented boulevard that would serve as the park's central spine, as well as park amenities that included a ferry

dock, parade grounds, a public beach, a canal system, and, along the western edge of the island, a pier and gallery oriented to the city, offering panoramic views and enhanced connectivity.

Olmsted's relationship with the city was strained from the beginning. Although his proposal was initially accepted, the city would veto his proposed gallery the following year. Olmsted considered the gallery essential to enhancing connectivity and supporting the myriad proposed park uses. This was the only major structure proposed by Olmsted for the site and even though he would lobby intensely for its retention, in the end the city deemed it too expensive. This was unacceptable to the elder Olmsted and in 1885, a little more than two years after his proposed plan was approved, he resigned from the project. In an interview at the time he stated, "I know nothing of that place." In 1917 Frederick Law Olmsted Jr. was contacted for assistance

Above left: The James Scott Memorial Fountain; Frederick Law Olmsted Jr. was on the jury to select the winning design. **Above right:** View from Belle Isle toward downtown Detroit. **Below right:** The MacArthur Bridge, completed in 1923, was the only land crossing from the city to the island at the time, designed in consultation with Olmsted Brothers.

in enlarging a copy of the plan and John C. Olmsted responded to the letter, because his brother was out of town, noting that he had worked on the project with his father.

Following Olmsted Sr.'s involvement, a park construction boom began around the turn of the century. This resulted in the current Italianate Detroit Boat Club (1902), the Field House (1898) and its associated thirty-six acres of athletic fields, and the Belle Isle Zoo (1895). In 1915, 200 acres of new parkland were added, the result of fill installed along the park's western tip. During this time, Albert Kahn designed several structures, including the Belle Isle Aquarium and Anna Scripps Whitcomb Conservatory in 1904 and the Livingstone Memorial Lighthouse in 1930. Other significant park features include the grand Beaux Arts–style James Scott Memorial Fountain, designed by Cass Gilbert and Herbert Adams (Olmsted Jr. served on the jury for the Memorial Competition Committee), and the Douglas MacArthur Bridge, designed in consultation with the Olmsted Brothers firm.

Although Olmsted Sr.'s involvement was brief, his impact on the park was significant. A review of the park today indicates that his proposed system of canals was accepted, as was the central spine of Central Avenue. His recommendations to aid in mosquito management, including selective thinning and the removal of understory plant materials in the park's woodlands, were carried out. And, in the end, a pavilion that integrated a gallery, as originally proposed, would be realized. Belle Isle Park, the largest park in Detroit, was listed in the National Register of Historic Places in 1974.

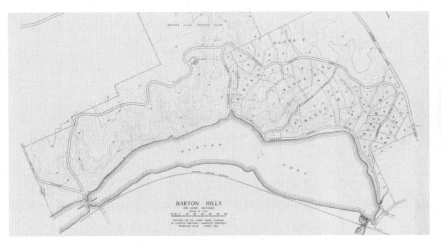

A 1922 plan showing the position of the dam and the topography of the lots.

A view across Barton Lake, revealing how houses on large lots are set back from the shore, maintaining privacy and preserving lakeside planting.

BARTON HILLS, ANN ARBOR

In conjunction with the construction of Barton Dam, a hydro-electric project on the Huron River in 1913, Alex Dow, president of the Detroit Edison Company, acquired the surrounding land, which he devoted to a variety of purposes: a demonstration farm, a resort for the company's women employees, a park, and a residential development centered on the steep ravines that were unsuitable for agriculture adjacent to the reservoir. Dow's land manager, William Underdown, solicited the help of the Olmsted Brothers firm, and their agent, George Gibbs Jr., visited the site in 1915, submitting a report on the proposed concept for the development several months later. The firm continued to refine the design over the next several years, with both John Charles Olmsted and Fredrick Law Olmsted Jr. weighing in on various aspects of the project. In 1919 the first holes of an associated golf course and country club were opened, and an expansion followed in 1922; noted golf course designer Donald Ross contributed to the layout of the course.

Commanding views of the lake from the finger-like ridges guided the plan, with the most valuable lots sited on high points. These significant vistas informed the platting, and as originally envisioned, plantings would have been carefully curated to frame the views; over time, however, natural succession has overtaken formerly open areas, diminishing the borrowed views. The lakeshore itself, and portions of the ravines, were reserved as parkland. Barton Shore Drive wraps along the water's edge, with a single community boathouse sited along the beach as the only major intervention. Much of the development was realized by the mid-1920s, with the Olmsted firm continuing to consult throughout the decade; a set of stone entry gates, designed by Edward C. Whiting, was one of the firm's last significant contributions.

A 1929 drawing for the approach to a suggested chapel and service building at Washtenong Memorial Park.

WASHTENONG MEMORIAL PARK, ANN ARBOR

In 1929 land manager William Underdown and the newly created Washtenong Memorial Association brought the firm back to Ann Arbor, this time asking Olmsted Brothers to design a cemetery on forty acres just north of Barton Hills. Once again, the acreage was mostly treeless, and the topography allowed for proper drainage. The association wanted the parcel of land divided into four, ten-acre parts, with the land along Whitmore Lake Road to include a main entrance, space for a chapel, interior drives, and walkways. The general plan, completed in 1931, used a curvilinear road system following the natural topography. An axis for a chapel, service area, and fountain visible from Whitmore Lake Drive cuts across the main interior curvilinear drives, providing a rectilinear counterpoint.

Interspersed among plots are groupings suitable for family lots or mausoleums. Pathways throughout were to be laid in gravel, or left as lawn, and groupings of evergreen plantings were used to direct views. The project was plagued by financial problems and while the drives within the ten-acre area along Whitmore Lake Road were built consistent with the plan, the remainder were not. The cemetery association added a chapel and an associated service building, but not in the recommended location. A detailed planting plan for those ten acres was executed under the direction of Harlow Olin Whittemore, chairman of the University of Michigan's department of landscape architecture. Correspondence between the Olmsted Brothers firm and Whittemore indicate that he had planted according to the location and species shown on the Olmsted plans. Some of the chosen evergreens were not thriving in the clay soils, leading Whittemore to seek advice and alternatives. As late as 1959, Whittemore, by then serving as a private consultant, was still in communication with the Olmsted Brothers firm about honoring the planting design intent.

MISSISSIPPI

Alcorn State University, Alcorn   167

University of Mississippi, Oxford   169

Many of the heritage trees in the Grove remain today.

ALCORN STATE UNIVERSITY, ALCORN

Alcorn State University, founded in 1871, is the oldest public historically Black land-grant institution in the United States. The site was originally Oakland College, a Presbyterian school established in 1828 on 225 acres. The campus, in Claiborne County, is about twenty miles south of the nearest urban area, Fayette, which has a population of 2200. The university is located within a largely forested area east of the Mississippi River and Louisiana border.

In 1878 Alcorn University became Alcorn Agricultural and Mechanical College, exclusively for males, until a dormitory for women was built in 1902. In 1974 Alcorn Agricultural and Mechanical College was renamed Alcorn State University. The campus has grown to 1700 acres and the facilities increased from three original buildings to more than eighty structures. The student body has likewise increased from 179 students to more than 4000.

When the Olmsted Brothers firm took on the project in the 1950s, there was already a large central green space with pedestrian walkways, surrounded by a tree-lined curvilinear main road. Secondary roads radiate from this thoroughfare in a pinwheel design. The firm was asked to lay out additional circulation routes associated with planned building sites, and to prepare the associated grading plans. Olmsted Associates remained involved in campus expansion projects through 1972. Features that were part of the 1960s-era campus plan—the lake at the entrance road, the curvilinear main road—as well as the proposed new roads and the athletic facilities have not been dramatically altered. Since the 1970s, the campus has expanded east of those features.

In 1982 the oldest section of the campus, which faces the large green and contains nine Greek and Colonial Revival buildings built between 1838 and 1939, was listed in the National Register of Historic Places.

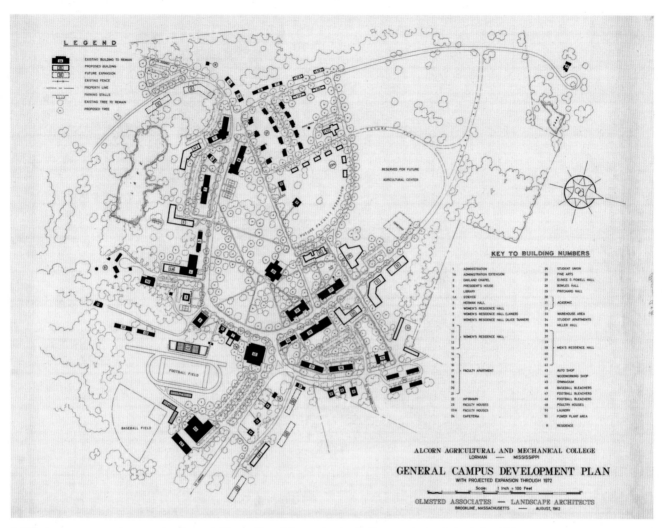

A 1962 plan for a proposed campus development; Olmsted Associates was involved in its expansion beginning in the 1950s.

The Lyceum, the university's most recognizable building, faces many heritage trees like the one at left.

UNIVERSITY OF MISSISSIPPI, OXFORD

The Mississippi State Legislature chartered this university in 1844. In 1848 architect William Nichols laid out the institution's original campus plan. The design was composed of a parklike octagonal space encircled by institutional structures, including the university's flagship white-columned building, the Lyceum (also by Nichols). A century later, university officials hired the Olmsted Brothers firm to develop a general plan for the 640-acre campus to accommodate an anticipated future enrollment of 5000 students. With work overseen by Carl Parker, the east–west axis was established along a central ridge. The design honored Nichols's original plan with a series of open quadrangles interconnected via a system of axes and cross-axes. Roadways and areas for parking were relocated to the periphery to better define the campus's pedestrian-oriented core. The planting plan emphasized placing varieties of dogwoods, oaks, and fruit trees across campus.

The historical central green core, known as the Circle, is a shaded lawn with brick paths radiating out from a central flagpole, providing a foreground for the Office of the Chancellor building. Adjacent to the Circle is the Grove, a ten-acre sloping lawn, which was shown on the 1959 Olmsted plan, crisscrossed by paved pedestrian pathways and populated by 160 oak, magnolia, and elm trees. Moving west beyond the core, a series of campus landscapes are arranged along the central ridge, including the Library Quad and Magnolia Mall. A network of vehicular roads connects the core to additional quadrangles, formal lawns, and recreational facilities. Olmsted Brothers, and its successor Olmsted Associates, remained involved with the university for more than forty years. The campus now encompasses 1200 acres, serving 24,000 students. The Circle was designated a National Historic Landmark District in 2008 due to its significance in the university's infamous desegregation battle in 1962.

MISSOURI

LIBERTY MEMORIAL, KANSAS CITY

Soon after Armistice Day in November 1918, civic-minded Kansas Citians formed the Liberty Memorial Association (LMA), its purpose to create a lasting monument for those who served in what was described as the "war to end all wars." Led by lumber tycoon Robert Anderson Long, the LMA successfully raised more than $2.5 million from 83,000 contributors in its first ten days. With city council approval, on February 9, 1920, an elevated, blighted site was selected just south of Jarvis Hunt's Beaux Arts–style Union Station (1914). This space would become a memorable first view of Kansas City for innumerable rail travelers.

An invitational design competition for the memorial was won by New York architect Harold Van Buren Magonigle, to work collaboratively with landscape architect George Kessler. Three years after the Armistice, in November 1921, the site was dedicated, with over 200,000 in attendance.

Construction over the next seventeen years brought the memorial structure to completion in 1926, while the complex landscape work continued until 1938. The design team who brought the memorial to fruition included Magonigle, augmented by local architects Wight and Wight and landscape architect Kessler until his 1923 death. Hare and Hare and the Olmsted Brothers firm, including Frederick Law Olmsted Jr. with partner Percival Gallagher and assistant E. M. Prellwitz, completed the landscape.

Built on more than forty-seven acres, the Liberty Memorial, in the Egyptian Revival style, showcases a monumental central shaft rising twenty-one stories from a memorial courtyard, bordered on the east by Memory Hall and on the west by a museum. Two monumental limestone sphinxes face south, flanking the staircases on each side, which descend in stages to the terminus of the south end of the Memorial Mall. Parallel parkways, with a central grass panel, stretch a quarter mile southward toward Penn Valley Park. Delineated by double rows of sugar maples and pin oaks according to the 1937 Olmsted firm plans, this area marks the main vehicular and pedestrian entrances. At the southern end of the mall, two groves of memorial trees remain with plaques, although the more elaborate Olmsted planting plans were never executed. Dense tree planting, including cottonwoods, were placed along the streets east and west of the memorial, with ground cover over the steep slopes.

To the north, below the memorial courtyard, a large wall contains the *Great Frieze* by sculptor Edmond Amateis, depicting war and peace with dedicatory inscriptions. From this wall a complex of stepped terraces with dual fountains meets an elliptical, sloping lawn descending the hillside, shaped by paths and steps on either side. At the bottom, the Dedication Wall (1934), with bronze busts of military leaders, forms the backdrop to a street-side plaza across from the station. These spaces, envisioned by Kessler, were refined by Olmsted Jr. with assistant Prellwitz, in collaboration with Wight and Wight.

This compelling memorial was rehabilitated beginning in 2000 and rededicated in May 2002. It continues in its historical use as a monument to World War I, with the library, archives, and museum in operation. It was designated a National Historic Landmark in 2006.

Left: The Egyptian Revival–style Liberty Memorial, completed in 1926. **Bottom:** An aerial view of the memorial grounds shows double rows of sugar maples and pin oaks, as well as a grove of trees at the southern end of the landscape, according to Olmsted plans from 1937.

NEW HAMPSHIRE

Phillips Exeter Academy, Exeter   174   Swasey Parkway, Exeter   176

The current campus retains the circular green bisected by Front Street, seen toward the bottom of the image, plus the internal quadrangles suggested by Olmsted in 1907.

PHILLIPS EXETER ACADEMY, EXETER

In 1781 Elizabeth and John Phillips established the Phillips Exeter Academy in Exeter, New Hampshire. At the turn of the twentieth century, the board of trustees was contemplating acquiring various parcels of land in and around the campus. They contacted Frederick Law Olmsted Jr. for assistance in the location of a new library, dormitories, and an auditorium to hold assemblies that would accommodate the future complement of 500 students. The

board was aware that John Charles Olmsted had sited a dormitory for the Phillips Academy in Andover, Massachusetts, in the 1890s and the work was greatly appreciated.

During the initial discussions, the academy emphasized the cordial but prickly relationship with the Town of Exeter. Exeter was incorporated in 1683 and while small in scale, was proud of its existing buildings and had, over the years, accommodated

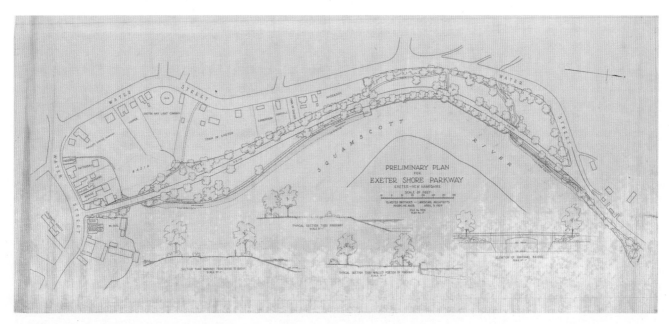

Preliminary plan for the Exeter Shore Parkway, 1929.

the academy, even letting students use the local public library. But there were concerns that rumors about land purchases might give the impression that the school was taking over the town. The core of the campus was bisected by Front Street and interspersed with residential properties in various states of repair. Expanding the existing quad design was only possible if certain properties could be acquired. The 1906 correspondence between the trustees and John C. Olmsted, who took on the project, clarifies these issues as well, indicating which views should be maintained to best respect the existing colonial style and character and setting of the campus buildings.

John C. Olmsted and Edward Whiting prepared initial sketches for the location of the proposed library. In his lengthy evaluation of the site, Olmsted argued that certain properties should be acquired, regardless of cost, and that existing elm trees should be preserved where possible to provide the appropriate setting for the library. He noted the necessity of fireproof buildings (the Dunbar Building burned down during the discussions) and that an overall plan would best serve the interests of academy. The plan was received with mixed results

and work ceased. During the 1920s, the firm was asked to prepare planting plans and in 1929, the firm built a model of the campus including athletic buildings and fields proposed for an expansion to the east across the Exeter River. Later work overseen by Percival Gallagher included planting plans, grading plans, and studies for athletic fields, as well as a design for a memorial garden near the principal's house. The firm continued to offer guidance until 1952.

Today, the academy covers 673 acres and educates 1000 coed students. The campus still retains the large circular green bisected by Front Street as well as the interior quad organization shown on Olmsted's 1907 sketch. The doubling of the student body from the 500 planned for in 1906 has resulted in more dormitories and academic buildings around the quads than originally envisioned.

The Front Street Historic District, listed in the National Register of Historic Places in 1973, covers an area of 200 feet on both sides of Front Street, from Gale Park Memorial to Spring and Water Streets, and includes bisected frontage of the Phillips Academy.

Above: The parkway is still a dominant feature of the town of Exeter. **Right:** The Swasey Parkway under construction in 1930, showing the careful retention of heritage trees.

SWASEY PARKWAY, EXETER

Seeking to beautify the working waterfront of Exeter along the Squamscott River, which inventor and philanthropist Ambrose Swasey traversed daily from his Fort Rock Farms homestead, Swasey proposed the creation of a waterfront parkway for the city in the mid-1920s. He hired Warren H. Manning, who had previously consulted on his estate, to prepare plans for the parkway, which would be constructed through an industrial neighborhood. Manning charted the alignment of the roadway, a design which the Olmsted Brothers firm largely followed when they took on the project. The firm, however, incorporated a less formal approach to the proposed plantings than the allée of English elms suggested by Manning. The firm also proposed a more ambitious reclamation of the adjacent marsh and waterfront for parkland. Construction proceeded quickly, and the parkway was dedicated in November 1931.

Stone walls mark both ends of the half-mile-long corridor, distinguishing it from the urban landscape to the south and the more rural setting to the north. An open lawn dotted with trees lends a parklike character to the space, providing opportunities for passive recreation. The riverbank is highlighted as a feature of the parkway, with an existing wharf utilized as an overlook, and a second overlook constructed to the north. Walkways connect the parkway to surrounding streets, enabling pedestrians to engage with the landscape and the water's edge.

NEW JERSEY

Essex County Park System 178

Branch Brook Park, Newark 179

Eagle Rock Reservation,
    West Orange-Verona-Montclair 183

South Mountain Reservation,
    Maplewood-Millburn-West Orange 184

Lawrenceville School, Lawrenceville 186

Cadwalader Park and Cadwalader
    Heights, Trenton 187

Union County Park System 188

Warinanco Park, Elizabeth 190

Echo Lake Park, Mountainside 190

Rahway River Parks, Rahway 190

Watchung Reservation, Mountainside 192

Weequahic Park is a pastoral hideaway just a couple of miles west of Newark Liberty Airport.

ESSEX COUNTY PARK SYSTEM

In 1867 Frederick Law Olmsted Sr. and Calvert Vaux were invited to explore possible parkland for Newark, a growing industrial city in Essex County across the river from their pioneering creations for Central Park and their early Brooklyn work for Prospect Park. For the New Jersey site, they chose a 420-acre tract with scenic potentials for a good approach route and pastoral space to allow "an enlarged sense of freedom," away from city intrusions. (Some of the acreage from this site would eventually become Branch Brook Park.) With a county system of government in New Jersey, this park for Newark alone was rejected as too expensive for the county.

The park idea continued to simmer in Essex County long after this circa 1870 rejection. The American park movement

had progressed in cities across the country, including an innovative idea for a metropolitan-based system emerging around Boston to develop regional parks and connective parkways, regardless of city jurisdictions. This concept, created by Charles Eliot, by then a member of the Olmsted firm, provided a good model for Essex County. In 1895, after forming the Essex County Park Commission, the county again consulted with the Olmsted office, among other firms. At that time, John Charles Olmsted, representing Olmsted, Olmsted, and Eliot, submitted a comprehensive report detailing the public health and economic benefits of a park system as well as the duties of a park commission, and praising the county's scenic opportunities. However, the park commission initially chose the firm of (John) Bogart and (Nathan) Barrett to lay out a countywide system of diverse park spaces. After two years with little system-wide implementation, the commission returned to the Olmsted firm, now called Olmsted Brothers. John Charles Olmsted developed and implemented a comprehensive and viable system, respectful of natural resources while meeting community needs. This solidified a relationship with the Olmsted firm that lasted six decades and involved park sites across the county, from small city squares to parks of all sizes and characters, including extensive reservations (as Eliot had conceived in Massachusetts). The intended network of connective parkways designed by the firm was only minimally implemented, with much acreage gradually being acquired by state highways.

Today the county park system encompasses more than 6000 acres and is composed of thirty parks and reservations stretching from the town of Fairfield to the city of Newark. The system includes a series of waterways, scenic overlooks, and a network of trails. Though natural in appearance, many of the system's expansive views and landscape features, including landforms, lakes, and plant materials, were in fact designed by the Olmsted Brothers firm. Today, the system is managed by the Essex County Department of Parks, Recreation and Cultural Affairs. Although the entire system is not listed in the National Register of Historic Places, a number of individual parks are, including Anderson (listed in 2009), Branch Brook (1981), Lincoln (1984), Military (2004), Riverbank (1998), Washington (1978), and Weequahic Parks (2003).

One of Branch Brook's masonry bridges, accommodating traffic above and pedestrians below.

BRANCH BROOK PARK, NEWARK

When Nathan Barrett and John Bogart were hired to develop a park system, the Essex County Park Commission had already commenced land acquisition for the acreage to become Branch Brook Park, facing formidable barriers in the area they were contemplating. From the sixty acres given by the water board around a circular stone reservoir to the south of the site, their possibilities included an oddly shaped linear strip to the north

that was trisected by two major roads, Park and Bloomfield Avenues, limited on the west by the old Morris Canal (which became the subway tracks) and on the east by expensive residential land. This topographically irregular land, left over from quarrying, contained woods, a former ice pond, and what was known as Old Blue Jay Swamp. After two years of elaborate gardenesque work, partially implemented in southern Branch

View of the south part of the lake under the Barrett and Bogart gardenesque scheme, circa 1899.

Brook Park, it became clear to the commission that Barrett and Bogart's schemes were destructive of natural features and economically unfeasible.

After lengthy negotiations, the commission acquiesced to the Olmsted firm's experienced business procedures and comprehensive vision for planning the entire system and, in particular, their transforming of Branch Brook Park's challenging landforms into a cohesive park asset for Newark. Their skillful sequencing of active and passive spaces was especially appreciated. John Charles Olmsted sought to retain some of the disconnected Barrett and Bogart gardens and architectural underpasses by Carrère and Hastings to separate travel ways in the southern section. He reintegrated these elements into an overall design and shaped the pond into a linear multiuse lake, reaching into the park's middle section, with waterside paths

and meadows where he placed terraces, overlook shelters, and a music pavilion. To knit the three divisions of the park together, the intervening streets were carried on designed "flyover" bridges, under which the park drive, accompanying paths, and waterway seamlessly connected the sections, enhanced by textured plantings. Although the southern division had ice-skating and later roller skating and boating on the lake, most of the activities here were more contemplative. Active recreation, ball fields, and a swimming beach in the early days were found in the middle division, while in the more pastoral northern division, John Charles Olmsted and assistant Percy Jones shaped a path beside a sinuous brook, crossed by individually designed, small rustic bridges shaded by canopy trees for an orchestrated scenic passage alongside a bucolic meadow. The meadow was eventually converted for sports.

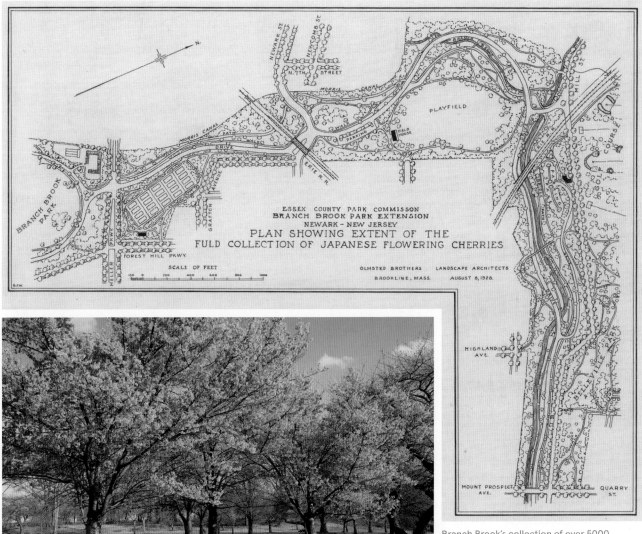

Branch Brook's collection of over 5000 flowering cherry trees, planned in 1928 to rival the display in Washington, DC, continues to attract visitors every spring.

Beginning in the mid-1920s, Branch Brook Park was expanded to 360 acres and extended north into Belleville to abut that township's parks, and to incorporate a parkway along the wilder but degraded Second River which, in turn, connected to Passaic County. This work was planned by Percival Gallagher (who was simultaneously working to the south in Union County), and involved complicated engineering for channelizing the river, for bridges, for paths, and for parkway and recreational spaces along the banks. This new area provided much of the locale for a Branch Brook Park attribute, its notable collection of Japanese cherry trees. Begun by Caroline Bamberger Fuld in 1928 (who was advised by Gallagher), this collection of single- and double-flowered forms now numbers over 5000 planted throughout the whole park, but particularly along the slopes of this extension, bringing thousands of visitors yearly to the park. The trees' original purpose was to rival those along the Potomac in Washington, DC. Branch Brook Park was listed in the National Register of Historic Places in 1981.

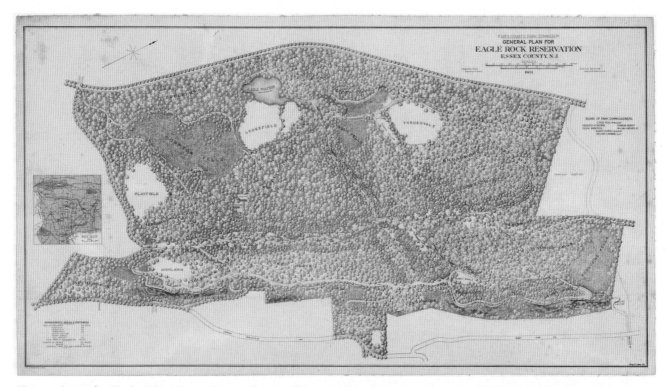

Above and opposite: The Eagle Rock Reservation provides over 400 acres of natural space in northern New Jersey; visionary thinking and a land acquisition campaign guided by Olmsted Brothers saved it from almost certain private development, due to its proximity to New York City.

EAGLE ROCK RESERVATION, WEST ORANGE-VERONA-MONTCLAIR

This region, defined by the Watchung Mountains, was populated by the Lenni-Lenape Indigenous peoples before the arrival of European colonists. During the Revolutionary War, the Continental Army used the mountain overlooks as observation posts. In the nineteenth century, the Watchung's First Mountain became known as Eagle Rock due to its nesting eagles. Nearby, Union Army officer Llewellyn Haskell began assembling the considerable acreage that would become the desirable residential community of Llewellyn Park. By the 1870s, the area had become a resort destination, with a trolley line to Eagle Rock Avenue laid out in 1884. In 1894 the newly formed Essex County Park Commission asked Olmsted, Olmsted, and Eliot (among other firms), to advise on a comprehensive plan for the acquisition of parklands. Their report praised the scenic opportunities of the Eagle Rock area. Although in 1895 the commission hired the Bogart and Barrett firm to design the park system, the Olmsted Brothers firm replaced them in 1898 and quickly began to guide land acquisitions to develop this area as a reservation. Working with the engineers, John Charles Olmsted carefully planned well-graded but subtle drives, bridle paths, and trails throughout the steep slopes and valleys in this ruggedly beautiful wooded landscape, endeavoring to take full advantage of interesting interior views across streams and bogs. He recommended hemlocks and pines to enrich the boldness of valleys, with native rhododendrons, laurels, and ferns to texture the trails. He placed shelters at suitable stopping points to capture the remarkable views across the river, advising on the stone for requisite walls to blend with the extant ledges. By 1911 an open shelter with Italianate arches known as the Casino was built at a scenic overlook at the crest of Eagle Rock—later to be enclosed to become the Highlawn Pavilion Restaurant.

This 408-acre park lies between the towns of West Orange, Montclair, and Verona. The entrance to the park at Eagle Rock Avenue is fronted by an expansive green, which leads to a scenic overlook that affords panoramic views of the Manhattan skyline. The crest overlook became, after 9/11, the site for a donated memorial, dedicated in 2002. Designed by sculptor Patrick Morelli, the bronze memorial consists of a granite wall inscribed with the names of the 9/11 victims and several figurative elements, including an eagle perched on a tree.

Once the reservation was established, the Olmsted firm worked to remove the scars of previous human incursion, using "aesthetic forestry" to manage the land, while helping it to appear wild.

SOUTH MOUNTAIN RESERVATION, MAPLEWOOD-MILLBURN-WEST ORANGE

Of vital concern for the Essex County Parks Commissioners in 1895 was to set aside and protect for public benefit the wild woodland slopes and stream valleys between First and Second Mountains of the Watchung range. This area, to be called South Mountain Reservation, was historically and culturally significant—associated with the Indigenous Lenape peoples; with Continental army outposts during the American Revolution; and with essential early industries. It was also significant for its scenery and its geological, ecological, horticultural, and hydrological resources (the Rahway River flows through the reservation, creating a dramatic waterfall at Hemlock Falls). As custodians of the public funds, the commission began to acquire parkland parcels in this area through purchase or gift, to prevent destruction through speculative ventures. As soon as the Olmsted Brothers firm was hired in 1898, John Charles Olmsted, along with Percival Gallagher, explored this diverse terrain, advising the commission

on what to purchase in order to retain the entirety of landscape "units." This was a slow process—to put together the over 2000 acres, covering several townships and multiple jurisdictions, and then shape the land into a cohesive reservation, interwoven with user amenities of trails, roads, paths, shelters, picnic groves, and overlooks. All were carefully graded and unobtrusively located, to highlight the diverse scenic opportunities that would seemingly appear removed from civilization.

Over the next decade or so, most of the parcels were accumulated, generating considerable efforts by the Olmsted firm's professionals to erase the scars of previous farming, overgrazing, and timbering, and to judiciously thin the woodlands, avoiding monotony and tameness for scenic and effective management reasons. Unsurprisingly, this engendered as much resistance then as such practices do today. Their next step in this process, which John Charles Olmsted referred to as "aesthetic forestry,"

Passaic River Park in the early morning mist.

was to "assist nature" by carefully replanting for healthy forested areas, some as "open woodland," others as "closed woodland," and underplanting the upper canopy with appropriate native flowering trees, shrubs, and herbaceous materials. Specialized areas of the reservation were given distinctive names, both as a means of wayfinding and as descriptive of the enhanced character (including Mayapple Hill, Laurel Wood, Tulip Meadow, Hemlock Falls, Summit Hill, and Painter's Point). There were swamps to be cleared for mosquito control, views looking in and out to be revealed, connecting roads and their entrances to be developed, and playgrounds and camping grounds to be added.

The construction, forestry work, and even land acquisitions for this reservation continued well into the 1920s, managed by Gallagher and James Frederick Dawson, with Hans J. Koehler evaluating the plantings. During the Great Depression, projects were funded by WPA money with encampments of Civilian Conservation Corps (CCC) to carry them out. In the post–WWII years, attitudes toward an extensive reservation changed with new activities introduced into the park. The Codey Skating Arena opened in 1958, followed by the Turtle Back Zoo in 1963, and then miniature golf, a restaurant, and other features, creating an ever-expanding recreation complex. One of several bodies of water encompassed by the reservation since the nineteenth century, the Orange (township) Reservoir, which was enlarged and reshaped to enhance its scenic effects in the early twentieth century by John Charles Olmsted, was abandoned as part of the water supply system circa 2000, during which time it, too, was repurposed for recreation. With this emphasis on active recreation, the core purpose for setting aside this unique and scenic park space has been diminished, and less attention and funding have been dedicated to the renewal and management of the park's remarkable woodland resources.

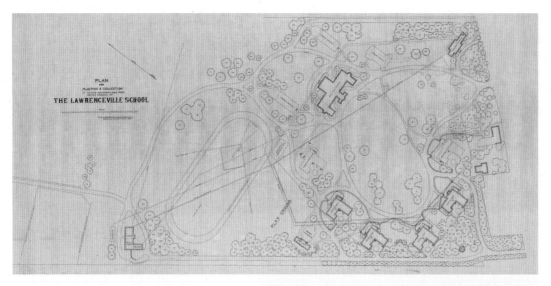

The diversity of trees planted at Olmsted Sr.'s urging to use the campus itself as a "museum of dendrology" is clearly seen in the 1886 planting plan **(above)**, as well as on the main grounds today **(right)**.

LAWRENCEVILLE SCHOOL, LAWRENCEVILLE

One of the first preparatory boarding schools in the United States, Lawrenceville School was founded in 1810 as the Maidenhead Academy. Hired by its board of trustees in 1880, Frederick Law Olmsted Sr. created a campus master plan predicated on fostering a vibrant academic community. Working closely with architects Peabody and Stearns to carefully site a dozen buildings, Olmsted Sr. drew from the English campus system, with buildings arranged around a central green. Known as the Circle, this kidney-shaped lawn is ringed by several residence halls, the Edith Memorial Chapel, and administrative buildings built in the Neo-Romanesque style. Olmsted created a living "museum of botany and dendrology" for the students' edification, with 371 species of trees planted throughout the landscape, arranged by genus for easy comparison. Campus additions in the 1920s by Delano and Aldrich left the Circle untouched, instead expanding the grounds to include more housing, classrooms, and extensive athletic facilities. Olmsted Brothers served as the consulting landscape architects during this expansion.

The Lawrenceville School campus now comprises 700 acres of parklike land and is the setting for a golf course, arts center, sports complex, and a thirty-acre solar farm. The school administers an endowed fund to maintain the integrity of the largely intact historic designed landscape. Eighteen acres of the campus within the parameters of Olmsted Sr.'s design were designated a National Historical Landmark in 1986.

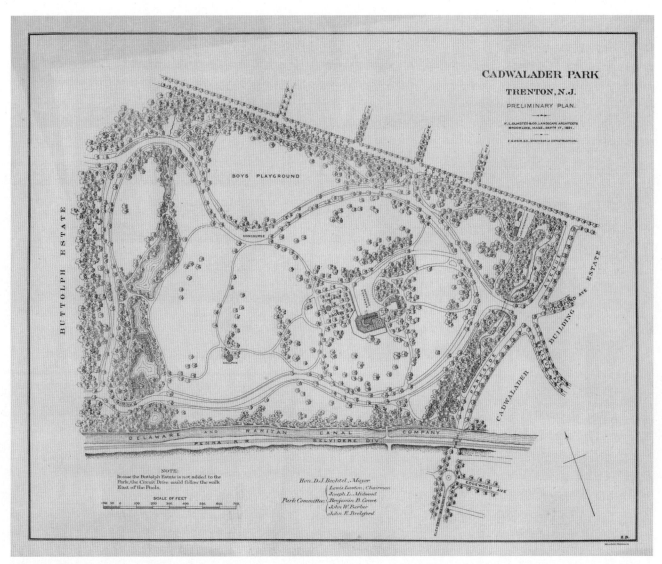

Preliminary plan for Cadwalader Park, 1891.

CADWALADER PARK AND CADWALADER HEIGHTS, TRENTON

Following the 1888 acquisition of the Ellarslie Mansion and surrounding lands, the City of Trenton consulted with Frederick Law Olmsted Sr. in 1890 about redevelopment of the site as a public park. Design proceeded rapidly, much of it under the supervision of John C. Olmsted, and a looping carriage drive, pathways, and plantings were quickly installed in the following years. The existing mansion was the focal point of the design,

to be repurposed as a refectory, and new approach drives and paths provided connections to it. Complementing this structure were a vine-covered terrace and concert grove, which provided outlooks to the tree-dotted lawn beyond. In 1892, political changes in Trenton resulted in decreased support for parks, and the Olmsteds lost the commission. While park progress continued to follow the broad contours of the Olmsted firm's plan, monuments and zoo enclosures were introduced into the pastoral landscape against the firm's recommendations.

Though they did not direct influence over the park's design during this period, Olmsted Brothers, in 1905, did implement a subdivision plan for the land opposite the park's eastern edge, which their father had speculated on in the park's initial planning. John C. Olmsted prepared designs for the Cadwalader Heights property of businessman E. C. Hill with curving streets that extended the curvilinear character of the park's drives out into the surrounding neighborhood, blending it into the rectilinear grid of the city. In 1910 the firm was again retained to work on the park, this time to design an addition to the south, which included a wading pool for children, tennis courts, and refinements to the approach to the main park. The Mansion House was listed in the National Register of Historic Places in 1973, with little reference to the park.

UNION COUNTY PARK SYSTEM

By 1921 the population of Union County had surpassed the 200,000 needed to support a parks commission. Once appointed, the new commission acted quickly to engage Percival Gallagher of the Olmsted Brothers firm for a countywide reconnaissance, evaluating the potential for a well-distributed expansive network of parks and riverside corridors, linked by cross-county parkways. Anticipating that Union County's good transportation systems and gently rising pastoral topography interlaced by rivers would ensure its continued residential growth, Gallagher looked to set aside land of all types for recreation—active and passive—while also protecting especial landscape features and water resources for public enjoyment. For their second countywide park-planning endeavor (the first having occurred two decades prior in Essex County), the Olmsted firm's plan was to create several large park units with special recreational or unique scenic opportunities to serve the entire county, as well as smaller parks for locally accessible community needs. Their goal was to always harmonize landscape values with active recreation, to enhance vistas and enrich diverse plantings, all with clear regard for successful connectivity as neighborhoods grew around the parks.

Working closely with Union County Engineer-Secretary W. R. Tracy, and assisted by Olmsted firm associate Carl Rust Parker (who took over after Gallagher's death in 1934), Gallagher shaped a remarkably varied park system, prescient in its regional environmental concerns for watersheds and flood mitigation and for horticultural diversity. Upon his death, the park commission paid tribute to his "wide vision, far-flung experience and high knowledge of the beautiful and the practical," leaving a park system as a memorial where "laughter of happy people will ring for years to come."

By gift, purchase, and some condemnation, Union County had acquired nearly 4000 acres of land by 1930, distributed among ten parks that the Olmsted firm was then planning, a number which grew as the work increased and diversified over the decades. The Elizabeth and Rahway Rivers served as major spines for the park system, while to the west, the slopes of the Watchung Mountains provided wilder acreage for a large reservation, similar to the Essex County system. Along the riverine corridors, linear parks with accompanying parkways grew into several separately named parks as additional lands were acquired and protected. New Deal money helped sustain construction, especially after the destructive flooding of the Great New England Hurricane of 1938. The Olmsted firm continued to advise Union County well into the 1960s. Today, the Union County Department of Parks and Recreation, which includes Cultural and Heritage Affairs, manages 6200 acres of thirty-six diverse parks.

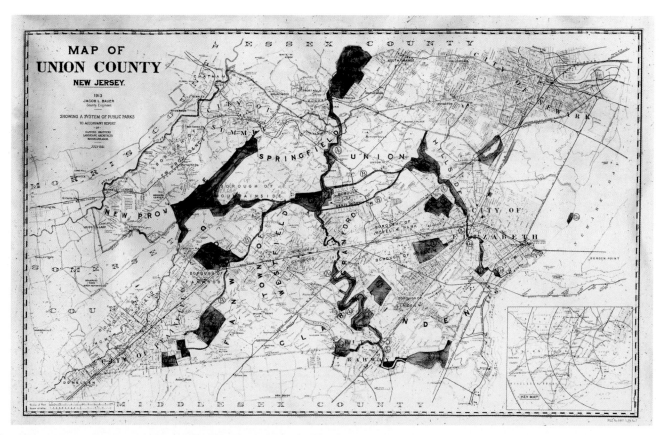

A 1913 plan for interconnected public parks that reach residents across the district.

A 1956 drawing for gates to what is now Warinanco Park's Caxton Brown Memorial Azalea Garden.

Warinanco Park's lagoon winds through much of its 204-acre site.

WARINANCO PARK, ELIZABETH

Warinanco Park, in Elizabeth, was one of the first parks to be acquired and designed for the Union County system; the flagship pleasure ground was crafted to demonstrate good design principles. The park balanced scenic attributes and a large interior meadow and lake, with recreational facilities, a stadium, track, ball fields, playgrounds, and the park administration building on the periphery of its 204 acres. Named for a Lenape sachem, this park contains specialized planted areas: a magnolia grove, an azalea garden, and a memorial herbaceous garden. Centrally located, Warinanco is one of three Olmsted brothers–designed parks for this city, the other two along the riverine corridor—the Elizabeth River Parkway (forty acres), a series of linear parks abutting the watercourse to the northwest, and Mattano (eighty acres) to the southeast, its once pastoral fields now major sports and skateboarding venues.

ECHO LAKE PARK, MOUNTAINSIDE

Echo Lake Park, originally 128 acres, was another early acquisition, a scenic mill race in a wooded valley along Nomahegan Brook, which was dammed to form two lakes for boating. There were meadows, picnic groves, and some peripheral ball fields with drives to connect to Rahway River and Watchung Reservation. This green space has greatly expanded with the abutting, privately run Echo Lake Country Club.

RAHWAY RIVER PARKS, RAHWAY

Originally 900 acres, the Rahway River Parks comprise a series of scenic green spaces of various sizes to both enhance and protect the banks of this very circuitous river and its tributaries. Originating in Essex County, the Rahway River flows into Arthur Kill. The Olmsted firm prepared plans for linked parklands, providing wooded walks and trails and an accompanying drive, widening several individual parks into larger places to accommodate various recreational and environmental opportunities.

Echo Lake Park today retains much of the same character shown in this vintage postcard, with the peaceful pond, shoreside walkways, and heritage trees.

Rahway River Park provides opportunities for recreation under heritage trees as well as protecting its namesake waterway.

In fall, the Watchung Reservation provides quintessential Northeast color.

WATCHUNG RESERVATION, MOUNTAINSIDE

Watchung Reservation, which started at 1800 acres and has now been increased to over 2200, is a wooded preserve sequestered from the cities. It contains sites of geological, historical, and cultural significance intersected by trails and bridle paths, with Surprise Lake for water recreation. In the 1980s, Route I-78 cut through the northern section.

NEW YORK

Buffalo Park and Parkway System	195
Niagara Reservation, Niagara Falls	198
Brooklyn Park and Parkway System	200
Prospect Park, Brooklyn	201
Fort Greene Park, Brooklyn	204
Ocean and Eastern Parkways, Brooklyn	205
Brooklyn Botanic Garden, Brooklyn	207
Central Park, Manhattan	209
Morningside Park, Manhattan	211
Riverside Park, Manhattan	213

Fort Tryon Park, Manhattan	215
Forest Hills Gardens, Queens	217
Gold Coast Estates, North Shore of Long Island	218
Rochester Parks System	220
Highland Park, Rochester	222
Genesee Valley Park, Rochester	223
Seneca Park, Rochester	224
Thompson Park, Watertown	225

Above: The Bow Bridge has become one of Central Park's most iconic features. **Right:** Downing Park is the only project where two generations of Olmsteds and Vauxes worked together.

Frederick Law Olmsted Sr.'s career as a designer of landscapes began in Manhattan, New York, when the Greensward Plan—the original plan for Central Park on which he and architect Calvert Vaux collaborated—won the 1858 design competition for a publicly funded, centrally located park for the city. Within ten years, two other major projects in New York State, Prospect Park in Brooklyn (1866) and the Buffalo Park System (1868), set the standard for urban parks and park systems throughout the country. These projects exemplified the comprehensive planning which Olmsted Sr. and Vaux brought to their tasks, anticipating needs for emergent centers to have accessible and diverse green spaces for respite from urban bustle. Whether within one extensive location separated from city clamor or spread throughout a growing city in varied yet interconnected individual units, their park designs revolutionized how the urban fabric was shaped in the late nineteenth century. More than manipulating landforms purely for decoration, their designs worked within natural conditions to offer sequenced spaces. Such sequencing allowed for different experiences, whether water, woodland, or greensward. In turn, conflicting routes were minimized among pedestrian, equestrian, and carriage visitor, as well as between those seeking spirited exercise and those seeking quiet contemplation. Architecture was subordinated within the verdant surrounds.

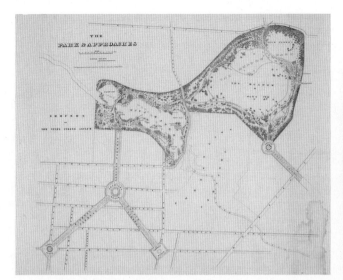

Delaware Park in Buffalo features meandering walkways and rustic bridges through a landscape of mature trees.

BUFFALO PARK AND PARKWAY SYSTEM

Designed between 1868 and 1915, this network of interconnected parks and parkways was among the first of its kind in the United States and is exceptional for its comprehensive scope, inspiring numerous other systems. Though initially asked to select one site for a large park in Buffalo, Frederick Law Olmsted Sr. proposed the acquisition of a large, undeveloped parcel outside the city to be connected to other smaller parks by a system of parkways. Working with Calvert Vaux to create recreational space to temper Buffalo's urban conditions, Olmsted developed the 350-acre "park" from existing agricultural land. Closer to the urban core, "The Front" was situated on a bluff overlooking Lake Erie and included an amphitheater, a formal terrace, and a network of carriage drives. Overlooking the city, "The Parade" initially accommodated military drills and included a public hall but was later redesigned by John Charles Olmsted with aquatic features. Augmenting the parks, an interconnected system of parkways, boulevards, and avenues was developed, forming a northerly arc around the city. Punctuated by residential squares and circles, the tree-lined streets with wide setbacks, planted medians, and landscaped central areas added 125 acres of parkland to the system.

Increased industrialization and population growth strained the capacity of the early parks. The Olmsted firm was again engaged at the end of the 1880s to extend park planning into the problematic southern section of the city where railroads now crisscrossed the low-lying swampy areas. Olmsted Sr. had hoped for a large park fronting Lake Erie, but it was deemed too expensive. Instead, large neighborhood recreational parks, Cazenovia and South, the latter including an arboretum, were planned by John Charles Olmsted and added to the system, as well as significant changes to the Parade, renamed Humboldt.

Established in 1869, the Buffalo Board of Park Commissioners provided nearly fifty years of administration regarding the acquisition and development of the system. Comprising eight parks, eight circles, and nine parkways, the so-called Olmsted Parks and Parkways Thematic Resources was listed in the National Register of Historic Places in 1982. Recognizing that only two such systems were designed by Olmsted and Vaux (the other in Brooklyn), the Buffalo Olmsted Parks Conservancy was established in 1995 to oversee the management of more than 850 acres of parks, parkways, and circles. Beginning in 2004, the conservancy took on the maintenance and operations of the entire park and parkway system.

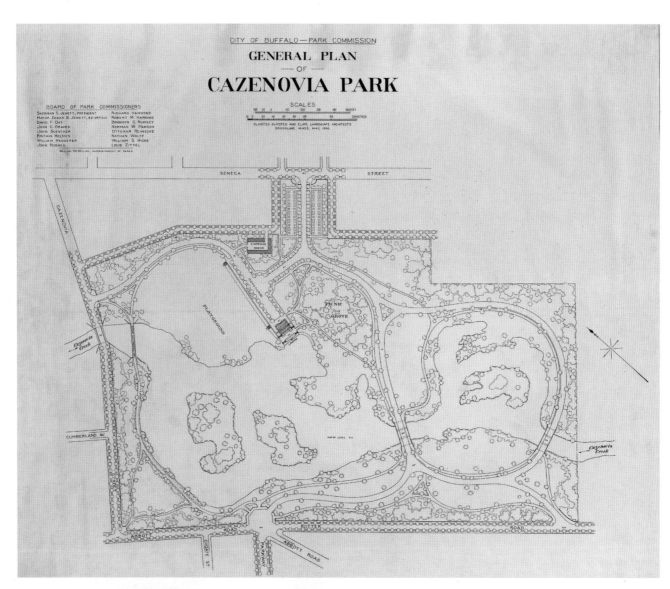

General Plan of Cazenovia Park

Top: Cazenovia Park plan, 1896. **Above left:** Buffalo's South Park features an arboretum displaying trees that can thrive in Western New York as well as a glass conservatory by Lord and Burnham, now the Buffalo and Erie County Botanical Gardens. **Above right:** Many consider the water feature in South Park Olmsted Sr.'s best.

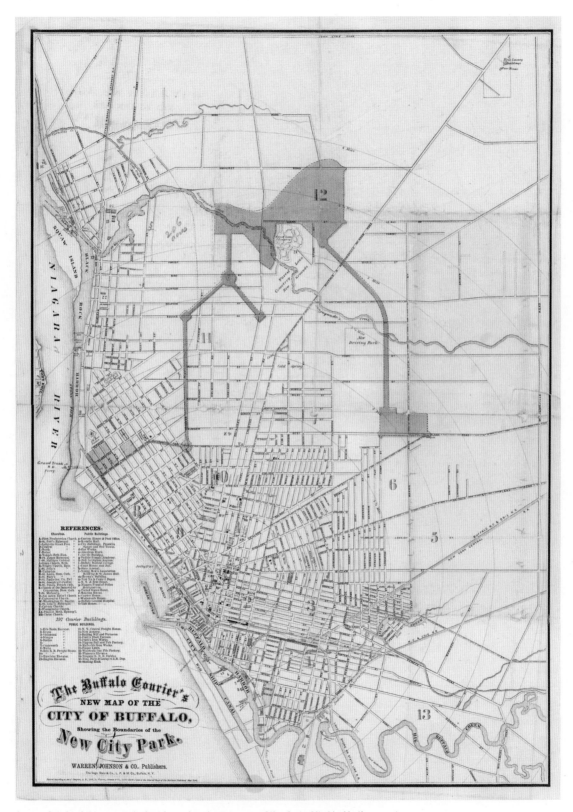

A map showing interconnected parks and parkways—one of the first of its kind in the country.

Above: Diagram used in demonstrating how hydroelectric power's impact on the landmark site could and should be minimized. **Left:** Plans for improvements to the Niagara recreational area, 1887.

NIAGARA RESERVATION, NIAGARA FALLS

During planning for the Buffalo park system, Frederick Law Olmsted Sr. became increasingly alarmed by the rampant commercialization above the falls along the rapids of the Niagara River, which included Goat Island, Three Sisters Islands, Robinson Island, Bird Island, Brother Island, and Green Island. He felt that these areas of spectacular scenery and unique geology—formed during the most recent ice age and ranging from the dramatic rapids to the intricacy of Goat Island's unusual vegetation (a result of the misty conditions), were national and global treasures, like Yosemite. They deserved special protection. An 1880 report, written with James T. Gardner (with whom he had worked in Yosemite), stated the case for removal of various intrusive businesses along the banks, and the creation of a reservation. In this, they were echoing earlier preservationists, such

Above: Conditions at Niagara Falls circa 1908 make it evident that visitors could benefit from a safer viewpoint. **Right:** The pedestrian bridge to verdant Goat Island crosses vigorous rapids preceding the chute.

as artist Frederic Church, who had long crusaded for protective measures. As a result of the vigorous campaign they mounted, amalgamating journalists, writers, political leaders, and many concerned citizens, Niagara was designated New York's first state park in 1885. Olmsted, Vaux, and Company was hired in 1887 to design the necessary amenities for public use.

The challenge for Olmsted and Calvert Vaux was to provide for a circulation system without undue intrusion into this delicate environment. To bring the visitor to the unique viewpoints: above the falls, along the rapids, and on the islands, they carefully wove subtle curvilinear drives and paths throughout the wooded property. Shelters and benches at appropriate stopping points always ensured that the scenic values were highlighted. On the other side of the border, this reservation planning spurred the Canadian government to adopt similar measures, founding a commission in 1885 and Queen Victoria Park in 1888. Olmsted Sr. did not pursue the 1887 request for an advisory visit. However, between 1914 and 1928, both Olmsted brothers, John Charles and Frederick Law Olmsted Jr., provided

advice concerning park development for this commission. Queen Victoria Park today is known as much for its carpet bedding as it is for its river and falls scenery.

The Olmsted Brothers firm was also involved in other projects affecting the scenery along the Niagara River. In particular, Olmsted Jr. advised the Niagara Falls Hydraulic Power and Manufacturing Company on minimizing the impact of its installations along the banks.

Increasing tourism to experience this world wonder has resulted in a continuing struggle over the preservation of historic and scenic values versus additions needed for the reservation to accommodate public demand. Niagara Reservation was designated a National Historic Landmark in 1966.

Prospect Park in fall, along the shores of the lake.

BROOKLYN PARK AND PARKWAY SYSTEM

In 1868, as they worked on park designs in the then rural borough of Brooklyn, Frederick Law Olmsted Sr. and Calvert Vaux expanded their thinking to propose planning on an unprecedented scale for a network of parks and radiating roadways throughout the borough. The planning extended to the beaches to the south and across the East River to Central Park. Inspired by the grand parks and boulevards of Haussmann's Paris and by Berlin's *Unter den Linden*, Olmsted and Vaux coined the term "parkway" in the design of this project, imagining scenic, tree-covered passages for carriage rides rather than dusty, crowded streets. Long before comprehensive city plans and zoning regulations were standard practice, their parkway concept aspired to stimulate the growth of heathy, spacious neighborhoods with ample recreational open space on contiguous lands.

Aided by the politically powerful president of the Brooklyn Park Commission, James Stranahan, Olmsted and Vaux were able to complete several significant components of the plan, including Prospect Park (1867); Eastern Parkway (1870), which begins from the northern tip of the park by Grand Army Plaza (1867) and runs east for 2.5 miles; and Ocean Parkway (1876), which begins at the southwest corner of Prospect Park and runs south for nearly six miles to Coney Island.

Smaller parks suggested by Olmsted and Vaux in the greater Brooklyn system include the thirty-acre Fort Greene Park (1867) and the nearly eight-acre Tompkins (now Herbert Von King) Park (1870), among others. In the 1890s the Olmsted firm returned to expand park planning, now advised by John Charles Olmsted. They worked on developing further greenways throughout the borough, particularly along the water's edge, such as Bay Ridge Parkway-Shore Road (1893–1897) along Gravesend Bay, and on plans for small parks—Sunset Park (1894); Bushwick Park (1895); Dyker Beach (1897), Highland Park (1894), and Brooklyn Forest (1897). The last two became part of the borough of Queens in 1898.

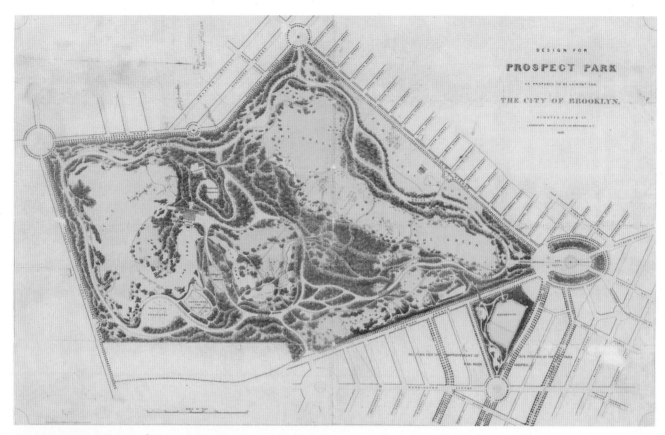

An 1868 plan for Prospect Park.

PROSPECT PARK, BROOKLYN

Negotiating with the Brooklyn Park Commission, Calvert Vaux had already ensured an irregularly shaped 650-acre land parcel for the Brooklyn park before commencing design in 1866 with partner Frederick Law Olmsted Sr. This land held potential for a more interesting combination of desired elements—woods, water, greensward—than could be accomplished in Central Park's linearity. In the north, ninety acres of undulating land allowed them to create their iconic pastoral ground, the Long Meadow, defined by textured evergreen and deciduous borders, intersected by paths graded to be invisible. Varied tree groupings contributed to a subtle shadow play on the lawn, producing an inviting inducement to explore. In contrast, on the east they structured the rugged, rock-filled Ravine, with densely wooded slopes, through which a constructed stream meandered, finally

spilling over falls down to the Lullwater. This narrowed water body eventually emptied into the larger Prospect Lake at the park's southern end, with a complex shoreline of bays and headlands. A concert grove, with a carriage concourse and a music island, enlivened one area of the shoreline. Throughout these spaces pedestrian and equestrian paths and drives curved under bridges of differing characters, while shelters, benches, and other furnishings were sited to take full advantage of varied vistas. Near the northeast entrance to the park, in a low area, they created an area for children's activities, the richly planted "Vale of Cashmere," with a pool for model boats and an intended playground.

By the end of the 1880s the scenic rurality that Olmsted and Vaux envisioned for Prospect Park began to be disrupted.

Prospect Park, as seen from above, stands out as a clear oasis from the built environment surrounding it.

With the appointment of Stanford White as architect for the park, various sculptural features by noted artists and formal structures, such as the Boathouse and entrances, were inserted, along with embellishments such as the balustrade that surrounded the intended children's pool. Most significant, the imperious Soldiers and Sailors Arch at Grand Army Plaza cast a different mood at point of entry. Such changes continued in the mid- to late twentieth century under Parks Commissioner Robert Moses, the Works Progress Administration, and later park administrations, as new demographics brought new requirements for playgrounds, sports fields, a zoo, a bandshell, and a skating rink that obscured the graceful Concert Grove.

With the appointment in 1980 of a separate administrator for Prospect Park and the creation of the Prospect Park Alliance, ongoing research-based rehabilitation efforts took hold to restore features. As financial support would allow, buildings, bridges, and shelters were repaired or rebuilt; compacted woodlands were set aside to organically regenerate once detrimental invasive vegetation was eradicated; an innovative new skating facility enabled the lakeside Concert Grove to resume its intended character. Most recently, the intricacy of the Endale Arch was restored and recaptured. Prospect Park was designated a New York Scenic Landmark in 1975 and listed in the National Register of Historic Places in 1980.

Above center and above: Balustrades and urns were part of recent restoration work along Prospect Park's lakeside.

Enjoying the Long Meadow, circa 1916.

Spaces like the Long Meadow provide a pastoral mood.

Fort Greene Park's stately trees create a ribbon of green canopy between Downtown Brooklyn, with the Manhattan skyline beyond, and surrounding streets of brownstones.

FORT GREENE PARK, BROOKLYN

Designated as parkland in 1847, these thirty acres on a hill had been the setting for Revolutionary War fortifications, also used in the War of 1812. Frederick Law Olmsted Sr. and Calvert Vaux in 1867 laid this space out for both commemoration and recreation, with an intended observatory and structures on the hilltop to capture the splendid skyline views. Below the hilltop were tree plantings on hillsides, a plaza for gatherings, lawns, and playgrounds on the lower ground. In 1908, a prominent memorial designed by McKim, Mead, and White, accessed by a grand stairway, was installed on the hilltop, to honor the men and women who died on British prison ships in nearby Wallabout Bay during the Revolutionary War. A great uncle of Olmsted's had been among those victims.

Today, the park retains its original Olmsted and Vaux character, with winding pathways, sloping lawns, and numerous mature trees, including a grove of stately sophoras and three dozen elm trees—including a 135-year-old English elm. The park also hosts active uses, with basketball and tennis courts and two playgrounds, and accommodates many neighborhood gatherings. Today, the Fort Greene Park Conservancy provides programming, maintenance, and advocacy to advance the park's stewardship.

Ocean Parkway serves as an instant front yard to thousands of Brooklyn residents along its nearly five-mile length.

OCEAN AND EASTERN PARKWAYS, BROOKLYN

Part of Frederick Law Olmsted Sr. and Calvert Vaux's larger design for a Brooklyn parkway system, Ocean Parkway, along with Eastern Parkway, was built from what was originally planned as four legs radiating from Prospect Park. Built concurrently with the park and completed in 1876, this approximately five-mile parkway was the first of its kind in the United States. Modeled after the *Avenue de l'Impératrice* in Paris (now *Avenue Foch*) and *Unter den Linden* in Berlin, but on an even grander scale, the parkway served both scenic and practical purposes. At a massive 210 feet across and stretching from Park Circle (now Machate Circle) near the southwest corner of Prospect Park South to Coney Island, the parkway separated roadways by type of use—private carriages in the inner lanes, with tree-shaded bridle and pedestrian paths. After 1894, the byway also included the first bicycle path in the country. Commercial vehicles were assigned to the outer edges, to be closer to the houses they would service. The route was marked by engraved stones every half mile and buffered on both sides by greenswards planted with triple rows of trees (today primarily maple, oak, sycamore, elm, and a few ginkgo trees). Satisfying the Olmsted-Vaux design intent, the pedestrian paths are lined with long rows of benches and playing tables, to serve as an active park edge for

Eastern Parkway buffers surrounding Prospect Heights and Crown Heights residents from six lanes of traffic, while providing them with shady pedestrian malls.

the surrounding neighborhood. Until the 1970s, when the bridle path was removed, there continued to be an equine presence on the parkway, although racing generally came to an end in 1908 when betting became illegal.

Over the eras, the abutting neighborhood evolved from one of rural farming to one of private homes for middle-class Eastern European and Jewish immigrants, to a fashionable neighborhood of high-rise apartments. In the 1950s the northernmost half mile of the parkway was demolished and replaced by Robert Moses's Prospect Expressway. Ocean Parkway was listed in the National Register of Historic Places in 1983.

Eastern Parkway was constructed between 1870 and 1874, intended to create a link between New York City and the outer boroughs and act as both a transit link and pleasure drive. Olmsted and Vaux's original design intent was for a citywide park system linked by scenic roadways. Eastern Parkway would pass across Prospect Park, extending to Central Park via a bridge

and then on to the Hudson River, while Ocean Parkway would connect from Prospect Park to the Atlantic Ocean. John Culyer, who supervised the parkway's original construction, repair, and maintenance from 1870–1874, designed a two-mile extension from 1890 to 1893, linking Prospect Park to Highland Park.

Now one of the busiest roads in the city, originating at the northern tip of Prospect Park, Eastern Parkway consists of a broad, six-lane roadway flanked by two tree-lined pedestrian malls that also serve as bike lanes, and two service roadways for slower local traffic. It runs just under four miles—from Grand Army Plaza, east to Ralph Avenue, curving north to Broadway, and then extending to Bushwick Avenue. The section between the Plaza and Ralph Avenue was designated a National Historic Landmark in 1978, and still retains much of its original character as a place for strolling, leisure, and recreation. Both Ocean and Eastern Parkways were designated as New York City Scenic Landmarks, in 1975 and 1978, respectively.

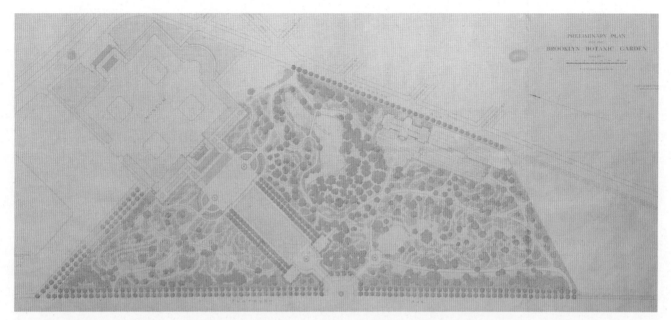

An early plan by the Olmsted Brothers for the Brooklyn Botanic Garden reveals how the space features formal areas adjacent to the museum and conservatory, then quickly becomes less formal as meandering paths bring visitors close to various plantings.

BROOKLYN BOTANIC GARDEN

Purchased by the City of Brooklyn along with land for the adjacent Prospect Park, this once-glaciated, marshy, thirty-nine-acre parcel was a municipal dump until 1897. In 1909, the project commenced with a contract between the City of New York and the Brooklyn Institute of Arts and Sciences.

The institute's director, Franklin W. Hooper, and the garden's first director, Charles Stuart Gager, contracted with the Olmsted Brothers firm to prepare a general plan for the rubble-strewn site, to include the grading for the now-landmark Administration Building, by McKim, Mead, and White, along with locations for other specialized buildings and gardens.

The Olmsted plan covered four distinct areas, each with a different character, separated and framed by trees with connective turf walkways: border plantings along the inner edges of paths; a terrace and lawn with shrubs extending from the Administration Building (later the Magnolia Plaza and Lily Pool Terrace); small botanical displays set among trees and large shrubs; and flat areas of long, narrow beds framed by tall foliage. The plan, supervised by Olmsted Jr. with Percival Gallagher, Percy Jones, and Hans J. Koehler, also included a pond, an esplanade, and a plaza at Flatbush Avenue. Horticultural propagation and display buildings are generally still located as originally planned.

The garden opened on May 13, 1911, highlighting native plant species found within 100 miles of the city—the first collection of its kind in a North American botanic garden. Harold Caparn, who was appointed landscape architect and grounds manager in 1912, designed subsequent sections, including additional acreage, often in conjunction with the Olmsted Brothers firm and others.

While Brooklyn Botanic Garden retains Olmsted Jr.'s intended spatial framework, many of the interior, eclectic, sub-garden spaces have evolved, although many are still connected by original winding paths. This sensitivity has safeguarded the Olmsted

The Brooklyn Botanic Garden's Cherry Esplanade provides formal structure and shade even when not in bloom.

Brothers firm's vision of the pastoral and their intended idea of "elsewhere," away from urban congestion and noise.

The three-acre Japanese Hill-and-Pond Garden, designed by Takeo Shiota, opened in 1915 as one of the first Japanese-style gardens in an American public park. It was followed in 1917 by the Rock Garden, utilizing glacial boulders; the Shakespeare Garden (1925); and the Cranford Rose Garden (1928), designed by Caparn with over 1000 varieties. In the 1930s, Works Progress Administration laborers helped build the Herb Garden and the original Horticultural Garden was developed into the three-acre, Italian Renaissance–style Osborne Garden. Landscape architect Alice Ireys created the tactile Fragrance Garden in 1955 to facilitate access to plants through the senses of smell and touch.

The Steinhardt Conservatory (1988), extending south from an original display house, serves as the Palm House. The Olmsted firm's esplanade, originally meant to connect to the Brooklyn Museum of Art with a grand Neoclassical staircase, was not realized as conceived, although remnants can be found in the garden's stately Cherry Esplanade. Recent projects have replaced aging infrastructure with modern technologies and greener, more accessible practices, allowing for expanded educational and cultural programs.

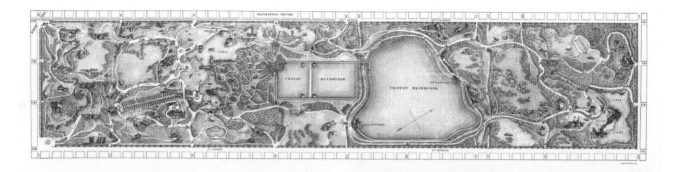

Top: A detailed map for Central Park, after the original Greensward Plan, circa 1860. **Above left:** Bethesda Terrace and Bethesda Fountain, designed by Jacob Wrey Mould and featuring the sculpture *Angel of the Waters* by Emma Stebbins—the first woman to receive a public art commission in the city—commemorates the opening of the Croton Aqueduct in 1842, which brought fresh water to New York City. **Above right:** Olmsted and Vaux included large boulders as a reminder to city dwellers of the area's geology, as development erased most signs of Manhattan's natural topography.

CENTRAL PARK, MANHATTAN

With their precedent-setting, prize-winning entry, the Greensward Plan for New York in 1858, Frederick Law Olmsted Sr. and Calvert Vaux envisioned a transformation of the 750-acre site—from irregular topography, challenging schist outcroppings, bogs, and windswept fields encompassing the Croton Reservoir, into expanses of lush pastoral meadows, shadowy woodlands, reflective lakes, and impressive boulders, interlaced by curving paths and ample park drives. Behind perimeter walls backed by dense plantings, the park space could offer peaceful withdrawal from the city's hard edges. With their ingenious design for sinking the transverse roads, even the crosstown

vehicular traffic could be isolated from park visitors. Designed with strong artistic intent, Olmsted and Vaux looked to create varied and intriguing passages of scenery for the visitor moving throughout the park, whether perambulating or by another mode of movement. Necessary architectural elements—buildings and shelters to offer visitor amenities, bridges to keep the travel ways separated, walls and steps for ease of travel—were all subordinated by grading or vegetation to landscape values.

Certain features were purposefully highlighted—the formal Central Park Mall as a gathering place, the bandstand, and the Bethesda Terrace, with its central fountain and views across

Central Park is justifiably famous for its great variety of bridges, totaling thirty-one for pedestrians, not including the small rustic bridges in the wooded areas.

the lake to the contrasting Ramble, a place for more solitary explorations. With the undulating topography along circuitous paths, all these spaces offered orchestrated experiences, whether singular or gregarious, to stimulate or soothe the visitors' sensibilities. Major goals for the park via its unrestricted meadows were to enhance an "enlarged sense of freedom" so often truncated by bustling city streets, and to encourage visitors' awareness of the delicacy, textural variety, and abundance of nature. Olmsted and Vaux, imbued with the romantic values of their time, saw such sensory "unbending" and intermingling of people of all classes as a way to encourage a healthier, more creative citizenry—more able to engage in their patriotic, commercial, or social endeavors.

Notable figures associated with the park's nineteenth-century development included sanitarian George E. Waring, who ensured the proper drainage for the park; architect Jacob Wrey Mould, responsible for many bridges and the Bethesda Terrace; horticulturist Ignatz Pilát, who oversaw the textured plantings; and landscape architect Samuel Parsons Jr., who continued this work and safeguarded the Olmsted-Vaux design legacy through 1911.

Gilmore Clarke, Thomas Price, and Betty Sprout introduced the Conservatory Gardens in the 1930s, while in the 1960 to 1980s period, landscape architects Richard Dattner and M. Paul Friedberg added innovative adventure playgrounds and play spaces. A separate administrator was appointed for Central Park in 1979, followed in 1980 by the founding of the Central Park Conservancy, to oversee park management. The conservancy augmented city services and provided a much-copied model for management and public-private partnerships. At 843 acres, Central Park became a National Historic Landmark in 1966. It was designated a New York City Scenic Landmark in 1974.

A small waterfall tumbles into the pond at the edge of Morningside Park's imposing cliff.

MORNINGSIDE PARK, MANHATTAN

Spanning thirty linear acres in Harlem that surround a jagged schist cliff, this park was conceived in 1867 by Andrew Haswell Green, commissioner and comptroller of Central Park. Frederick Law Olmsted Sr. and Calvert Vaux prepared complex plans in 1873, which included a large building for tropical plants and small lagoons, but an economic recession postponed construction. Fifteen years later, collaborating with architect Jacob Wrey Mould, Olmsted Sr. and Vaux, no longer formal partners but working together, instead developed a wide esplanade along Morningside Drive, supported by a monumental retaining wall with semi-octagonal belvederes and several broad staircases descending to the lower ground. To enliven the dramatic ledge, they placed a profusion of prostrate plants tumbling down the slope. Broad paths, graded for accessibility, meandered around the outcroppings and the lower planted or meadow areas.

At the turn of the twentieth century, the park became a repository for monumental sculpture by noted artists, including Frédéric-Auguste Bartholdi's statues of Lafayette and Washington, the Carl Schurz Memorial by Henry Bacon and Karl Bitter, and the Seligman Fountain by Edgar Walter. From the 1930s onward, more active recreation opportunities—playgrounds, a baseball diamond, basketball courts—were added to the eastern and southern portions of the park. In 1968, the construction of a gymnasium for Columbia University students was begun on this parkland but halted after vigorous community opposition; the excavated hollow was transformed into an ornamental pond with a waterfall in 1990. The Thomas Kiel Arboretum, situated at the 116th Street entrance and modeled on an 1858 arboretum design created by Olmsted and Vaux for Central Park that was never implemented, opened in 1999. Morningside Park was designated a New York City Scenic Landmark in 2008.

Top: Rugged stairs traverse Morningside Park to mediate its elevation changes. **Above:** At the top of Morningside Park's massive retaining wall, a walk places visitors in the canopy of trees growing below.

Riverside Park stretches four miles, with broad pedestrian promenades running continuously through much of it.

Rustic boulders and naturalistic plantings help the park feel apart from the city, although it runs in a narrow strip between just 100 and 500 feet wide.

RIVERSIDE PARK, MANHATTAN

Stimulated by the success of Central Park, park commissioners turned their consideration for making more parkland toward the sloping terrain with its riverine vistas along the upper Hudson River waterfront, from about West 59th Street northward. Rising above the working docks and railroad tracks lining the water's edge, this land, some of which was already occupied by expansive country seats, appealed to Frederick Law Olmsted Sr. as an opportunity to design an extensive promenade for carriages, with bridle and pedestrian paths, accompanying parks, and unparalleled views—spaces with both recreational and residential prospects. From 1874 until he was ousted in 1877, he transformed the former Riverside Avenue between 72nd and 125th Streets into wide, tree-lined Riverside Drive, with sloping linear parks retained by stone walls along the western edge, ending in a grand concourse. Colleagues Calvert Vaux and Samuel Parsons, among others, continued development of Olmsted Sr.'s concepts with varying success into the early twentieth century, shaping the roadway around grounds for the various monuments sited along this scenic parkway.

In the following decades, the railroads' need to expand and the citizens' increasingly vocal desire to protect and expand this park and parkway space resulted in numerous planning schemes, many of which involved Frederick Law Olmsted Jr. With architect Arnold Brunner and New York City Parks Department's landscape architect Charles D. Lay, the younger Olmsted worked between 1912 and 1916 to plan for the northern extension and expansion of Riverside Park by roofing the tracks and train yards to create more parkland. Olmsted Jr. vociferously defended "park values" in these proposals, to prevent damage to naturally picturesque conditions, such as the boulder outcroppings at historic Fort Washington Park (later Fort Tryon Park). These schemes went largely unfulfilled. With the reign of Robert Moses, beginning in 1934, assisted by WPA labor and the "West Side Improvement" plan designed by Gilmore Clarke, Michael Rapuano, and Clinton Loyd, the park expanded on filled land toward the river, for the Henry Hudson Parkway. Numerous recreational facilities, architectural embellishments, and the esplanade were added to existing spaces, bringing some of the Olmsteds' vision to fruition, albeit at a greatly expanded scale. In 2000, a seven-acre tract, Riverside Park South from 68th to 72nd Streets, was added to Riverside Park. In 1980 the 171-acre original section of Riverside Park was designated a New York City Scenic Landmark.

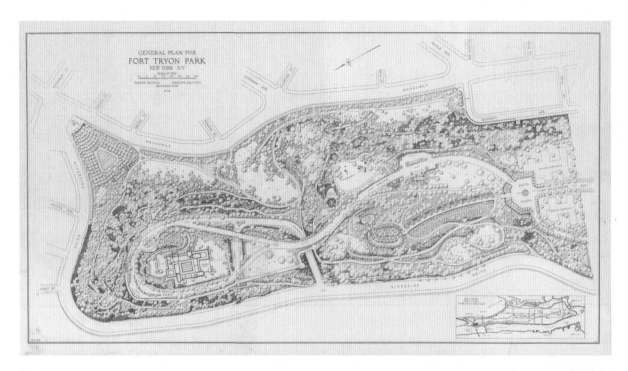

Top: Fort Tryon Park plan, Olmsted Brothers, 1935. **Above:** View looking south from Fort Tryon Park, 1932.

The 1931 sketch for Fort Tryon, showing the ambling promenades, overlooks, and terraces that take advantage of famous views.

Fort Tryon Park's position on a high point in Upper Manhattan gives it enviable vistas over the Hudson River and to the Palisades.

FORT TRYON PARK, MANHATTAN

Recognizing the scenic and historical importance of this beautiful but precipitous schist outcropping that dominated the northwestern end of Manhattan, John D. Rockefeller Jr. began purchasing land as early as 1916 to gift to the city for a park. This rocky promontory, important to the Lenape people and the location of a major Revolutionary War battle, was in the early twentieth century the site of several country estates. The most notable of these belonged to Cornelius K. G. Billings and was called Tryon Hall. It featured an Italianate landscape by Charles Downing Lay and housed the studio and medieval collections of sculptor George Grey Barnard. The latter became the core of the Cloisters, a branch of the Metropolitan Museum of Art, to which four acres was dedicated and would become part of Fort Tryon Park. Since the sixty-seven acres of the Rockefeller purchase came with stipulations, the city rejected

the offer. It would take until around 1926 for Rockefeller and the city to come to an agreement. By that time, Rockefeller had also acquired the Palisades, on the facing side of the Hudson River in New Jersey, to be set aside as parkland, thus preserving a critical vista.

Between 1927 and 1935, Frederick Law Olmsted Jr. and the Olmsted Brothers firm, particularly Henry V. Hubbard and James F. Dawson, were fully engaged in transforming this topographically challenging but commanding site into a functional park. Deliberate considerations were given to views out from within the park and to the park from various venues, including the then-proposed George Washington Bridge. Noting its potential for "luminous" open space contrasted with intimate sylvan scenery, the firm toiled to capture the inexpressible quality of "a rock-perched

Above: Robust rock walls share a design vocabulary with the Cloisters buildings. Below: The Cloisters tower rises dramatically out of surrounding Fort Tryon Park.

fortress of the old world" with accessible roads and paths, while meeting community needs for recreational spaces. Olmsted Jr. saw his challenge as fitting together units of design, some symmetrical and geometric, others more eccentric, like a "large Gothic composition," with terraces to capture the sweeping Hudson River views and textured plantings and gardens to enhance buildings and structures. Overcoming innumerable engineering challenges, steps and paths were carved into the stone escarpment for woodland passages. Retaining walls of local stone with great arches for pedestrian and automobile passage were also aligned to frame significant vistas. Taking an aesthetic cue from the great arcade remnant of the Billings Estate along the Henry Hudson Parkway, the Olmsted firm and Rockefeller's engineers designed the monumental arch over Margaret Corbin Drive, linking the park with the parkway. The flatter northeast corner, abutting the local neighborhood, provided the playground, pool, and other recreational opportunities.

Beyond providing the city with a unique park and museum, this massive project, mostly underwritten by Rockefeller, created employment during the difficult Depression years. Deeded

to the city after 1931, the park opened to great acclaim in 1935, four years after the George Washington Bridge and three years before the Cloisters was completed. Listed together in the National Register of Historic Places in 1978, the Cloisters and the park were also designated as Individual and Scenic New York City Landmarks in 1974 and 1983.

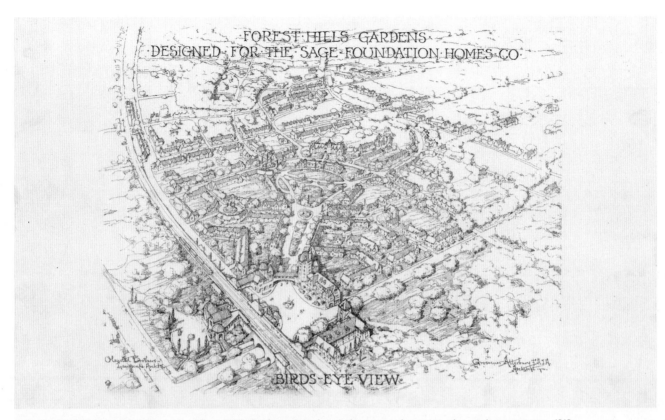

FOREST·HILLS·GARDENS·
DESIGNED·FOR·THE·SAGE·FOUNDATION·HOMES·CO

BIRDS·EYE·VIEW·

A drawing for the planned development—at Forest Hills Gardens a broad central avenue and common, plus ample green space—1910.

FOREST HILLS GARDENS, QUEENS

Between 1901 and 1910, the construction of the Queensboro Bridge and the Long Island Rail Road tunnels spanning the East River made central Queens a viable bedroom community. In 1906, the Cord Meyer Development Company amassed 600 acres of farmland with the intention of creating Forest Hills, a middle-class residential neighborhood. Three years later, the corporation sold 142 acres to the Russell Sage Homes Foundation, founded by Margaret Olivia Sloan Sage, a fan of Ebenezer Howard's *Garden Cities of To-Morrow* (1902), who sought to create an idyllic garden suburb. Sage hired Frederick Law Olmsted Jr. of Olmsted Brothers and architect Grosvenor Atterbury for the general plan.

Modeled after a traditional English village, the plan features a shopping section along the parcel's southern boundary and two small parks, Flagpole Green and Station Square, plus a distinctive town center with a commuter train station and a hotel. The tree-lined residential streets, laid out by 1910, were made curvilinear to discourage through traffic; sidewalks promoted pedestrian use. The landscaped housing lots were substantial, and only Tudor or Georgian houses were to be constructed, of masonry or concrete, with either red tile or slate roofs. Atterbury used standardized precast concrete panels in his house designs. Today the community consists of over 800 single-family homes, townhouses, and garden apartment buildings.

In 1913, the West Side Tennis Club, which hosted the US Open Tennis Championships between 1915 and 1977, relocated to the northeast section of Forest Hills Gardens. One of America's earliest garden cities, the development is managed by the Forest Hills Gardens Corporation.

Top left and right: Two views of the William Coe Estate grounds, circa 1924. **Above left:** The Coe Estate pool has been well maintained by the Planting Fields Foundation. **Above right:** The Otto Kahn Estate, now Oheka Castle, is a case study in formal landscape design.

GOLD COAST ESTATES, NORTH SHORE OF LONG ISLAND

The North Shore of Long Island has an ideal combination of scenery, climate, and soil. The rolling topography and little peninsulas jutting out into the Long Island Sound are well situated for large estates, country and sporting clubs, and cemeteries. Starting in the 1870s until the late 1930s, the area between Little Neck Bay east to Northport Bay became known as the Gold Coast as large tracts of land were transformed into gracious private estates for wealthy corporate moguls. Of the more than 500 such properties developed between 1890 and 1940, the Olmsted

firm was involved in 200 of them, about forty of which were for cemetery "rooms," the ultimate residence, for these civic leaders and their families.

Over the decades, properties fell into disrepair, burned, were subdivided, or were adapted for other uses. A few of the Olmsted-designed properties are extant and accessible to the public: the Bayard Cutting Estate, an Olmsted Sr. design, now a New York State Arboretum and CSA farm; the William Coe Estate in Oyster Bay, known today as Planting Fields Foundation; the Otto

Kahn estate, in Huntington, now Oheka Castle, reconstructed as a resort hotel and special events venue; and the former Harold Pratt Estate in Glen Cove, a partial ruin, managed as the Welwyn Preserve, with the Holocaust Memorial and Tolerance Center of Nassau County housed in the mansion. Properties still privately owned are occasionally accessible, such as the former John Aldred Estate, Ormston, now Saint Josaphat Monastery in Glen Cove, and the two cemeteries with Olmsted designs, Memorial Cemetery of Saint John in Oyster Bay and Locust Valley Cemetery.

Many of these grand properties were characterized by a dignified entrance drive with orchestrated vistas, an impressive entry court at the main house set among mature trees, notable plantings, and expansive lawns. Garden "rooms," mostly in the formal style, radiated out into the grounds, decorated with fountains, pools, and sculpture, or designated for specialized plantings, such as roses. Outdoor amenities included tennis courts, swimming pools, and walking and bridle paths; ancillary buildings such as stables and farmsteads were inconspicuously tucked away. Some properties were vast, such as Welwyn at 1000 acres, and included their own cemetery designed by Olmsted Brothers; others, such as Ormston, were of a relatively modest scale.

Design challenges for the Olmsted Brothers firm included coordination of this palette of projects, many of which were ongoing simultaneously. The plans had to respond to specific site conditions, satisfy clients' and architects' tastes and budgets, and provide individualized and noteworthy landscape settings.

Of those that survive today, the Bayard Cutting Arboretum State Park was listed in the National Register of Historic Places as part of a historic district in 1973, while the former Coe and Aldred estates were listed in 1979.

Top, center, and above: The Harold Pratt Estate, now the Welwyn Preserve, featured extensive horse paddocks and now encompasses a nature preserve for a stretch of the bay's shore.

Lower Falls in Rochester's Maplewood Park were laid out to feature the Genesee River.

ROCHESTER PARKS SYSTEM

The provision of public space has a long tradition in the city of Rochester, whose early development was organized around several public squares that served as community gathering places in the early 1800s. With further growth spurred by the routing of the Erie Canal through the city, additional squares were established, along with landscaped burial grounds like Mount Hope Cemetery, established in 1838. By the 1880s, the desire for true public parks, comparable to those being established in other cities, led some local landowners to donate property for this purpose, and to the establishment of a board of park commissioners in 1888. Following proposals from five of the country's

leading designers, including Frederic Law Olmsted Sr.'s former partner Calvert Vaux, the Olmsted firm was selected to lead the development of a comprehensive park system.

As proposed by Olmsted Sr., the Rochester system is composed of three large parks: Highland Park (the former Ellwanger and Barry Nursery, which would retain its horticultural character, including an arboretum), Genesee Valley Park (a Naturalistic-style landscape south of downtown with gently rolling terrain along its riverbanks), and Seneca Park (north of downtown with its dramatic, Picturesque-style character and more rugged terrain along three miles of both sides of the

Genesee Valley Park, with quintessential Olmsted-spaced trees over gently rolling greensward.

Genesee River). Collectively, these parks, which range from twenty acres to 800 acres, were intended to capture some of the region's major distinctive landscape characteristics and scenery.

Olmsted Brothers, under John Charles Olmsted, continued involvement in the development of the system after Olmsted Sr.'s retirement, and by the early 1900s, the park system expanded with the addition of four major new parks, two small new parks, two street malls, and dozens of playgrounds. The majority of these commissions were for existing parks, including Brown Square, Jones Square, Caledonia Square (Lunsford Circle), Franklin Park (Schiller Park), and Washington Square. Of those, new or revised plans for Brown Square, Jones Square, and Madison Square (Susan B. Anthony Square) were prepared, as were designs for two squares acquired by the city: Riley Triangle (Anderson Park) and the Maplewood Grove. The firm generated plans for park

connectors: Genesee Valley Parkway, Seneca Parkway, and Lake View Parkway. In his 1911 report, *A City Plan for Rochester*, prepared for the Rochester Civic Improvement Committee, Frederick Law Olmsted Jr., together with Arnold Brunner and Bion Arnold, recommended additional neighborhood parks, reservations, and parkways, as well as a system of outlying parks. The firm continued to consult on the system's development until 1915, when the independent board of park commissioners was dissolved and replaced by a city parks department. The City of Rochester, along with the City of Louisville, have the only park systems in which all three Olmsteds were involved in the design. In 2003, the Municipal Park System of Rochester, including many of these parks and squares, was listed in the National Register of Historic Places while Seneca Parkway was included in the Seneca Park East and West Historic District nomination of the same year.

Highland Park's original planting plan dates to 1893; its origin as a nursery and arboretum is still apparent in places.

HIGHLAND PARK, ROCHESTER

As previously referenced, in 1883 George Ellwanger and Patrick Barry gave the City of Rochester twenty acres of their nursery, still containing significant plant collections, for use as a park. The Rochester Parks Commission hired the landscape architecture firm F. L. and J. C. Olmsted to design the park as an arboretum. The firm created a Picturesque-style park that incorporated the adjacent city reservoir and afforded scenic views of the city. Their plan saw Pinnacle Hill planted with pine trees to the north and arrangements of shrubs to the south. An adjacent meadow was framed by shrubs and trees. A winding drive ascended the hilltop to the park's focal point, the three-story Children's Pavilion designed by Shepley, Rutan, and Coolidge. Park Superintendent Calvin Laney and horticulturist John Dunbar helped realize the park's design. Over time, Dunbar changed the park's planting palette to emphasize ornamental flora. The Lamberton Conservatory was added to the park in 1911, in addition to two land parcels, including the estate of Horatio Gates Warner in 1951. The Children's Pavilion

was destroyed in 1963, and the Lamberton Conservatory was reconstructed in 2007.

Early twentieth-century residential subdivisions and the Mount Hope Cemetery frame the 150-acre park. Both Reservoir Avenue and Highland Drive divide the park north to south. A curvilinear walkway follows the Olmsteds' original circulation system to encircle the reservoir before summiting the hilltop and descending the park's southeastern slope. The path winds down the hillside through plantings of magnolia, lilacs, and pansies, crossing Highland Avenue to reach a series of memorials, including the Vietnam Veterans Memorial of Greater Rochester and the AIDS Remembrance Garden. East of Pinnacle Hill is a wooded park area that includes a lily pond, a natural amphitheater, and a bandshell known as the John Dunbar Memorial Pavilion and Warner Castle, with its sunken gardens designed by landscape architect Alling DeForest and added in 1930. Highland Park is a contributing feature of the Municipal Park System of Rochester, listed in the National Register of Historic Places in 2003.

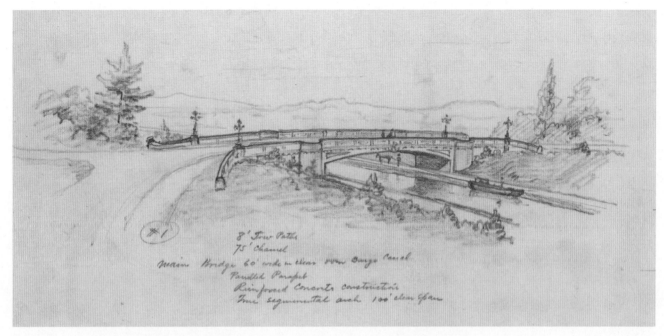

Genesee Valley Park's barge canal necessitated a plan for three pedestrian bridges; this drawing is from 1910.

GENESEE VALLEY PARK, ROCHESTER

Originally known as South Park, this landscape is part of the Rochester Park System designed by the Olmsted firm between 1881 and 1912. Frederick Law Olmsted Sr. chose the 543-acre site, divided by the Genesee River, for its natural incorporation of water with wooded, rolling terrain. Recreational facilities were placed west of the river, while the opposite bank was transformed into a pastoral setting complete with a meadow, deer park, and picnic groves encircled by carriage routes. Between 1889 and 1898, 62,500 trees were planted along a bordering railroad line and the adjacent Westfall Road, while shrubs and willows were embedded along the park's riverbanks and within the woods. During this time, John Charles Olmsted oversaw the placement of additional recreational facilities, including a golf course that supplanted the meadow. A donation of 120 acres expanded the park in 1908. When the park was divided north to south by the Erie Canal in 1918, Olmsted Brothers mitigated the disruption to the site by creating a bridge that reunited the landscape. The park was further divided in the late twentieth century by the I-390 Expressway.

Surrounded by a mix of residential and urban development, this park is bound between Elmwood Avenue and Crittenden Road to the north and south, respectively, with the Genesee River forming much of the western boundary. The expressway and Erie Canal divide the park north to south and cross perpendicular to the river. Along the eastern riverbank, Moore Road winds south through wooded terrain and across the canal, connecting park features that include a historical pavilion, a deer park, picnic groves, and the Genesee Valley Golf Course. Adjacent to Elmwood Avenue, on the western shoreline, are a number of recreational facilities that include a boathouse and ice rink. Concrete bridges span the canal, while a network of trails provides scenic viewsheds of the river. The park is a contributing feature of the Municipal Park System of Rochester, listed in the National Register of Historic Places in 2003.

Seneca Park runs for three miles along a forested river gorge.

SENECA PARK, ROCHESTER

These 297 acres are a component of the Rochester Park System designed by Frederick Law Olmsted Sr. beginning in 1888, with a general plan created in 1893. Olmsted designed the park to provide public access to the Genesee River while also preserving the area from encroaching development. His original master plan called for tree-lined carriage drives on both sides of the canyon, and a circulation network of paths that sensitively minimized disturbance from grading. Dense plantings along the gorge served to prevent erosion and reduce the risk of falling debris. A series of overlooks provided scenic views from 200 feet above the river. In the early twentieth century, park leaders, influenced by the City Beautiful movement, installed new recreational assets, including swimming pools, playgrounds, and a zoo (established beginning in 1894). The additions were in part overseen by John Charles Olmsted, who sought to integrate these features with the aesthetic established by his father.

This linear park frames three miles of steep banks on both sides of the Genesee River. East of the river, a one-way carriageway curves through rolling woodland and loops around the artificial Trout Lake, created by damming a natural spring. The road and lake, situated on a plateau and bordered by picnic groves and meadows, were both designed by Olmsted Sr. Trails with occasional descents to the river follow the edge of the gorge. To the north, trails are surrounded by a wilderness of sassafras, hickory, maple, oak, and horse chestnut trees, while to the south a pedestrian bridge spans the river to connect both sides of the park. Located on a ridge, the Seneca Park Zoo, expanded in the 1930s, is visually separated by its higher elevation and perimeter woodland plantings. Seneca Park was listed in the National Register of Historic Places as Seneca Park East and West in 2003.

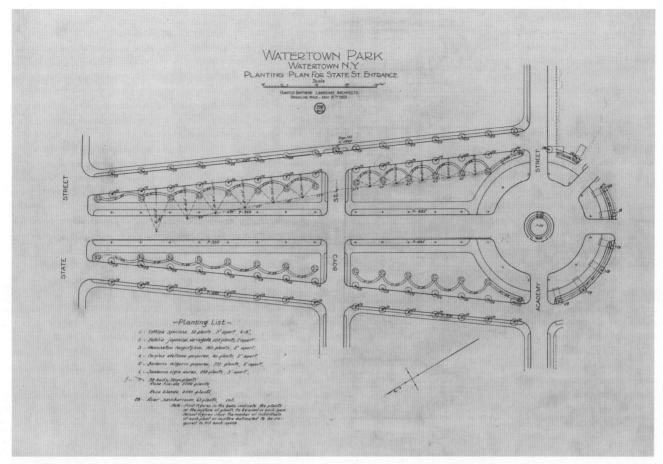

Planting plan for the original entry boulevard to what would become Thompson Park, 1901.

THOMPSON PARK, WATERTOWN

In 1899 John C. Thompson, president of New York Air Brake Company, located in Watertown, contacted the Olmsted Brothers firm about creating a park as an anonymous gift to the city. With his office in New York City, Thompson was very familiar with Olmsted park work. Under the advice of John Charles Olmsted, he secretly acquired more than 700 acres of woods and fields encompassing Pinnacle Hill, with its scenic vistas over the growing city and toward Lake Ontario, in order to lay out a park with suitable approaches. Contiguous land for residential development was also part of the acquisition. Producing a "General Plan" by 1901, over the next two decades John Charles Olmsted supervised construction on this challenging, rocky site. He planned a formal tree-lined boulevard as the primary entrance from State Street, connecting to roads and accompanying paths curving upward through the park to its summit. To mitigate the steepness, he designed walls, overlooks, shelters, and steps ascending the slopes (built from stone quarried on-site)—all accompanied by textured plantings. At the summit, a water tower intended to be a lookout anchored one end of a formal axis, with a monument square at the other end. For children's

The Thompson Park Pool, receiving heavy use in 1902.

recreation, a particular concern of Thompson's, he provided playgrounds, a wading pool, and a pavilion. The hillside slopes were to be treated as pastoral meadows with ponds.

Ownership and responsibility for maintenance was transferred to the city in about 1916. The donor's identity remained a secret until Thompson's death in 1924 when his purpose, to provide healthy recreation and a sense of ownership for Watertown families—whether worker or manager—was revealed.

In 1920, a zoo was constructed on thirty-two acres, and later, the park's sweeping meadows became an eighteen-hole golf course, now privately managed. In July 2016 a sculpture, Honor the Mountain Monument, was installed on the summit square to celebrate the sacrifices of the 10th Mountain Division and the civilian workforce located at nearby Fort Drum.

Rustic shelters function as overlooks from the top of Pinnacle Hill, photographed here in 1902.

NORTH CAROLINA

Biltmore, Asheville   228   Village of Pinehurst   232

Duke University, Durham   231   Capitol Square, Raleigh   233

An aerial perspective shows how Biltmore's formal gardens are set in the context of the surrounding landscape and mountains.

BILTMORE, ASHEVILLE

At 125,000 acres, George W. Vanderbilt's Biltmore was one of the largest residential commissions ever undertaken in the United States. Between 1889 and 1895, the self-sufficient estate, complete with working farm and fully integrated horticulture, forestry, and land management programs, was designed by architect Richard Morris Hunt and landscape architect Frederick Law Olmsted Sr. Olmsted saw this commission as an opportunity to demonstrate to the public, without extravagant decoration, the transformation of rugged, forested land into tasteful grounds to enhance the architecture and the natural scenery.

The mansion is accessed by a three-mile approach road, winding through densely planted woodlands with orchestrated vistas, including a dramatic glimpse across a meadow of the mansion atop its hill. Roadside views are punctuated by rocky outcrops and rustic bridges across a meandering stream which widens into small lagoons. A long, formal lawn esplanade lined with a tulip tree allée precedes the east-facing front of the château-style mansion, so sited as to hide the major scenic vistas. Olmsted's plan reserves the full panorama of rolling terrain, woodlands, and distant mountain views for those enjoying a sunken lawn terrace on the southern side. Below this terrace, Olmsted created other

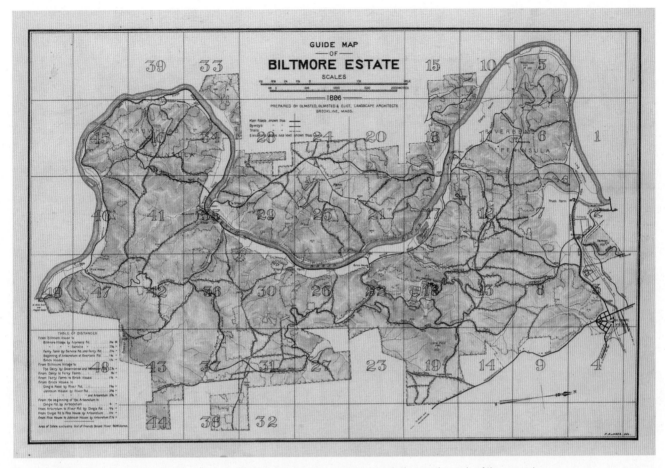

The map of the Biltmore grounds, with the residence itself toward the bottom right, reveals the massive scale of the property.

garden "rooms," each with distinct character: a terrace of geometric lily pools and lawn panels; a ramble of paths winding down a slope around textured plantings; a four-acre walled cutting and vegetable garden with grape arcade; and a glen of seasonal plant groupings, in particular the spring azalea garden leading into the near woods. Chauncey Beadle worked with the Olmsted Brothers to design and manage the gardens and woodlands, with their network of bridle and walking paths, until his death in 1950.

Extending his plan to develop a scientific arboretum of native plant materials for the estate, an "outdoor museum" with supportive microclimates, Olmsted's innovative recommendation

was for Vanderbilt to acquire an additional 120,000 acres of Mount Pisgah woodland. For this endeavor, Vanderbilt hired Gifford Pinchot to scientifically manage this commercial forest enterprise, eventually establishing the US Forest Service and later developing the nation's first forestry education program with Carl Schenck: the Biltmore Forest School.

85,000 acres of the estate are now part of Pisgah National Forest. The property was first opened to the public in 1930 and was designated a National Historic Landmark in 1963. In 2002 the designation was expanded to recognize Chauncey Beadle, Edith Stuyvesant Vanderbilt, and her attorney, Julius Green Adams.

Above: The five-mile-long approach road to the main house at Biltmore. **Below:** View across the lagoon.

The quadrangle for the campus features axial paths and many heritage trees that create an enviably leafy canopy.

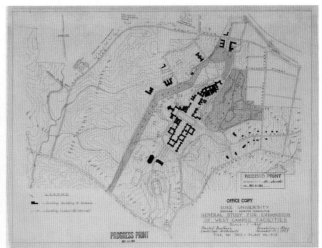

A 1959 plan shows Olmsted Brothers situating the campus carefully within the existing topography and landscape while reinforcing geometric circulation plans.

DUKE UNIVERSITY, DURHAM

This research university grew from humble beginnings as a one-room schoolhouse founded in 1838 by a community of Methodists and Quakers in Randolph County. Hoping to attract more students and by then called Trinity College, the school was relocated to Durham in 1892. Originally occupying ninety-seven acres on the east side of the burgeoning city, the college became a full university in 1924 with a major endowment by James Duke, which spurred the creation of a new, larger campus further west. Today, Duke University comprises nearly 9000 acres, spanning three contiguous campuses.

Beginning in 1925, Olmsted Brothers, led by Percival Gallagher, designed the campus grounds, including a circulation system and quadrangles for both the Georgian-style East Campus (the site of the original Trinity College) and the Collegiate Gothic–style West Campus, in collaboration with architects Horace Trumbauer and Julian Abele. Olmsted Brothers skillfully manipulated the irregular terrain to insert academic and residential building complexes within the unifying forest canopy, balancing symmetry and irregularity, axial vistas and secluded courtyards, to create a campus of unique character and charm within a vibrant city. In 1938 the Sarah P. Duke Gardens were established, with a design by landscape architect Ellen Shipman.

The Olmsted Brothers affiliation slowed after Gallagher's death in 1934, only to resume in 1945, again in conjunction with the Trumbauer office, and continued sporadically through the 1960s under Olmsted Associates. Until the 1990s, demands upon the university contributed to haphazard growth, which was finally addressed by renewed campus master planning. While several landscape architecture firms have contributed to a more cohesive environment to meet the university's demands for the twenty-first century, the strong design imperatives set forth by early Olmsted firm planning remain the character-defining aesthetic for the Duke campus.

Pinehurst's village green feels more like an arboretum than a traditional town square, thanks to rich plantings featuring pines.

VILLAGE OF PINEHURST

In 1895 James Walker Tufts of Boston commissioned Olmsted, Olmsted, and Eliot to plan a winter resort community to promote good health in the rolling North Carolina pine woods. Olmsted assistant Warren H. Manning carried out Frederick Law Olmsted Sr.'s plan for a scenic, self-sufficient rural village nestled among rich plantings, accessible by railroad. After 1896, as an independent landscape architect, Manning continued to work with Pinehurst and the Tufts family for forty-six years.

Settled across broad ridges and valleys, the 100-acre resort centers around a village green planted with pine trees. Concentric and radial curvilinear streets are lined with a diverse range of cottages, boarding houses, and small hotels, each set thirty-six feet back from the street with wide, street-side planting beds which serve as gutters. Sandy soils complicated implementation of this parklike setting, requiring considerable work to install more than 225,000 native evergreens and spring-blooming plants. Diverse opportunities for tennis, croquet, and other recreational activities were provided, including a significant early golf course, introduced in 1898.

Today, Pinehurst is a major resort with a grand hotel and numerous condominiums, widely recognized for its well-preserved Golf Course Number 2, designed by Donald Ross, and for Golf Course Number 4, which was the work of Robert Trent Jones and Rees Jones. Other site features include an equestrian center, pine grove, and deer park. Pinehurst was designated a National Historic Landmark in 1998.

The North Carolina Veterans Monument, **(right)**, set apart from Capitol Square grounds in an oval, lies on the north side of the capitol building.

CAPITOL SQUARE, RALEIGH

The largest of the five original squares laid out in William Christmas's 1792 plan for the City of Raleigh, these six acres continue to be at the geographical heart of the city's downtown. Over the course of its first century, the square hosted a series of smaller governmental buildings. At its center was the first capitol, a simple two-story structure replaced in 1833 by a Greek Revival building designed by architects Ithiel Town and Alexander Jackson Davis. The capitol building is sited at the intersection of the four major avenues of the Christmas plan, reinforcing the axiality of the street grid. Added throughout the nineteenth and twentieth centuries, more than a dozen monuments dot the landscape alongside mature oaks and hickory trees. A statue of George Washington was the first to be installed in 1857, situated opposite Fayetteville Street at the south entrance to the capitol. Erected in 1990, the North Carolina Veterans Monument dominates the north side of Capitol Square, with a forty-foot-tall structure within a paved oval plaza.

In 1928 Olmsted Brothers created a master plan for the capitol grounds, transforming the surroundings from piecemeal development into formalized, publicly accessible green space. The firm designed a parklike setting with curvilinear pebbled paths leading through geometric lawns. Though the paths have been repaved over time, in most cases the Olmsted-planned routes have been preserved. The firm realigned several statues to create a more orderly layout and introduced landscape features, including a stepped plaza with two small fountains at the capitol's east entrance. The Capital Area Historic District, encompassing Capitol Square and several blocks to its east and west, was listed in the National Register of Historic Places in 1978.

The North Carolina State Capitol Grounds' square plan (n.d.).

OHIO

Fine Arts Garden, Cleveland Museum of Art   237

NCR Projects, Dayton   239

Denison University, Granville   241

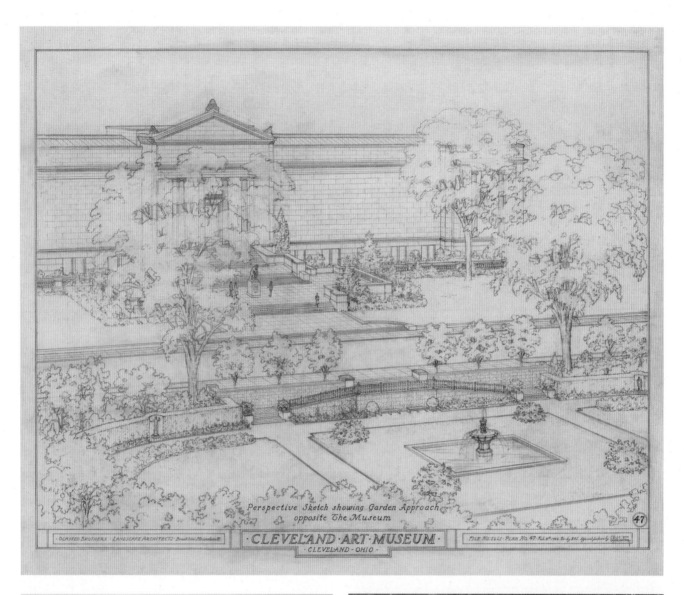

Perspective Sketch showing Garden Approach
opposite The Museum

47

· OLMSTED BROTHERS · LANDSCAPE ARCHITECTS · Brookline Massachusetts ·   · CLEVELAND · ART · MUSEUM ·   FILE NO 5621 PLAN No 47 Feb 8th 1926 By 881 Approved June by Olmsted

· CLEVELAND · OHIO ·

Top: A 1926 sketch for the approach to the Cleveland Museum of Art. **Above left:** The formal garden for the museum was first completed in 1928. **Above right:** A view across the lagoon and to the museum, seen from the corner of Martin Luther King Jr. Drive and Euclid Avenue.

FINE ARTS GARDEN, CLEVELAND MUSEUM OF ART

This garden occupies land that was originally part of a seventy-three-acre parcel donated, in 1882, to the City of Cleveland for use as a park by industrialist Jeptha Wade. A smaller adjoining segment, initially withheld as a reserve, was donated by Wade's grandson, Jeptha Wade II, to the city for the creation of the Cleveland Museum of Art, which opened in 1916. The Olmsted firm was first contacted by architect Benjamin Hubbell in 1912 and again in 1916 concerning landscape treatment around the building. Warren Manning had submitted Naturalistic-style designs to include Wade Park which were less formal than the Beaux Arts structure required. The museum's building committee decided not to employ a landscape architect at that time, and the grounds languished. Finally, in 1925 the Garden Club of Cleveland hired Frederick Law Olmsted Jr. of Olmsted Brothers to beautify the institution's setting and coordinate it with the surrounding parkland, with the city carrying construction expenses. The firm's design, developed by Olmsted Jr. together with Edward Clark Whiting (whose cousin, Frederic Whiting, was the museum director) and Leon Zach in 1928, included a two-tier formal garden descending from the museum's southern facade along a central axis into Wade Park.

The first tier, the Zodiac Garden, is a lowered terrace, defined by an oval lawn, its shape reinforced by marble curbing and a border of yew hedges. Fronting this hedge are twelve stone plinths, representing the signs of the zodiac, carved by Chester Beach who is also responsible for the formal central fountain, named *Fountain of the Waters*, a bowl with a tall water jet, surrounded by classical figures. Beach and Olmsted worked collaboratively to ensure the correct proportions for these decorative elements.

The second tier is a central grass mall, punctuated by parallel topiary and enclosed by side hedges descending a ramped slope which connects at its base with the path around Wade Park Lagoon, located in a hollow. The Olmsted plan decoratively refines the stone-lined pond edges into bays and headlands, accentuated by plant groupings and benches, all with an eye to the reflective qualities of the water. The surrounding descending slopes are a careful modulation of lawn and tree and shrub groupings. On axis with the museum's entrance, at the southern end of the lake, another step-ramp with central lawn panel ascends the slope to a terrace with a central sculpture by Frank Jirouch, *Night Passing the Earth to Day*. Formal stairs on each side ascend from this level to an upper marble terrace with a balustrade fronting on Euclid and Chester Avenues.

Listed in the National Register of Historic Places in 1982, the Fine Arts Garden is a contributing component of the Wade Park District along with the Liberty Boulevard Greenway and the Wade Oval, all of which provide a setting for some of the city's most significant cultural institutions.

National Cash Register Company ~ Dayton, Ohio ~ Plaza at Old River Park

Olmsted Brothers
Landscape Architects
Brookline, Mass.

A 1937 plan for the National Cash Register Corporation Plaza.

Carillon Historical Park, an open-air museum celebrating the achievements of Daytonians.

NCR PROJECTS, DAYTON

The Olmsted Brothers were involved in 279 projects in Ohio, of which 153 were in Dayton. Hired in 1896 by John Henry Patterson, founder of National Cash Register Corporation (NCR), the firm, initially under John Charles Olmsted and later involving Frederick Law Olmsted Jr., Henry V. Hubbard, and Carl Rust Parker, provided consulting services to this corporation, its leaders, and other associated clients for over sixty years. Early twentieth century Dayton became a hub for American industrial innovators, which included the Wright Brothers; Edward A. Deeds and Charles Kettering of the Dayton Engineering Laboratories Company (DELCO); and Thomas J. Watson of IBM, once an NCR sales manager.

Olmsted firm projects included NCR headquarters, recreational grounds, and landscaped housing for the employees and families; a public park system with improved riverside parkland; numerous subdivisions and street extensions; and private property designs for the Pattersons and their associates. Notable

sites still accessible to the public include Hills and Dales Park, the Wright Brothers Hill, and Carillon Historical Park.

In 1906 John Patterson purchased 500 acres south of the Miami River, authorizing the Olmsted Brothers firm to design a subdivision and park. John Charles with associate Percy Jones oversaw road and lot layouts for the residential areas and for a park accommodating active and passive recreation with meadows, bridle trails, a golf course, campgrounds, and fishponds. In 1918, Patterson gave 294 acres to the city as Hills and Dales Park. In 1920, Dayton expanded the public golf course from nine to thirty-six holes, eliminating much of the Olmsted Brothers design, leaving the remainder as a fifty-seven-acre park.

To celebrate the Wright Brothers' achievements, Edward Andrew Deeds, the third CEO of NCR and friend of the Wrights, commissioned Carl Rust Parker of Olmsted Brothers in 1938 to design a memorial park. An earlier attempt under John C.

Above: Dogwood Pond in Dayton's Hills and Dales MetroPark, featuring an Adirondack-style overlook shelter. **Below:** The Wright Brothers Memorial, commissioned by NCR CEO Edward A. Deeds, and completed in 1940.

Olmsted's direction after Wilbur Wright's 1912 death was left incomplete due to 1913 flooding. Located on a hill overlooking Wright-Patterson Air Force Base and burial mounds of Native American Adena culture, this park opened in 1940. It consisted of a circular design centered around a seventeen-foot granite shaft, surrounded by plantings, enclosed by low walls with interpretative plaques, noting both the significance of Indigenous peoples and aviation history. At the same time, Deeds conceived of Carillon Historical Park as a museum complex showcasing the region's industrial innovations and transportation achievements. Designed by Carl Rust Parker on difficult riverside terrain, this sixty-five-acre park, with its 151-foot carillon, opened in 1942. Both sites are listed in the National Register of Historic Places—Wright Brothers Hill in 2016 and Carillon Park in 2005.

Old River Park, planned by Olmsted Jr. and colleagues beginning in the late 1930s, served as a recreational area for NCR employees. It included a swimming pool, athletic fields, and playgrounds with specially designed structures (bridges, gazebos, fountains, etc.) Today, the park is owned by the University of Dayton and is used for ecological studies. In 2009, NCR moved its headquarters to Atlanta.

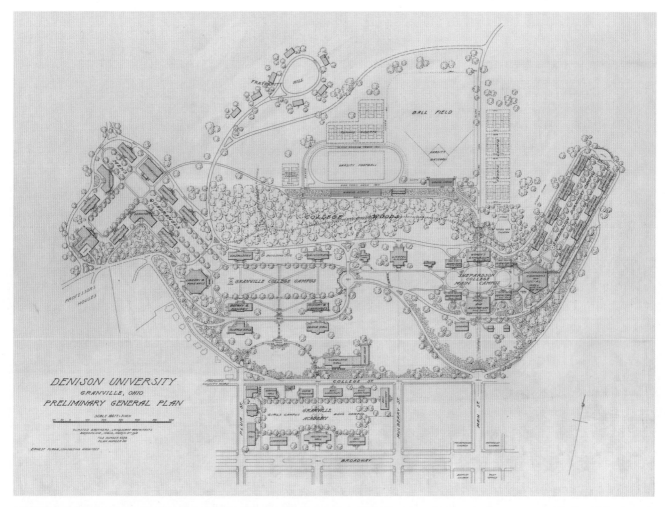

A 1918 campus plan for Denison University, notable for the graceful way quads on different axes create one cohesive campus, and for the retained woods that buffer the main campus from the athletic facilities.

DENISON UNIVERSITY, GRANVILLE

Founded in 1831, Granville Literary and Theological Institution, located thirty miles east of Columbus, was one of the earliest colleges to be established in the Northwest Territory west of the Ohio River. In the mid-1850s, it was renamed Denison University, and moved to the village of Granville. Female students attended the Granville Female Seminary in 1832, renamed Shepardson College for Women in 1886. Shepardson College was incorporated as part of Denison in 1900.

Transforming and enlarging the original 200 acres of wooded ridges with dramatic elevation changes into a cohesive campus was an expensive challenge. This work involved the relocation of Shephardson College; creating new residential and

Historic buildings surround open, grassy quadrangles on Denison's main campus.

academic buildings, gymnasia, and athletic fields; and housing for professors and fraternities. The planning was largely underwritten by Edward A. Deeds, 1897 Denison valedictorian, and a manager of National Cash Register Company (NCR) and founder of Dayton Engineering Laboratories (DELCO), who had worked with John Charles Olmsted and Percy Jones of Olmsted Brothers on numerous projects for NCR. By 1916, John Charles Olmsted, together with New York architect Ernest Flagg, was engaged to prepare layout proposals for anticipated growth. Collaborative, but stylistically different, their planning also had to contend with donor-driven tastes for particular structures. The 1918 General Plan, representing much of John C. Olmsted's vision to site buildings in harmony with natural conditions and with each other, consisted of a series of terraces along the existing contours, nesting the academic quad in the heart of the campus between the men's and women's colleges. The centrally located academic core was adjacent to the anticipated chapel and the 1910 Swasey Observatory. (In 1924, trustee Ambrose Swasey, also an Olmsted client, provided funds for the chapel.) Athletic fields were located north of the quads where the relatively flat terrain best accommodated such use. Curvilinear drives throughout the campus linked residential areas on west and east ridges back to the central core and downhill into the village, all enhanced by attractive plantings.

By 1919 architect Arnold Brunner of New York had replaced Ernest Flagg and, with the death of John Charles Olmsted in 1920, Frederick Law Olmsted Jr. stepped into the planning together with Edward Clark Whiting. Under this team, many practical and aesthetic issues were resolved concerning materials (brick instead of stone), Colonial rather than Gothic style, location of utility buildings, and the use of retaining walls (and eventually bridges) in road planning to adjust steep grades.

Today the spatial organization of the Olmsted-led design remains mostly intact, with later expansions respectful of John C. Olmsted's balanced arrangement of buildings around open quads, attentive to dramatic vistas out and up to the main campus on its hilltop. The original 200-acre campus has grown to 1100 acres, including a 400-acre biological reserve.

OREGON

Elk Rock Garden at the Bishop's
Close, Portland   244

Portland Park System   246
Terwilliger Parkway, Portland   248

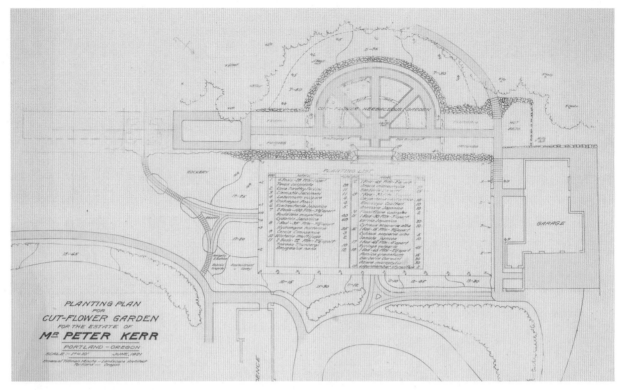

A 1921 planting plan for Elk Rock Garden.

ELK ROCK GARDEN AT THE BISHOP'S CLOSE, PORTLAND

Situated atop the cliffs overlooking the Willamette River, in the Abernethy Heights neighborhood south of downtown Portland, Elk Rock Garden is among the oldest, largest intact private gardens in the state.

In 1888, Peter Kerr, a Scottish immigrant and entrepreneur, arrived in Portland, where he soon started a successful grain business. In the early 1890s Kerr used the profits from his burgeoning business to purchase a modest parcel of land. By 1906, the Kerr family had bought three of the property's adjacent lots, increasing the site's total size to over thirteen acres. In December 1909, Kerr hired landscape architect John Charles Olmsted and architect D. E. Lawrence to design and construct a house and garden. In addition to laying out roads and pedestrian paths on the property, Olmsted sited the residence with vistas of Mount Hood. Upon the house's completion, Kerr, an avid amateur gardener himself, began implementing his plans for a sprawling hillside garden. From 1916 to 1919, Kerr and Olmsted began to realize

a Picturesque-style garden, utilizing intertwining paths and streams to portray a wild, albeit highly manicured and idealized, version of the natural landscape. In 1917, Kerr hired Emanuel T. Mische, a former Olmsted firm plantsman and former superintendent of Portland's parks, who designed much of the landscape we see today—one with expansive lawns immediately surrounding the house, and a hillside garden with pathways and vistas that take full advantage of the views of the Willamette River toward the town of Milwaukie.

Olmsted's association with the design would end in 1919 and Kerr would continue to spend another thirty-eight years meticulously planning and maintaining the garden until his death in 1957. Kerr ultimately planted an eclectic mixture of Scottish species (sentimental reminders of his homeland) and Pacific Northwest natives. Following his death, both the house and garden were given to the Episcopal Diocese of Oregon, with the stipulation that the property be open to the public.

Top and above: The Bishop's Close enchants, both with vistas out through a lawn and across the adjacent river, as well as with densely planted, meandering paths

Top left: Sellwood Park runs along the banks of the Willamette River south of downtown Portland. **Top right:** Firwood Lake in Laurelhurst Park is surrounded by carefully chosen trees meant to give the impression of being natural. **Above left:** Kenilworth Park is notable for its grove of large Douglas fir trees. **Above right:** The reservoirs atop Mount Tabor Park no longer provide drinking water, but adjacent paths provide views all the way to downtown Portland.

PORTLAND PARK SYSTEM

The Portland Board of Park Commissioners decided in 1903 to expand and link together parks that had been part of the city's first plat map in 1852 but were never connected, including a continuous line of parks called the Park Blocks and two city blocks named the Plaza Blocks. In the intervening years, the city beside the Willamette River had also acquired City Park, Columbia Park, and Willamette and Governors Park, plus additional land on King's Hill at the west end of downtown, near Balch Creek in the northwest hills of the city, and close to Ladd's Addition on the east side of the river. Parkland totaled 205 acres, significantly less than in the neighboring city of Seattle, which had a smaller population.

While John Charles Olmsted was already in Portland in 1903 to plan for the Lewis and Clark Centennial Exposition (to take

Peninsula Park in north Portland features a formal rose garden.

place in 1905), the board asked him to develop plans for the park system. His published report became a model for establishing responsibilities for park boards and for developing comprehensive systems of open space.

Olmsted developed an eighteen-point plan with varied parks and boulevards, taking advantage of the views of the natural mountain scenery and adjoining rivers. It focused on the area between the West Hills, Columbia Boulevard in the north, 40th Avenue on the east, and the Multnomah-Clackamas County border to the south. In the area he called South Hillside Parkway (now Terwilliger Parkway), Olmsted proposed a scenic drive; of the four parts of the city covered in the plan, the South Hillside/ Terwilliger Parkway was the only one fully realized.

The ambitious proposal anticipated Portland's future growth. In 1908 John Charles Olmsted recommended Emanuel Mische, who had worked at the Olmsted Brothers firm, for the job of park superintendent. In the job, Mische continued implementing the plan, with Olmsted serving as a visiting consultant. Later that year, Mische designed Peninsula Park, then Kenilworth Park (1909), Sellwood Park (the former City View Park, 1910), Laurelhurst Park (1910), and Mount Tabor (1911), all based on Olmsted's initial recommendations. In 1912, the city commissioned further work by Edward Bennett, based on his extensive city planning in Chicago. Many aspects of Bennett's Greater Portland Plan followed John Charles Olmsted's original proposals. Where Bennett proposed elevated roadways over the Willamette River, instead of landscaped parkways, the city ultimately adopted Olmsted's suggestions that natural features be as accessible as possible, with a park ribbon adjoining the river.

Today, the city's public parks and parkways span about 12,500 acres with much of its acquisitions and development guided by the 1903 plan by the Olmsted Brothers firm.

Originally referred to in John Charles Olmsted's 1903 report to the Portland Park Commissioners as South Hillside Parkway, the land (named Terwilliger Parkway since 1912) was proposed as one of the main scenic drives leading south out of the city. The Board of Park Commissioners had commissioned Olmsted to design a system of connected parks and parkways at a time when the city did not yet have main boulevards that would serve arterial traffic. Olmsted envisaged a forty-mile loop trail system that included the parkway on the western part of the city, inclusive of two forest reservations that would preserve some of the characteristic hillside landscape and afford views of the river, downtown, and snow-peaked mountains.

The parkway adjoins the River View Cemetery property that was gifted to the city in 1854 by one of Portland's first permanent white settlers, James Terwilliger. Following Terwilliger's death in 1892, and the city's subsequent acquisition of adjoining land, his family deeded a right-of-way through their property in 1909. The deed specified that the land was to be used as a boulevard or parkway for the benefit and use of the public, which helped preserve and protect its wooded character and unobstructed views during several construction stages in subsequent years.

Although the Olmsted Brothers firm had sketched preliminary plans for the roadway development, the final plan was drawn by the superintendent of parks, Emanuel Mische, John Charles Olmsted's recommendation for the position. The parkway opened in 1912 and was formally dedicated two years later.

The current parkway of about 115 acres winds from downtown along the west hills, passing through the neighborhoods of Marquam Hill, Southwest Hills, and Burlingame, and by Lewis and Clark College before ending at Oregon Route 43 in Lake Oswego. The parkway width includes about 100 feet of land on both sides of the road. It also boasts a parcel donated by Charles and Thelma Norris in 1992, including numerous rhododendrons that Mrs. Norris had planted while a member of the

Much of Terwilliger Boulevard's seven-and-a-half-mile length follows the contours of Portland's western hills, giving the pedestrian pathways enviable views out across the Willamette Valley.

American Rhododendron Society. The Friends of Terwilliger Parkway was established in the early 1990s with a mission to protect the historic, natural, and recreational character of the parkway. In 2021 they were instrumental in listing Terwilliger Parkway in the National Register of Historic Places.

PENNSYLVANIA

FDR Park, Philadelphia	251	Stoneleigh, Villanova	254
Vandergrift Town Plan	252	Kirby Park, Wilkes-Barre	256

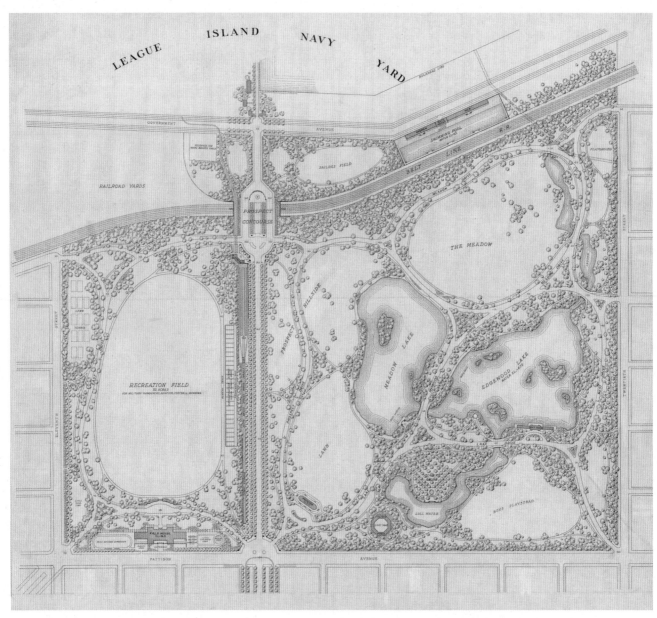

Olmsted Brothers' original 1915 plan for FDR Park.

The boat house and classical rotunda were both included in the park's original plan.

FDR PARK, PHILADELPHIA

The initial concept for FDR Park, originally known as League Island Park, was established by Samuel Parsons Jr., the winner of an 1899 design competition for the site. This concept was further refined in a 1908 study by the City Parks Association of Philadelphia. It showed a broad concourse in the center of the park, which is bisected by Broad Street, connecting to Marconi Plaza to the north and eventually to city hall. A winding perimeter drive wrapped around the park, with a meadow in the eastern portion and a ball ground to the west. Two lakes, illustrative of the site's history as marshland, were located in the northwest corner of the park. In 1912 the Olmsted Brothers were asked to further improve the park. Their scheme reversed the park's program, and instead relegated active recreation to the smaller eastern half of the park, while increasing the complexity of the drives, paths, meadows,

and lakes that structured its passive functions. A grand boulevard connected to the plaza, and the concourse was shifted to extend over railroad tracks on the park's southern edge; further Picturesque-style treatments provided a link to the nearby station.

FDR park was largely complete by 1915, but the design was not to last long. Philadelphia City Architect John Molitor reconfigured the park again to host the city's Sesquicentennial Exposition of 1926. The recreational elements in the park's eastern half were replaced with a large stadium, a military camp was placed in one of the meadows, and pavilions for various states and countries were located throughout the park. Marconi Plaza, which the Olmsteds had designed with a central formal concourse and framed by more informal greens, was selected to host a giant replica of the Liberty Bell.

Vandergrift's streets of varied Victorian homes and mature plane trees are still well tended by residents today.

VANDERGRIFT TOWN PLAN

At a time of labor unrest in the late nineteenth century, George McMurtry, chairman of Apollo Iron and Steel Company—a large manufacturer of rolled steel in southern Pennsylvania—went to France, Germany, and England to explore planned factory villages. Partnering in the steel company with entrepreneur J. J. Vandergrift, who, in turn, was associated with John D. Rockefeller's burgeoning oil business, McMurtry was expanding to a new plant on hilly farmland along the Kiskiminetas River. Beyond improved living environments, McMurtry was considering enabling workers to buy, not rent, their homes as a means of ensuring a committed labor force. In 1895 he requested a visit from Frederick Law Olmsted Sr.

to develop this plan for "better than the best." Since Olmsted Sr. had essentially retired by then, John Charles Olmsted took the lead.

The Olmsted plan, which evolved for part of the Apollo-owned land, located railroad and factory buildings on flatland by the river, while placing the main business street and residential areas on higher ground above the smoke and noise. There were to be wide, paved streets for good drainage, ample and deep lots, and small parklets, all curving around the hillside. This curvilinear street pattern, and the railroad's location, carved out what should have been the central core—the village green—with its abutting municipal building, the casino, to be offset to the northern edge of the town.

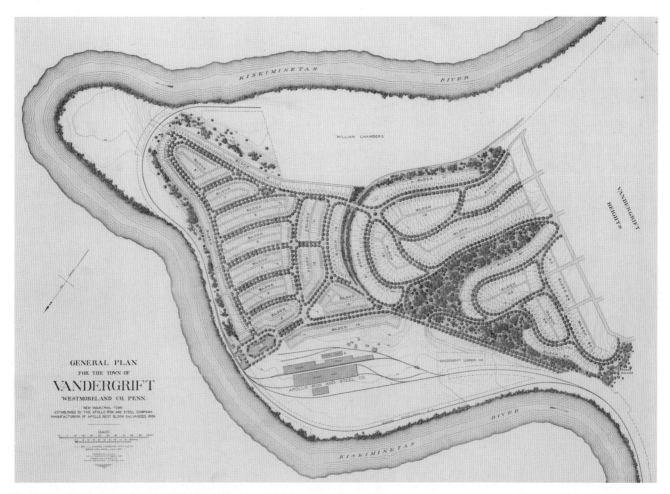

General plan for the town of Vandergrift, circa 1900.

What emerged in 1896 from this quickly implemented plan were architecturally varied and individualized Victorian homes, with indoor plumbing, along treelined streets. Churches, schools, parks, and independent businesses were situated along Grant Street. Although the intended Olmsted lot sizes were reduced to accommodate more house sites and roads were narrowed, their well-engineered drainage and paving systems were retained. Lots sold quickly when bidding began, some to investors but most to skilled workers. For the lower-paid and foreign-born workers, Vandergrift Heights and East Vandergrift were developed, not by the Olmsted firm but as an engineer-designed community of smaller, affordable lots on gridded, steep streets with fewer amenities. McMurtry's real estate gamble paid off, when, during the labor troubles around 1901, his workers supported him because they liked their modern town. In 1917 John C. Olmsted noted that the lesson learned from Vandergrift was to have iron-clad restrictions limiting lot sizes and one family per lot.

Although the mill ownership and product changed over time, and the community has weathered serious economic challenges, there is a strong sense of pride of place today. Vandergrift was listed in the National Register of Historic Places as a historic district in 1995.

Perspective drawing of Stoneleigh's pool, garden building, and surrounding area, circa 1908.

STONELEIGH, VILLANOVA

Stoneleigh's history as an estate began in 1877, when Pennsylvania railroad executive Edmund Smith acquired sixty-five acres, constructing a large stone house and laying out the grounds with the aid of Charles Miller. In 1901 Samuel and Eleanor Bodine acquired the property and continued to develop it as a country place, rebuilding the mansion as a Tudor Revival manor and hiring a succession of designers to refine the grounds. The firm of Pentecost and Vitale introduced dramatic Beaux Arts gestures, including a circular flower garden and pergola, elaborate terraces around the house, and an axial entry court. In 1908 the Bodines turned to the Olmsted Brothers firm, who continued to consult on the property's development, maintenance, and eventual subdivision. The firm also provided advice to the Bodines' son William, who built his own home on the northern portion of the property. The remainder of the estate was acquired by Otto and Phoebe Haas in 1932, following Samuel Bodine's death; they too called on the Olmsted firm for advice on the care of the grounds. The firm's involvement was one of their longest associations for an estate landscape, spanning a half century.

The formal circular drive approaches the Tudor Revival–style main house, clearly emulating great English estates.

The pergola at Stoneleigh was influenced by English precedents, perhaps Hestercombe.

The Olmsted Stoneleigh work, which softened the Beaux Arts plan, was overseen by firm principal Percival Gallagher. They retained the circular garden but replaced its interior with an open lawn. The formal entry sequence was replaced by a curving drive, while pasturelands between the stable and Willow Cottage were converted into a paddock, and ultimately a great lawn. A careful manipulation of the grading and planting (for example, between the house and Spring Mill Road) ensured continuity between the earlier work and the new. The service aspects of the estate were subordinated while new house construction was accommodated through a sensitive subdivision of the property. Beyond the house and gardens, curving walks and lawns afforded sweeping views from the preserved portions of the terrace.

In 1964 Otto and Phoebe's son John and daughter-in-law Chara acquired the property. In 1996 they placed the property under a conservation easement. Following John's passing in 2011 and Chara's in 2012, their children entrusted Stoneleigh to Natural Lands in 2016. Today the property is open to the public.

A large shelter, a meadow dotted carefully with a variety of deciduous trees, and a bucolic pond give Kirby Park a "country park" feel.

KIRBY PARK, WILKES-BARRE

In 1903 Warren H. Manning proposed parks for Wilkes-Barre, an industrial city along the Susquehanna River. At that time, he was planning a system of large and small parks for Harrisburg, the Pennsylvania capitol, farther south along the river, to include several sites on the waterfront. Manning's lengthy Harrisburg work led to the development of a parks commission and stimulated other projects along the river valley.

For Wilkes-Barre, a $250,000 donation from businessman Frank M. Kirby, following a donation of considerable acreage on the west side of the river, prompted the city to contact Frederick Law Olmsted Jr. of the Olmsted Brothers firm in April 1921 to design the park named for the donor. From the outset, a major concern was how to deal with frequent flooding of the park. Working with a limited budget, Olmsted was determined to first develop the uninterrupted "pleasant rural and sylvan scenery" of a country park to meet a variety of park uses, while studying alternative locations for a levee—preferably at the river's edge or along inland railroad tracks. A 1920 engineering study had recommended a levee that would bisect the site and consume the available funds.

The F. M. Kirby Park board agreed to defer the levee, allowing the Olmsted team to create a great undulating meadow offering long vistas, surrounded by broad spreading trees, including a WWI memorial grove. The meadow was designed to retain, then disperse stormwater with a runoff drain. A bandstand, picnic grove, and playgrounds were tucked into the woodlands while paved drives and pedestrian and bridle paths ringed the meadow. Opportunities for active recreation were located along the northern edge, closest to Market Street transportation. Intended regrading and planting of the steep riverbanks were interrupted by a spring flood in 1924, just before the official park opening, and again in 1936 with more devastating damage. When the levee was finally built, it separated and protected the inner park, now reduced to fifty-two acres, from its riverside acreage, leaving this as a wild area and causing the small riverside zoo, created in 1932, to be abandoned.

Today, Kirby Park is in great demand. The expansive meadow is now interrupted by four ball fields, a parking lot, tennis courts, a stadium, and several other sports facilities. A large irregular pond now occupies the southeast corner.

RHODE ISLAND

Newport City Plan	259	Blackstone Boulevard, Providence	263
Newport Estates, Newport	260		

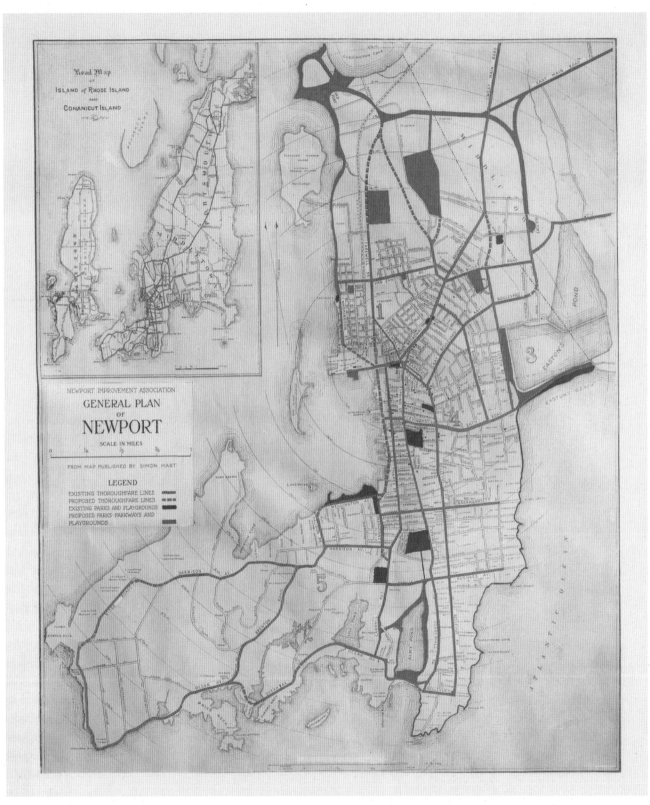

Proposed Improvements to Newport, circa 1913.

Cliff Walk runs for three and a half miles around the eastern and southern shores of Newport, giving precious coastal access to pedestrians.

Easton Beach, which is preserved for public use as an isthmus across Easton Bay.

NEWPORT CITY PLAN

In August 1913 Frederick Law Olmsted Jr. submitted a planning report to the Newport Improvement Association, titled *Proposed Improvements to Newport*. Olmsted Jr. observed the beauty and unique scale of historic Newport. He remarked on the shabbiness yet charm of its antique dwellings, the inconvenience of its crooked narrow streets, as well as the vulgarity of its oversized mansions.

The primary focus of Olmsted's planning recommendations and design work was to enhance the inherent character of the distinctive scenery. He emphasized the natural assets of distant or borrowed views of the shores and open waters due to the island's topography. (This led to targeted design recommendations for Ocean Drive, Cliff Walk, Easton Beach, Wellington Avenue, King Park, and Washington Street.) Secondly, recognizing the need to safeguard scenery found throughout the city's tree-lined streets, home grounds and villas, public and private gardens, and parks, Olmsted recommended building codes and street improvements. Olmsted took a revolutionary approach— to view the city as a dynamic cultural landscape offering a

holistic approach to its nature, scenery, and culture—all while preserving and protecting its unique scale and the individuality of its extant resources (buildings, streetscapes, and landscapes).

The younger Olmsted's report built upon the significant planning done previously in this scenic and multilayered community by his father and brother. Although the firm of F. L. and J. C. Olmsted was already shaping substantial residential grounds for some of Newport's notables, beginning in the early 1880s, their most important commissions at that time were for development conglomerates, such as the Newport Land Trust and others, adapting vast acreage on Aquidneck Island into residential enclaves while providing critical amenities. Well-drained roads curving around the boulder-strewn terrain provided access to distinctively designed lots, each shaped to capture scenery of ocean or bay or the rugged windswept moors. Their planning was ever respectful of Newport's natural assets of idiosyncratic topography, scenic shoreline, and abundant native plantings due to the beneficial climate.

Above: Olmsted Sr. made a dramatic stone bridge at Rough Point. **Top right and above right:** The formal approach to Ochre Court and dramatic bluffs at Rough Point..

NEWPORT ESTATES, NEWPORT

In town, the senior firm modulated the extravagant taste of Gilded Age moguls with quieter landscapes to settle Beaux Arts mansions, two of which are publicly accessible today. The grounds of Ochre Court (1888–1893), the Richard Morris Hunt mansion for Ogden Goulet, with its entrance allée and terraced bayside vistas, is now part of Salve Regina University. Farther down Bellevue Avenue is the F. W. Vanderbilt Estate (1887–1890), now owned by Newport Restoration Foundation. Here Olmsted Sr. enhanced the ocean-edge bluffs and outcroppings with a dramatic stone arch and wild plantings, while keeping the domesticated turf and shrubberies closer to the Peabody and Stearns Tudor-style mansion.

Olmsted Brothers worked on several projects in the public realm, some a result of a 1913 Olmsted Jr. report: the rehabilitation of Washington Square; relocation of the Oliver Hazard Perry statue by William Green Turner; and transformation of the utilitarian Bath Road into tree-lined Memorial Boulevard, with its pleasurable vistas of Easton's Beach. The report also recommended acquisition of parkland to protect Miantonomi Hill, important to the Narragansett nation, which was achieved in 1923 with the donation to the city of thirty-seven acres by the Stokes family, Olmsted clients and colleagues. In 1929 a McKim, Mead, and White memorial tower for WWI victims was erected.

In the private realm, the Olmsted Brothers, together with their partners James Dawson and Percival Gallagher, and associates, plantsmen Harold Hill Blossom and Hans J. Koehler, carried forth nearly thirty residential commissions, some lasting decades, for notable clients such as the Brown brothers from Providence (Harbor Court, now the New York Yacht Club, 1913–1926), the Auchincloss family (Hammersmith Farm, 1909–1946), and others. Today, some of these gardens and landscapes can be visited in whole or in part. Château-sur-Mer (1915–1918), the estate of George Peabody Wetmore, offers the textured lawns, trees, and shrub surroundings for a Bellevue Avenue mansion, while out on Aquidneck, the recaptured Blue Garden, a three-acre Italianate garden "room" of blue blooms remaining from the estate of Arthur Curtiss James, is available for visits by appointment.

The Olmsted Newport legacy is rich and diverse. As impressive as the public and private places are, it is the 1913 *Proposed Improvements to Newport* that has shaped the public mindset for more than a century—from respecting architectural scale and texture of the historic community, to protecting trees and tree canopies, to safeguarding viewshed corridors and panoramic vistas, the Olmsteds created a way of seeing and managing change that was innovative in its thinking about cities. Their vision proclaimed that historical fabric is as alive and dynamic as the people moving through it.

Top: At Château-sur-Mer, the Newport Wetmore estate, the High Victorian–style house with its mansard roof is nestled into a parklike entry sequence. It received an elaborate plan for a variety of espalier fruit trees by Olmsted Brothers in 1916. **Above:** The Blue Garden, from the James estate on Aquidneck and planned circa 1911, has retained much the same character and color scheme.

Blackstone Boulevard, planned with rows of elegant deciduous trees and a hardy understory, was Rhode Island's first designed parkway.

BLACKSTONE BOULEVARD, PROVIDENCE

Although the Olmsted firm involvement in the public realm in Newport was significant, it was less so in Providence, where much of the pioneering work was undertaken by H. W. S. Cleveland.

One project that the firm had a small role in was Blackstone Boulevard, which was the state's first designed parkway. Designed by H. W. S. Cleveland, the 200-foot-wide parkway was commissioned by the Swan Point Cemetery in 1886 to provide a more dignified arrival experience for the forty-year-old cemetery. Road construction commenced in 1892 and was completed two years later.

The boulevard was designed to run from Butler Avenue to East Avenue in Pawtucket and was composed of a grassy central park flanked by a pair of one-way roadways, tree-lined perimeter grass shoulders, and sidewalks. Planting of the boulevard's central park and the medians did not take place until 1904. With Cleveland's passing in 1900 the Olmsted Brothers firm was engaged to develop a planting plan that would be based on his original design for the length of the boulevard.

Specifically, John Charles Olmsted, who had undertaken the field work with Carl Rust Parker, proposed that the central parkland median and the perimeter shoulders be planted with deciduous trees that would have an understory of hardy perennials, in addition to broad mass plantings of flowering and evergreen shrubs. Although the planting design intent has diminished over time (for instance, understory plantings have been replaced by lawn and there is a diminished tree canopy), the boulevard has not been significantly altered.

In 1913 the Olmsted Brothers returned to Providence and prepared a plan for the western section of Swan Point Cemetery, which was largely realized.

Blackstone Boulevard quickly became a highly desirable address. The Blackstone Boulevard-Cole Avenue-Grotto Avenue Historic District, including 380 contributing structures, was listed in the National Register of Historic Places in 2009. The preservation and stewardship of the boulevard is advanced by the Blackstone Parks Conservancy working in partnership with Providence Parks and the Department of Public Works.

SOUTH CAROLINA

YEAMANS HALL CLUB, NORTH CHARLESTON

The rolling wooded acreage intersected by the sinuous Cooper River to be developed into a prestigious resort community came with a notable lineage. This 1000-acre site, a land grant from King Charles to Sir John Yeamans circa 1670 (where Yeamans is reputed to have built a mansion of imported English bricks), seems to have been then occupied by Landgrave Thomas Smith and his descendants until 1900. By that time, the old cemetery was in disarray and the mansion a ruin, damaged by an 1886 earthquake and subsequent fire. The surrounding landscape of huge live oaks dripping in moss, magnolias, hickories, hollies, and willows contained the natural beauty characteristic of this region. Supplied with ample fresh water from two springs and riverfront views, this land held great appeal for a fine tourist hotel, golf courses, yachting, and a sizable cottage colony. Once isolated, this still-rugged land was now just twelve miles from Charleston, easily serviced by train and motor.

Inspecting the ground in 1915 at the request of Charleston developer E. W. Durant, Frederick Law Olmsted Jr. praised the topography and vegetation as well suited for a first-class golf course with diverse cottages tucked along the edges and sites for other outdoor amusements. By 1923, with wealthy northern investors, development of the general layout for house sites, roads, small parks, and other amenities began under William B. Marquis from the Olmsted Brothers firm, collaborating with golf architect Seth Raynor on the location of fairways and greens, both designers ensuring attractive long vistas while retaining ample property screening. Olmsted firm plantsman Hans J. Koehler diversified the native vegetation by inserting azaleas and camellias as understory. With Southern Colonial set as the prevailing architectural style, New York architect James Gamble Rogers's design for the large clubhouse ran into vociferous opposition from preservation groups and club members, as it involved destruction of the Yeamans Hall ruin (although new buildings had already been placed in close proximity).

By 1928 a substantial clubhouse was built, which included a portion of a corner wall from the historical ruin, but development of the planned 200 house sites suffered a severe setback with the Depression. Maintaining consistent aesthetic oversight for both overall design and that of individual properties was a continuing struggle. Olmsted Brothers retained its advisory capacity until the late 1940s, when it counseled that management of surrounding woodlands for their landscape value was more critical than unprofessional timbering.

In 1996 the eighteen-hole golf course was restored by Tom Doak. Today, Yeamans Hall is a membership country club with a challenging golf course and an enclave of substantial private homes amid the developing communities of the North Charleston area.

The 1925 plan shows homesites interspersed around the golf course.

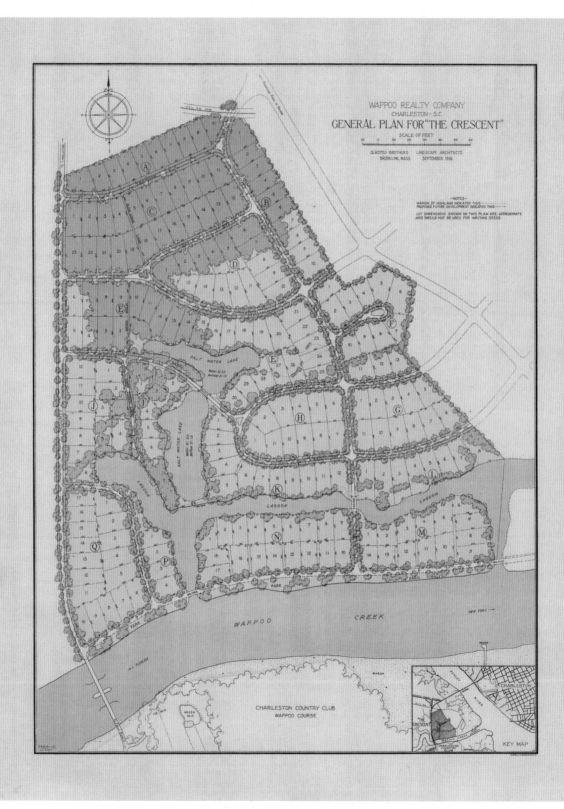

Plan for The Crescent development, also in Charleston, circa 1926.

TENNESSEE

Laura Spelman Rockefeller Memorial,
Gatlinburg   268

Woodmont Estates, Nashville   271
Fisk University, Nashville   271

The memorial is a popular stop for tourists on SC Highway 441.

LAURA SPELMAN ROCKEFELLER MEMORIAL, GATLINBURG

Preservation for public enjoyment of the southern Appalachian scenery of the Great Smoky Mountains, straddling the North Carolina and Tennessee borders, had long been of interest. This historically significant area, rich in horticultural biodiversity and old growth forests, also contains some of the highest mountains in the East. Most of the land, however, was in private ownership, used for logging. A twenty-year fundraising effort within both states, with some federal money and a $5 million gift from the Laura Spelman Rockefeller Memorial Fund, finally achieved the goal of establishing the Great Smoky Mountains National Park. President Franklin D. Roosevelt addressed the crowds from the terrace of the newly completed Laura Spelman Rockefeller Memorial in Newfound Gap at its September 1940 dedication.

This imaginative structure, by Olmsted Brothers partner Henry Hubbard, was designed at the request of the National Park Service, and inventively constructed by CCC labor between 1938 and 1940. Unable to find a suitable natural boulder setting where a tablet could be affixed near the two states' borders, Hubbard instead transformed the "nose of a little hill" into a spiral of two terraces climbing the slope. This scarred boundary hillside, near the Appalachian Trail, had been left after construction of the Blue Ridge Parkway.

A 1938 clay model of the proposed memorial, featuring the uppermost terrace, which was never completed.

Challenged by a limited budget of $20,000 in total and harsh winter conditions, Hubbard began design development in 1938 with a clay model of two semicircular stone block terraces hugging the hill face, connected by steps rising to an upper lookout. The memorial tablet to be attached to the wall, with words chosen by John D. Rockefeller Jr., "For the permanent Enjoyment of the People . . .", was to be designed by sculptor Paul Manship.

Hurrying to overcome considerable design and construction challenges by June 1939, the original dedication date, Henry Rice (a skilled superintendent borrowed from the Jefferson National Expansion Memorial in Saint Louis) and H. T. Thompson, National Park Service architect, consulted with Hubbard by mailed photographs and by phone.

The uppermost lookout was never constructed, leaving a scarred, bald ridge that was distressing to Hubbard, who continued to press for more surrounding planting. The terraces, however, he felt met the goals: to provide views on both sides of the notch in a structure to bear the plaque, well fitted to the hillside without ostentation. This memorial continues to be a major attraction for tourists along the parkway.

Inside the illustration (handwritten): *A. Proposed House of Distinction* "*Woodmont Estates.*" *Property of G. A. Puryear Et Al* — Olmsted Brothers Landscape A...

A 1937 photographic positive showing the house and rolling topograghy of the G. A. Puryear Estate, which would shortly be subdivided into the Woodmont Estates.

WOODMONT ESTATES, NASHVILLE

Inspired by their work on the Cherokee Gardens subdivision in Louisville, Kentucky, G. A. Puryear Jr., a Nashville banker, contacted the Olmsted Brothers firm in 1936 about subdividing the estate he had inherited from his recently deceased father. James F. Dawson led the design of the site, creating a winding network of streets following Sugartree Creek, which flows through the landscape. Plans for the site were completed by early 1937, and construction proceeded quickly. Marketing for lots followed shortly thereafter, and by 1938, several houses were completed or under construction. Pleased with the work, Puryear asked whether Dawson might design the grounds of his own new home in the community.

Valley Brook Drive follows a small tributary of Sugartree Creek down to the main branch of the stream. This tributary flows through the front portion of several of the larger lots of development, providing a scenic buffer between the large homes and the roadway. The plans called for a small reservation along the creek, bordered by a bridle path. The original design also called for a roundabout, named Puryear Circle, at the western end of the development. The circle, however, was not constructed; neither was a stream crossing in this area. And rather than the larger lots typical of the bulk of the community, smaller lots and tighter streets were built.

FISK UNIVERSITY, NASHVILLE

Fisk University was established in 1865 as the Fisk Free Colored School before being incorporated as an institution of higher learning in 1867. Originally located in what were once Union barracks near the present Union Station, the university relocated to the former site of Fort Gillem, a military base that it purchased in 1876. The first academic structures on the twenty-five-acre campus were Jubilee Hall (1876), the music annex (1876), and the memorial chapel (1892). Expansion to the south and east during the twentieth century created today's forty-acre campus. In the 1930s the university hired David Williston, landscape architect at Tuskegee University, and Percival Gallagher of the Olmsted Brothers firm, to develop a master plan for the campus, in conjunction with the design of a library by architect Henry Hibbs. Concerned that intersecting streets with their distracting noises would interrupt a cohesive campus, they recommended purchase of additional land to develop character of space for serious scholarship. They

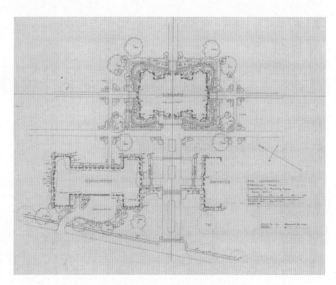

A 1933 plan shows Olmsted Brothers working to establish a master plan for the Fisk University campus expansion to include a mall, paths, and quads.

A unique limestone wall borders the Fisk University campus where it meets Meharry Boulevard, just south of Jubilee Hall.

intended to close off Seventeenth Avenue to eliminate traffic from the center of campus and to create a tree-lined turf mall on axis with the new library, continuing axial alignment of buildings for a Beaux Arts landscape. Unfortunately, lack of funds and the death of Gallagher in 1934 truncated the Olmsted planning.

Located two miles north of downtown Nashville, the university is bounded by Jefferson Street to the north and Jackson and Herman streets to the south. The axial relationships of the campus and its buildings are established by the orthogonal street grid, with the flagship Jubilee Hall perched on the crest of an incline. The landscape consists of six lawns oriented around Seventeenth Avenue, which forms the central spine of the campus, intersecting with Jefferson, Philip, and Herman

Streets before terminating in a tear-drop-shaped drive in front of Jubilee Hall. The Harry Elson Memorial Gate, located north of the intersection of Jackson Street and Seventeenth Avenue, marks the institution's formal entrance. Cement paths are laid out across many of the lawns in asymmetric patterns, occasionally bordered by irregularly shaped garden beds. Many trees, including cypress, dogwoods, and cherry, are interspersed across the grounds. A limestone wall, constructed in 1873, borders the campus between Jefferson Street and Meharry Boulevard, west of Seventeenth Avenue. Fisk University is part of the United States Civil Rights Trail, and the Fisk University Historic District was listed in the National Register of Historic Places in 1978.

UTAH

A contemporary aerial photograph shows both how the capitol was situated at the crest of a hill, as planned, and also how new buildings that did not figure into the original 1911 plan have since been built behind.

UTAH STATE CAPITOL GROUNDS, SALT LAKE CITY

Originally known as Arsenal Hill, the site for the new capitol building was selected by a Capitol Commission appointed in 1909 by Governor William Spry. In 1911 after procuring appropriations from the state legislature and securing a topographical map, the commission employed the Olmsted Brothers firm to provide a preliminary site plan that would include "advice in locating the building" prior to an architectural competition.

John Charles Olmsted spent nine days in the city sketching ideas and examining soils and elevations. He found the views outstanding and suggested using terraces to situate the building high enough to dominate the site. He recommended grading the north slope lower to allow views up to the building from all sides, carefully planting large trees to avoid obscuring the views. To achieve this effect, he urged the commission to consider land acquisition on the east to widen the site, allowing for a symmetrical plan. The commission eventually acquired additional land through gifts and purchases to accommodate the recommendations of both Olmsted and the winner of the competition, architect Richard K. A. Kletting.

The proposed boundaries for Olmsted's plan placed the capitol building in the center of the site at its highest gradient point, with surrounding oval pathways. He advised that the commission locate the electric car tracks coming from the west underground and included plans for a tunnel at the entrance of the west elevation to allow access to elevators.

The location of the capitol building was ultimately shifted 200 feet south on the property, which did allow for future buildings to the north. This change complicated the grading plan and siting of the building. The firm asked to be given an opportunity to prepare revised grading and planting plans, but their request was not accepted. However, the oval paths that Olmsted proposed were

constructed as tree-lined pedestrian corridors that are currently named for Philo T. Farnsworth, known as the father of television. Today, even though other public buildings have been added on the north side of the campus, the preeminence of the Utah State Capitol and the views from all sides, plus the judicious use of smaller trees, conveys much of Olmsted's design intent. The site was listed in the National Register of Historic Places in 1978 and is included in the Capitol Hill Historic District.

VERMONT

PRELIMINARY STUDY
OF PART OF PLAN FOR LAYING OUT THE
SHELBURNE FARMS ESTATE
OF
DR W.S. WEBB

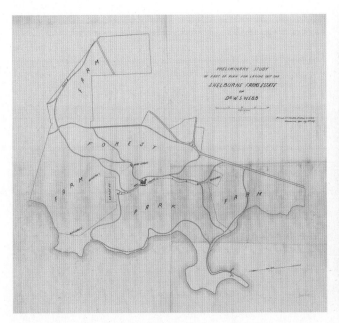

A simple but elegant drawing dividing up Shelburne Farms' functions.

The farm has been in continuous production and dedicated to the latest scientific practices since its inception. Today, that includes sound environmental practices.

SHELBURNE FARMS, BURLINGTON

Located south of Burlington on the shores of Lake Champlain, Shelburne Farms is a 1300-acre ornamental farm established in 1886 by Dr. William Seward Webb and his wife, Lila Vanderbilt Webb. The farm utilized the latest agricultural science practices to raise livestock, breed horses, and grow crops.

Between 1886 and 1889 Frederick Law Olmsted Sr. devised a tripartite, farm-forest-park plan, with two-thirds of the property used as working farmland punctuated by isolated stands of trees. Eleven miles of curvilinear, crushed-stone service roads and eight miles of walking trails were laid out in harmony with the existing topography to take advantage of the scenic views of the lake and the Adirondack and Green Mountains. Bordering the agricultural fields are 400 acres of hardwood and softwood

forests. In the center of the property lies the estate's parkland, which includes formal gardens and lawn and the vestiges of an 1894 golf course designed by Willie Park Jr. The property also includes twelve miles of pebble-beach lakefront and structures designed by Robert Henderson Robertson.

Since its inception, Shelburne Farms has been in continuous farm production. In 1972 descendants of the Webbs transformed the sustainable farm practice into a non-profit environmental education center, protecting the site with conservation easements and adapting the farm's structures for new uses to provide sustainable revenue (these include a notable inn and restaurant). The property was listed in the National Register of Historic Places in 1980 and designated a National Historic Landmark District in 2001.

Winding service roads situate Shelburne Farms' buildings within fields that gradually give way to surrounding forests and finally Lake Champlain.

VIRGINIA

A clay model for the memorial, circa 1922.

MASONIC MEMORIAL TO GEORGE WASHINGTON, ALEXANDRIA

Perched atop Shuter's Hill and commanding expansive views of the Potomac River Valley, this thirty-six-acre property surrounds the 333-foot-tall memorial, dedicated in 1932. Initially selected by an organization for the construction of a smaller memorial to Washington and a park, the site was purchased in 1915 by the Washington-Alexandria Lodge of the Masonic Order (chartered by George Washington in 1788) and an association was created to oversee the project. In 1922 architect Harvey Wiley Corbett was commissioned to design the memorial structure with Olmsted Brothers in charge of the landscape. Though young at the time, Carl Rust Parker was selected to lead the project, as he was a Mason.

Oriented to the east for ritualistic purposes and on axis with King Street, the memorial is sited above a terraced lawn. Parker's dramatic entry sequence included a curvilinear drive

The completed Masonic Memorial to George Washington.

and an axial stairway—both of which terminate at a grand plaza and a stone retaining wall on the upper terrace. Parker's general planting plan, presented in 1939, was never instituted. Various groups donated specimen trees, which accounted for the only real horticultural work on the site until landscape architect Kenneth Soergel developed a detailed plan in 1970, of which only a portion was realized. In 1982 a new entry was developed, featuring a concrete retaining wall inscribed with a quote and adorned with a sculpture relocated from the Washington Monument in 1976. In 1999 a 4000-square-foot Masonic compass emblem was installed upon the terraces fronting the memorial and in 2000 a program of dedicatory trees was instituted, resulting in the planting of more than 600 trees. In 2015 the memorial was designated a National Historic Landmark.

WASHINGTON

Thornewood, American Lake	283	Volunteer Park, Seattle	290
Washington State Capitol, Olympia	285	Lake Washington Boulevard, Seattle	291
Dunn Gardens, Seattle	286	Washington Park Arboretum, Seattle	292
Seattle Parks and Boulevard System	287	University of Washington, Seattle	293
Seward Park, Seattle	290	Park System of Spokane	295

The Tudor-style house and formal circular entry drive at Thornewood.

THORNEWOOD, AMERICAN LAKE

The expansion of the Tacoma Golf and Country Club along American Lake spurred the development of sizable country estates in the vicinity. By 1908, Banker Chester Thorne called upon John Charles Olmsted to shape his extensive property of woods and shorefront as a setting for a home in the English style, as desired by Mrs. Thorne. Olmsted, associate James Frederick Dawson, and other firm members were nearby in Seattle, planning the Alaska-Yukon-Pacific Exposition on the University of Washington campus, slated to open in June 1909. Olmsted was impressed by the Thorne property's scenery—the wild woods and vistas of mountain and lake. With special attention to resuscitate the surrounding natural woods damaged by previous lumbering, between 1909 and 1915 he developed a complex plan to accommodate all the features required of a grand country estate: gate-lodge and garage-stable, boathouse and waterfront, approach road and forecourt, tennis court, vegetable gardens and orchard with greenhouse, and elaborate multilayered garden rooms, some in the Elizabethan style. He oriented the formal gardens to frame the eastern vista of Mount Rainier (which he called Mount Tacoma), urging architect Kirtland Cutter of Spokane to do likewise with the main rooms of the mansion.

To repair the damage to the woodlands, varied native plants collected from the nearby higher mountain slopes were interplanted among the old-growth firs and cedars. For the formal gardens, Olmsted designed a sunken rectangular space enclosed by articulated walls with tea houses in the corners, the ornate herbaceous borders enhancing the distant view. Colors were

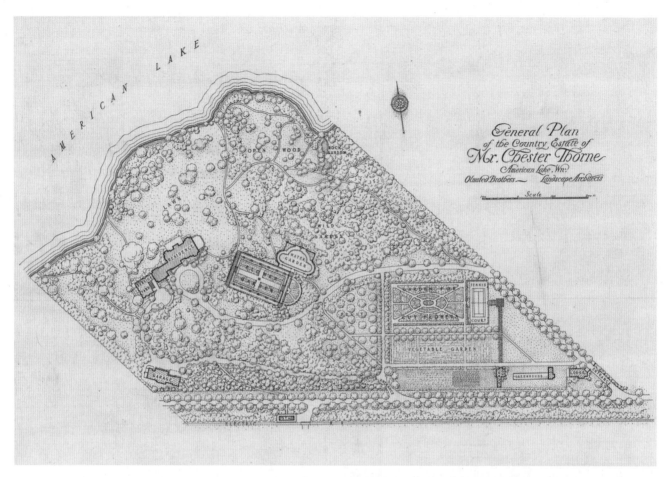

This plan shows how the house would be situated on the property, the arrangement of formal gardens, and tree placement to buffer the lot from the railway station on the southern edge (n.d.).

carefully orchestrated from pale hues in the center to darker shades with blues in the periphery. Out of the viewshed to one side, he placed a water garden with an elaborate wall fountain; elsewhere in the landscape were "rooms" for roses, cut flowers, vegetables, a wild garden of flower drifts, shrub-bordered lawn areas, and woodland pools meandering around a rock garden. The Olmsted firm designed or supervised the purchase of planters, benches, and garden statuary.

Though much heralded in print in its time and called "the most beautiful garden in America" in 1930 by the Garden Club of America, in 1959 Thornewood was subdivided after most family members had died. Most of the Olmsted "garden rooms" were dismantled, leaving only four acres, including the sunken

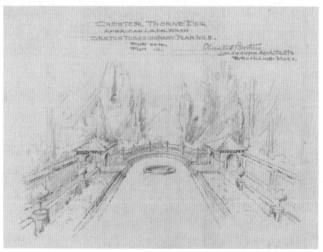

Sketch for the Water Garden, showing tea houses in each corner.

garden and some original trees around the mansion. Now a bed and breakfast, Thornewood was listed in the National Register of Historic Places in 1982.

The state capitol grounds today feature walkways, plantings, and distinct lawn areas that make it feel like a true civic campus.

WASHINGTON STATE CAPITOL, OLYMPIA

After Washington was admitted as the forty-second state in 1889, a competition was held to design its capitol, to be situated on a forested hilltop with dramatic views of the Olympic Mountains, Puget Sound, and the growing city. Ernest Flagg of New York won the 1893 competition, but only the foundation of his building was completed. In 1911 Walter Wilder and Harry White, with John Charles Olmsted consulting, created a master plan for six buildings, including the completed Flagg Legislative Building as the campus centerpiece on the west side of a fifty-four-acre campus. Controversy between architects and the landscape architect over building locations and aesthetic connections to the city center ended Olmsted's involvement at this time, although some of his ideas persisted. In 1927 Wilder and White recalled the Olmsted firm, led by James Dawson, to resolve the still problematic landscape issues of circulation and inconsistent building relationships. The 1928 Olmsted plan merged the drama of this unique site with needed formality for such important buildings. A parklike effect was created by sweeping lawns and layered plant groupings to set off the structures—some in formal tree allées for spatial definition, others as looser compositions of evergreen and deciduous material. A few areas were elaborate, such as the sunken garden.

Although campus buildings were completed in 1940 and a lake was constructed at the western edge of campus in 1951, some elements of the Olmsted plan, such as the west overlook, were never built. In the 1950s, development began on the East Capitol Campus, later shaped by Lawrence Halprin's landscape plan of 1967. There have been numerous subsequent master plan efforts, including a 2009 Vegetation Management Plan to address contemporary conditions while working to honor the character-defining features intended in the Olmsted design. Today, the campus operates as a civic center, with generous parkland, curvilinear walkways, and monuments and art installations. The campus was listed in the National Register of Historic Places in 1979.

Top and above: Dunn Gardens are characterized by the lush woodland garden. **Right:** The Olmsted Brothers firm's planting plan for the property, 1916.

DUNN GARDENS, SEATTLE

These ten-acre gardens were originally part of the country estate of Arthur and Jeannette Dunn, who purchased the land in 1914 as the site for their summer home. Commissioned to locate two houses and prepare landscape plans for the grounds, James Dawson, of the Olmsted Brothers firm, emphasized the natural features of the land: the gradual slope of the property that highlighted the sweeping views of Puget Sound and the Olympic Mountains, as well as a ravine on the southern edge of the property. Large, preexisting stands of second-growth Douglas firs were incorporated into the planting plan, which also included flowering shrubs and trees and extensive swaths of flowering bulbs. Stands of trees edged by perennial beds framed areas of open lawn. Arthur Dunn, an avid gardener, was responsible for implementing the plans.

After Dunn's death the property was divided, the original cottage demolished, and four new houses were constructed on the site. The original landscape remains, complete with curving paths and drives and a great lawn which sat below the original house, in addition to the E. B. Dunn Woodland Garden. Designed by Arthur's son Edward, the two-and-a-half-acre woodland garden was created on the former site of a garage and vegetable garden. It is forested with firs and deciduous trees planted by the younger Dunn, along with a variety of other woodland plantings. The estate and gardens were listed in the National Register of Historic Places in 1994.

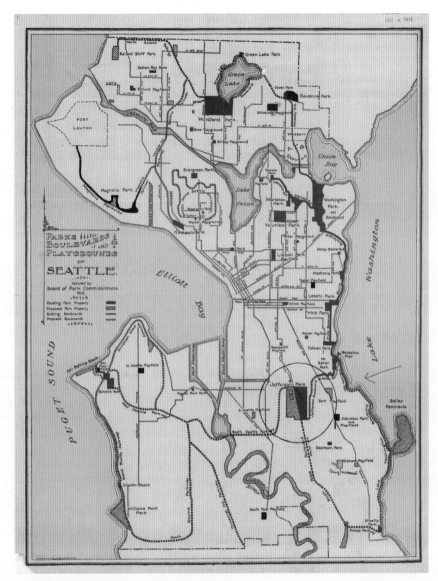

A 1909 plan shows parks distributed across the city.

SEATTLE PARKS AND BOULEVARD SYSTEM

In 1903 the Olmsted Brothers firm, under the leadership of John Charles Olmsted, developed *A Comprehensive System of Parks and Parkways* for Seattle's Board of Park Commissioners. So began a relationship between the city and the Olmsted firm that would span more than three decades, concluding with the firm's proposals for Washington Park Arboretum.

The original goal of the plan was to locate a park or playground within a half mile of every home, with a twenty-mile landscaped boulevard as both its dominant feature and connective tissue. Parks and parkways were located and shaped to maximize views of the spectacular features of a topographically complex landscape—snow-covered mountains, water vistas,

Top: Frink Park features roadways as well as rustic trails. **Center left:** Green Lake Park features a nearly three-mile path around the lake. **Center right:** A creekside trail with steps and a wooden bridge cross Ravenna Creek. **Above:** Interlaken Park and Boulevard roughly follow the earlier lines of an 1890s bike path and follow the natural curves of a ravine through dense woods.

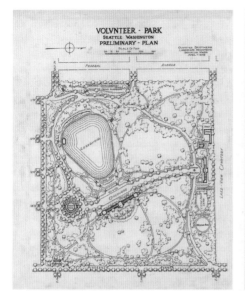

The 1909 plan for Volunteer Park.

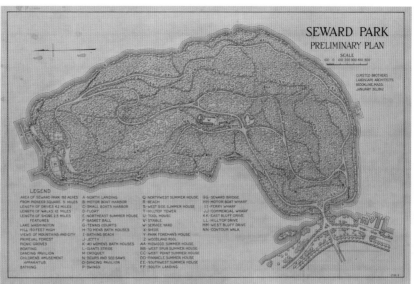

Seward Park Preliminary Plan, Olmsted Brothers, 1912.

or abundantly vegetated hollows. As testimony to the public support the plan generated, within ten years of its submission, most of the land was secured.

In all, the firm designed thirty-seven parks and playgrounds and twenty-three miles of boulevards and parkways, including Colman, Frink, Green Lake, Interlaken, Jefferson, Mount Baker, Seward, Volunteer and Woodland Parks, Lincoln Park (now known as the Bobby Morris Playfield), Washington Park and Arboretum, Hiawatha Playfield, plus Lake Washington,

Magnolia, and Ravenna Boulevards. Each park took advantage of the natural topography and features distinct to its particular location, with boulevards providing connectivity throughout.

Today, the Friends of Seattle's Olmsted Parks, a group founded in 1983 to promote awareness, enjoyment, and care of the city's Olmsted parks and landscapes, plays a key partnership role with the city. The Seattle Parks and Boulevard System was listed in the National Register of Historic Places in 2017.

Seward Park, which occupies all of Bailey Peninsula, juts out into Lake Washington.

SEWARD PARK, SEATTLE

In 1892 landscape architect Edward Schwagerl proposed that the city purchase Bailey Peninsula, a rare site where bedrock reaches the surface. At that time, Schwagerl's proposals were ignored amid suggestions that the peninsula was too far from town. An outcome of the Olmsted Brothers firm's Seattle report, the peninsula was acquired in 1911 for $322,000 and named Seward Park after William Seward, the secretary of state responsible for America's purchase of Alaska in 1867. Work began slowly at first on the 300-acre park; a few trails and picnic areas were constructed. Then in 1913, Lake Washington Boulevard was extended from Mount Baker to the park. In 1917 Lake Washington was lowered, creating a grassy meadow leading to a swimming beach; in 1927 a bathhouse was constructed. An old growth forest of virgin timber and vegetation covers 120 acres on the northern two-thirds of the peninsula today and is the largest such stand in the city.

VOLUNTEER PARK, SEATTLE

The city purchased this property above downtown Seattle for a park in 1876. Beginning in the early 1890s, Seattle's first superintendent of parks, Edward Schwagerl, made minor improvements to the park. In 1901 the name Volunteer Park was adopted to honor veterans of the Spanish-American War, and the city's first reservoir was built on the site. A water tower was added in 1906, with guidance from landscape architect John Charles Olmsted on its placement, style, and potential for future use as an observation deck. The 1909 design for Volunteer Park implemented an integral element of the Olmsted Brothers plan for Seattle's parks and boulevards. The design included both formal and pastoral elements, such as circuit paths and drives, lily ponds, a wading pool and playground, a pergola-music pavilion, shelter, and comfort stations, and an allée linking the water tower and a small conservatory. In 1933 the Seattle Art Museum opened in the center of the park, replacing the pergola and music pavilion. Other post-Olmsted additions include the insertion of a granite boulder to further honor Spanish-American War veterans in 1952, a play sculpture by Charles Smith in 1962, and the *Black Sun* sculpture by Isamu Noguchi in 1969. Volunteer Park was listed in the National Register of Historic Places in 1976.

Volunteer Park, perched atop Capitol Hill, provides views to downtown Seattle and features a brick water tower, lily ponds, and a glass conservatory.

LAKE WASHINGTON BOULEVARD, SEATTLE

Lake Washington is a glacially created freshwater lake. Pleasure travel along its shoreline was formalized in 1900 when the city's assistant engineer, George Cotterill, laid out a twenty-five-mile bicycle path system. With its spectacular views across the water to Mount Rainier and spanning just over nine miles, Lake Washington Boulevard was a key component of the Olmsted Brothers firm's plan. It would serve as the city's central north–south corridor, linking Ravenna, Magnolia, and Queen Anne Boulevards to Beacon, Duwamish, and West Seattle Boulevards. The boulevard was also designed to connect to the university and to major parks (Discovery, Green Lake, Woodland, Seward, Jefferson, and Lincoln Parks) while providing visual and physical access to significant water bodies (Puget Sound, Lake Washington, and Lake Union). The Olmsted firm made recommendations for the boulevard's complex road alignment with its scenic hairpin turns through Colman Park, including its width, road crowns, bridge design, edge treatments, guard rails, and even drainage inlets. Although there were no detailed plans for walks, plantings, or furnishings, these specifics were often included where the route overlaid park sites, such as at Washington Park (later the Washington Park and Arboretum). The site was listed in the Washington Heritage Register and the National Register of Historic Places in 2017.

67 — Scene on Lake Washington
Parkway, Seattle, Wash.

Lake Washington Boulevard as seen in 1909.

WASHINGTON PARK ARBORETUM, SEATTLE

Prior to the Olmsted firm's initial involvement with the city, the idea of an arboretum had already been conceived in tandem with the founding of the University of Washington, another landscape where the firm would later consult. In 1891 following the inspiration of Harvard University's Arnold Arboretum, legislation was introduced to create an arboretum that, like the Arnold, would be a partnership between the city and an academic institution, to display the diversity of plant materials in a scenic park setting. Washington Park, identified as a park site by both the Schwagerl and Olmsted proposals, remained largely undeveloped as parkland, except for a planted parkway running the length of the park, which the Olmsted firm designed in 1904–1906. Three decades later, the Seattle Garden Club donated $3000 to engage James Dawson and Frederick Law Olmsted Jr. to develop the arboretum's first planting plan that would encompass the entire park. That association was followed by another commission in 1938 for Azalea Way. Both schemes were only partially implemented as intended.

Located in a moist, maritime environment that allows for the cultivation of a greater plant palette than any other region in North America, the Washington Park Arboretum and Botanic Gardens are a living collection of deciduous, evergreen, and herbaceous materials, aesthetically arranged and maintained for purposes of education, conservation, research, and public inspiration. With over 4800 species and cultivars, the 230-acre park has a collection of international significance and acclaim.

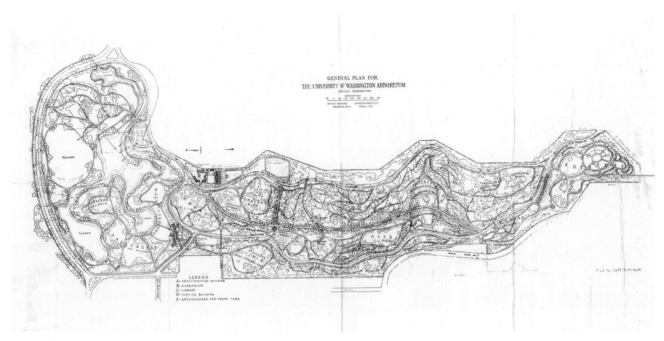

The 1936 plan for the Washington Park Arboretum, revealing how species are grouped.

UNIVERSITY OF WASHINGTON, SEATTLE

This university was founded in 1861 in downtown Seattle. In 1893 the university regents purchased 160 acres in Union Bay for the development of a new campus, and professor A. H. Fuller implemented a campus plan in 1900 by arranging buildings in a simple oval facing a central lawn. In 1903 the university hired the Olmsted Brothers firm to create a new plan. The firm redesigned the oval as the Arts Quadrangle (now the Liberal Arts Quadrangle) and installed the Science Quadrangle to the south. In 1906 the state chose this campus as the site of the Alaska-Yukon-Pacific Exposition. John Charles Olmsted and James Dawson created a system of avenues that linked circular courtyards and lush gardens to frame the Neoclassical buildings planned under John Galen Howard, architect for the exposition. The design's centerpiece, the Geyser Basin, anchors the Science Quadrangle. Iconic, open vistas provide views of Mount Rainer, Lake Washington, and Lake Union. In 1911 the Olmsted Brothers created a campus plan that integrated the exposition grounds. That plan was rejected in favor of a design known as the Regents Plan, by architect Carl Gould, which reduced the scale of the Olmsted Brothers' quadrangles while maintaining the principal axes and views. The Regents Plan placed a library plaza, named the Central Plaza, at the convergence of the quadrangles. In 1961 the high-spouting Drumheller Fountain replaced Geyser Basin at the head of the Rainer Vista.

Today, the campus reflects both the Olmsted and Regents Plans. Red Square serves as the institution's academic core. Four radial axes, including Memorial Way, the Liberal Arts Quadrangle, the Olympic Vista, and the Rainer Vista, extend from the core connecting the plaza. These plans have continued to serve as an armature for campus expansion with the introduction of new greens, gardens, courtyards, buildings, and wetlands.

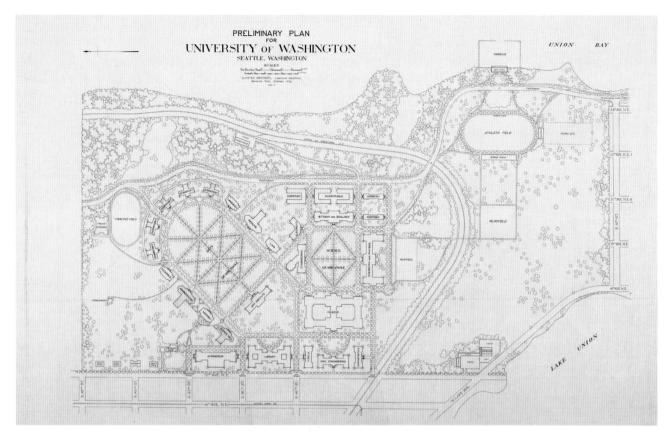

The 1904 campus plan for the new Arts and Science Quadrangles.

Cherry trees flourish on the quad in front of Raitt Hall.

Corbin Park's brilliant fall foliage display.

$$\overline{}$$

PARK SYSTEM OF SPOKANE

In December of 1906, John Charles Olmsted and associate James Dawson visited Spokane at the request of Aubrey L. White, president of the city's newly formed and independent Spokane Board of Park Commissioners (earlier park commissions, begun in 1890, were political appointees). With their extensive experience in the Pacific Northwest, including 1903 designs for park systems and institutions in Portland, OR, and in Seattle, the Olmsted Brothers firm was well positioned to manage comprehensive park planning for Spokane. With the city's rapid growth, by the time they returned nearly a year later to formalize their recommendations, railroad tracks had already overtaken certain areas that they had envisioned as part of the park system.

The Olmsted Brothers report, produced in 1908 but not officially released until 1913, followed their recommended components for a successful citywide park system, including large parks, local parks, parkways, boulevards, and playgrounds, as well as proposals for city planning and improvements to existing parks (many of which had been created as amenities in real estate speculations). Over the intervening years, Aubrey White led the parks commission to acquire more land to implement many of the firm's recommendations for park expansion to provide diverse recreational experiences for the developing city. Much of the work was overseen by John W. Duncan, who served as Spokane's first superintendent of parks from 1910–1942.

Clockwise from top left: Manito Park's wooded area, circa 1908. Manito Park, featuring formal parterres. Parkgoers' view looking west in Manito Park.

Taking advantage of picturesque natural features—the open land and wooded areas, the valleys and vistas—the plan recommended Gorge Park (now High Bridge) to highlight the large gorge and falls of the Spokane River; Upriver Park (now Felts) and Downriver Park to the northeast and northwest, and Latah Park (now Qualchan Hills) to the south for large areas away from the city center for active and passive enjoyment. Smaller parks and playgrounds, benefitting from the varied topography, together with tree-lined streets and wide boulevards, were planned for neighborhood amenities. Ahead of its time, the Olmsted firm's report stressed the importance of open spaces for a healthy population. Olmsted Brothers took care to identify geographically diverse locations, aiming for the equitable distribution of access to public park space.

They carefully preserved shorelines, created direct pedestrian access to the river's edge, and designed drives along bluffs and through wooded areas for scenic views.

By the 1913 public release of the Olmsted report, Corbin, Liberty, Adams (now Cannon Hill), and Manito Parks, as well as others, had been enhanced according to the firm's planning, with new plantings, drives, and varied recreational facilities. Olmsted recommendations for improving the city services, circulation, transportation, and recreation systems have continued to influence Spokane's growth. Select individual parks of the system have been listed in the National Register of Historic Places, including Corbin (as part of the Corbin Park Historic District) and Manito Parks in 1992 and 2015, respectively.

WISCONSIN

Town of Kohler   298

Washington Parks, Milwaukee   300

Lake Park, Milwaukee   302

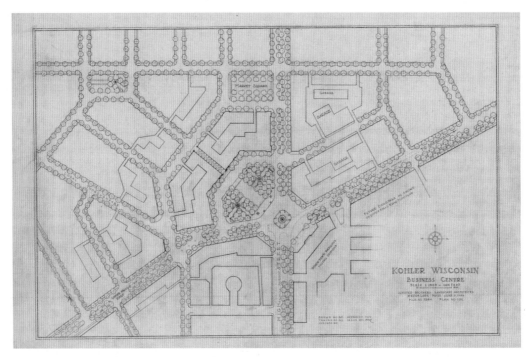

Kohler Business Center Plan, 1926.

TOWN OF KOHLER

Inspired by his European travels undertaken with his architect Richard Philipp, industrialist Walter Kohler Sr. undertook the development of a substantial garden city adjacent to his factory in 1916, consulting with planner Werner Hegemann and landscape architect Elbert Peets on the design. Unhappy with their work, Kohler hired the Olmsted Brothers firm for the town's expansion in the mid-1920s, having worked with them successfully on the grounds of his nearby estate, Riverbend, designed by Philipp a few years earlier. The Olmsted firm platted out "West II," as the new neighborhood was known, nearly doubling the size of the community. More ambitious plans for further expansion to the north and west—reminiscent of the firm's planned communities like Forest Hills Gardens in New York, went unrealized as the Great Depression set in. The firm continued to consult for the Kohlers into the 1950s, preparing concepts for new expansions of the village, designs for various public buildings, and concepts for a memorial highway along the north edge of the community, as well as planting designs for various sites and cemetery plans.

The most ambitious elements of the plans prepared by the Olmsted firm for Kohler Village included plazas anchored by businesses and civic institutions at the convergence of webs of axial streets. Curvilinear drives in the residential portions, if implemented, would have articulated the relationship of the village to the underlying landscape, including the Sheboygan River, which wanders along the southern edge of the village. West II bears signs of this grander vision, though at a smaller scale: a small common lies at the junction of three streets in the core of the addition, and a church fronts a small triangular park along Valley Road. Other signs of the Olmsted influence in the village include the lawn of the American Club (listed in the National Register of Historic Places in 1978), once a social institution and boarding house for the factory's workers, and the Nature Theater, an amphitheater inserted into Ravine Park, the community's primary open space.

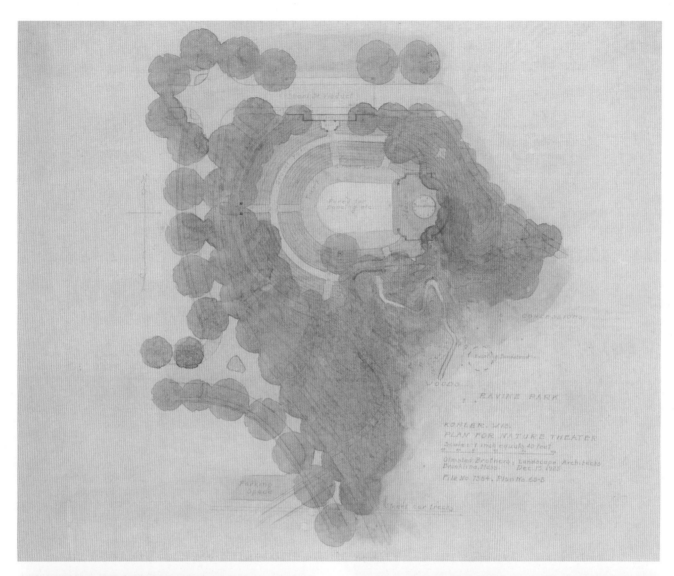

Clockwise from top: Plan for a "Nature Theater" for the residents, 1925. Kohler Company headquarters. Decent houses for workers were set back from the road by a plan to create front lawns under a generous tree canopy.

Above: A grove featuring many options for pedestrian circulation in Washington Park. **Above right:** New development continues to benefit from improvements made to Lake Park in the early 1900s **Right:** The entrance to the Lion Bridge in Lake Park.

WASHINGTON PARK, MILWAUKEE

Originally known as West Park, this land was acquired by the City of Milwaukee in 1891 and renamed Washington Park in 1900. The initial design by Frederick Law Olmsted Sr. included the layout of the park's circulation network of drives and walks and their integral bridges, the shaping and excavation of the ponds and lagoons, and extensive tree and shrub plantings. Very soon after Olmsted's initial involvement, the city's first zoo was added to the park's design, along with the construction of numerous athletic sports facilities. This included a one-mile horse racing track, lawn tennis courts, a toboggan slide with spectator grandstands, and a six-hole golf course (which eventually was razed to accommodate the zoo's expansion). Other additions to the 128.5-acre park include the Goethe-Schiller monument (1908) and the Art Deco–style bandshell, the Emil Blatz Temple of Music (1938). By the 1930s, the zoo was showing its age, and because of the lack of space to expand, a search began for a new location by 1947. In 1961 the zoo was reopened as the 184-acre Milwaukee County Zoo, which has since grown to 200 acres. The Washington Park Zoo closed for good in 1963.

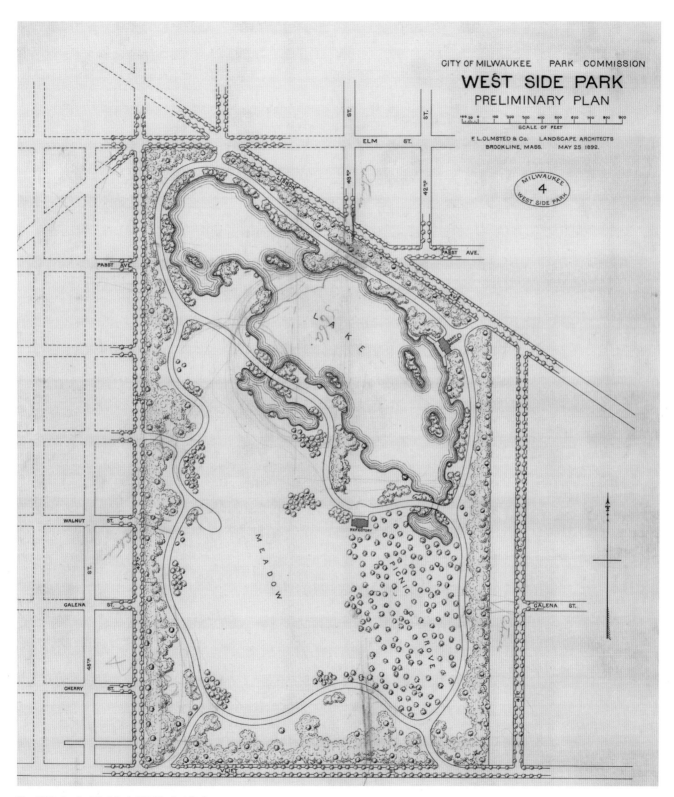

The 1892 plan for West Park-Washington Park.

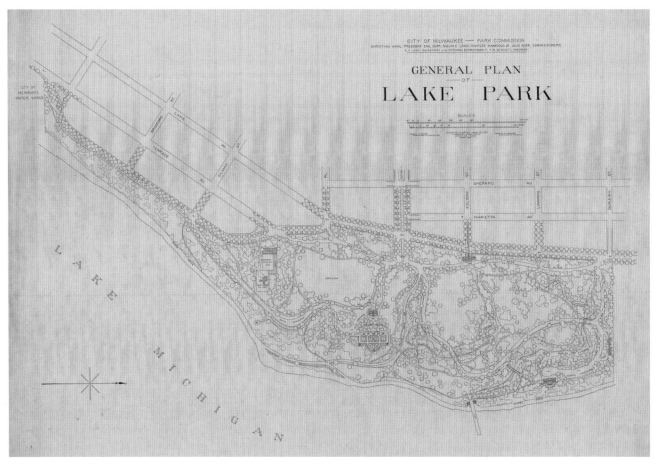

The 1895 plan for Lake Park, showing the locations of the music pavilion, Lion Bridge, and the lighthouse.

LAKE PARK, MILWAUKEE

Located along the shores of Lake Michigan, 140-acre (originally 124 acres) Lake Park was among the first five public parks acquired by the city in 1890. In 1892 Frederick Law Olmsted Sr. was engaged to develop a plan, to be bordered by the lakeshore bluff to the east and a road that would follow the adjacent city streets to the west. His design included a pastoral carriage road, bridges, and pedestrian paths that connected to diverse park destinations, including a refectory, music pavilion, belvedere, lagoons, and meadows. Following Olmsted's involvement in the early 1900s, additions were made to the park including a pavilion (1903) and a grand staircase (1907) designed by Alfred C. Clas, an architect and planner who also served on the original Milwaukee County Parks Commission. In recent years, development has emphasized recreation as testified by an eighteen-hole pitch-and-putt golf course, tennis courts, and athletic fields. Lake Park was listed in the National Register of Historic Places in 1993.

CANADA

Capilano Estates and the Lions Gate Bridge,
Vancouver   304

The Uplands, Victoria   307
Mount Royal, Montreal   309

A 1936 drawing for the Capilano Golf and Country Club.

CAPILANO ESTATES, VANCOUVER

In 1931 James Dawson, partner in the Olmsted Brothers firm, met with Alfred J. T. Taylor, engineer, entrepreneur, and Vancouver native, then working in London, to hear about an ambitious proposal. Looking to attract British capital to Vancouver, "the Gateway to the Pacific," Taylor was representing British Pacific Properties, Ltd., a syndicate that had purchased 4000 acres of sloping, thickly wooded land in temperate West Vancouver, from the Capilano River to Horseshoe Bay. Underwritten by numerous investors, the intention was to develop these panoramic parcels into varied high-end residential communities with amenities. The area was to be called Capilano, from a First Nations name meaning "beautiful river."

Dawson advised the syndicate to buy out "in-holdings" to have full control, and to acquire beachfront property for a range of opportunities. Between 1931 and 1937, the Olmsted firm, together with Canadian golf architect Stanley Thompson and local architects and engineers, laid out Capilano Estates and the Capilano Golf and Country Club on 1100 acres. A monumental project, curving north–south roads on manageable grades were carved out of virgin forests along the steep slopes, providing for uphill and downhill house sites, with views toward water or mountains. They retained acreage for schools and community amenities and protected watercourses with surrounding parkland. The Olmsted firm's layout essentially remains to this day.

Dawson insisted that there be a distinctive entry point for the development. He thus planned Taylor Way as an ascending, broad, straight, tree-lined boulevard, offering downhill vistas to the Lions Gate Bridge and across Burrard Inlet. He envisioned

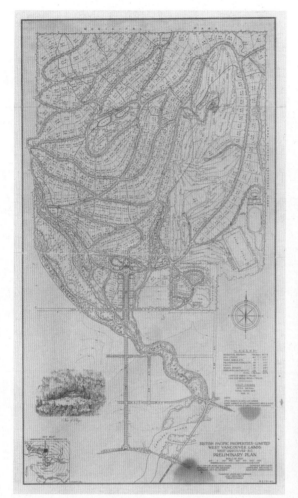

Above: Preliminary Plan for the Capilano Estates. **Above right:** Sketch for First Narrows Bridge. **Bottom Right:** The Lions Gate Bridge spans Vancouver Harbor and connects the city to Stanley Park.

a substantial architectural plaza as the uphill terminus. Such expenditure was rejected by the stockholders, resulting in the extant Taylor Way boulevard, now ending with a nondescript traffic circle. Full completion of the eighteen-hole golf course according to Thompson's renowned and demanding layout, with significant clubhouse facilities, was truncated by budgetary concerns, though the course remains a challenging par seventy-one with undulating greens lined with majestic firs.

The development of the Lions Gate Bridge, across the narrows from Stanley Park, was the determinant for the success of this enterprise. Without the bridge, access to West Vancouver relied on ferries. An engineering feat, this elegant and seemingly weightless steel cable suspension bridge, designed by Monsarrat and Pratley, was officially opened in 1939 by King George VI. At nearly 5000 feet long, the bridge stretches from a 364-foot height in Stanley Park, guarded by two carved Art Deco lions, to a long viaduct on the western side. Concerned that this bridge would increase commercial traffic through Stanley Park, the Olmsted firm made several recommendations from 1933 through 1937 to realign traffic interchanges, particularly around Lost Lagoon. Some of these changes are still reflected on the ground. The Lions Gate Bridge was designated as a Historic Site of Canada in 2004.

The Uplands plan provided for houses in a variety of architectural styles and at a variety of scales.

The Uplands development was intended to fit well within the natural surroundings, including views from Uplands Park southeast toward the Oak Bay Islands Ecological Reserve, where the Haro Strait meets the Salish Sea.

GIBSON CATLETT
CANADA.

THE UPLANDS, VICTORIA

Uplands is a 465-acre residential community of 600 homes in the northeastern part of Oak Bay, a municipality adjacent to Victoria, British Columbia. The development overlooks the Oak Bay and the Oak Bay Islands Ecological Reserve. It was designed between 1907 and 1908 by John Charles Olmsted for Winnipeg real estate developer William Gardner and is widely considered one of the first formally planned subdivisions in Canada.

Olmsted's design departed from the grid pattern of the adjacent Canadian subdivisions and featured a curvilinear street pattern. The main artery, Midland Road, was designed as a boulevard to accommodate streetcars and motorcars; the residential lots along this length of road were more rectilinear in shape than the lots along the secondary streets. Olmsted had a detailed survey prepared with five-foot contour intervals to ensure that the roads would work in harmony with the natural setting and that certain landscape features, such as the existing Garry oak trees and views out over the bay, were preserved and protected. On his many visits, Olmsted observed the evidence of traditional cultural practices of the Songhees First Nation, one of Canada's Indigenous peoples, in particular within the

Garry oak trees ecosystem, which indicated historical controlled seasonal burnings.

Olmsted prepared innovative guidelines for protective deed restrictions, including the buildings, to retain the carefully designed character. (The firm continued to use such an approach in later subdivisions such as at Palos Verdes.) Before construction began, the development faced insurmountable financial difficulties and most of the land was sold in 1911, although Gardner was able to require adherence to the design when the property changed hands. The municipality of Oak Bay agreed to take over the enforcement of the restrictions. Olmsted continued to make revisions while James F. Dawson managed the details such as streetlighting fixtures and grading revisions; telephone service was undergrounded to maintain the rural character. The Uplands Tramway, in service 1913–1947, was not built in the median of Midland Road as originally planned but within the roadbed; Midland Circle became the turnaround. The faint outline of the tramway is still visible in the Midland Circle pavement. The boulevard design along Midland Road to the intersection with Cotswold Road was never built and the recommended tree spacing conflicted with the tramway poles and wiring; those trees were not planted. The Olmsted firm ended their involvement in 1921.

In 1946 Gardner, who still retained an undeveloped seventy-six-acre area with direct access to Midland Road in the southeastern section (Blocks 23, 24, 29 and 31), sold the tract to the municipality for a public park. This section contained significant cultural landscape features, including Indigenous burial cairns and archaeological sites, plus Garry oaks, rocky crags, and panoramic ocean views. While there has been further subdivision of larger lots, the street network generally follows the original design plan of 1907. On August 19, 2019, the Government of Canada designated Uplands as a National Historic Site.

Mount Royal is known for its stunning fall foliage displays.

Beaver Lake, likely adapted from Olmsted Sr.'s original plan and adopting his use of organically shaped bodies of water within parks.

MOUNT ROYAL, MONTREAL

Beginning in 1874, Frederick Law Olmsted Sr.'s design for the nearly 700-acre Mount Royal was his first work on a major park project following the dissolution of his partnership with Calvert Vaux and is illustrative of his increasingly rich scenic vocabulary. This 750-foot-high monadnock, surrounded by a growing city, offered him the opportunity to organize the site into a series of distinctive picturesque experiences, connected by a continuous circulation route through orchestrated vegetation as the visitor traveled upward toward the summit. Progressing from lowland Piedmont with its deciduous trees, through the steep crags with their increasing wildness, to the summit, which Olmsted designated Upperfell, planted with scrubby northern species—pines and firs—to emphasize its rocky, exposed character, the visitor's sense of removal from the city was heightened.

Olmsted had hoped to create a summit promenade to enjoy the vistas, with areas below to meander down a glade of contrasting pastoral scenery. However, economically difficult times, the Panic of 1873, prevented full acquisition of needed land, and lack of understanding interfered with full development of his conception. Where this network of drives was to meet the city below, Olmsted proposed platting for surrounding houses, creating a gradual transition from the gridded streets to curving

blocks fronting common greens, like the *Côte Placide*, which featured tall shade trees characteristic of landscapes farther south.

Only the broadest strokes of Olmsted's framework were partially implemented beginning in 1875. His desire for gradual grades for both walkways and drives, including consideration for handicapped accessibility, were thwarted, with portions of the roadway realized only in a cruder fashion than the carefully choreographed topography and views to which he aspired. To express his frustrations, Olmsted self-published his report in 1881, detailing his design rationale. Park development continued beyond the turn of the century, and Frederick G. Todd—reputed to be Canada's first landscape architect, and a former Olmsted Brothers apprentice from 1896–1900—designed several additions to the park, including a cafe structure in 1905 and Beaver Lake in the 1930s. The latter intervention, near the site of a fleur-de-lis-shaped reservoir in Olmsted Sr.'s plan, features an organic shoreline, suggesting that Todd applied Olmsted's intended vision for naturalistic waterbodies in his approach to park improvements. Mount Royal is, along with Iroquois Park in Louisville, Kentucky, one of only two mountain parks designed by Olmsted Sr. In 2005 the Government of Quebec created the Mount Royal Historic and Natural District, a first in the province of Quebec.

MOUNT ROYAL

· DESIGN MAP ·

1877

Scale of Meters.

Scale of Feet.

The 1877 design map for Mount Royal, featuring the now-famous overlook at left.

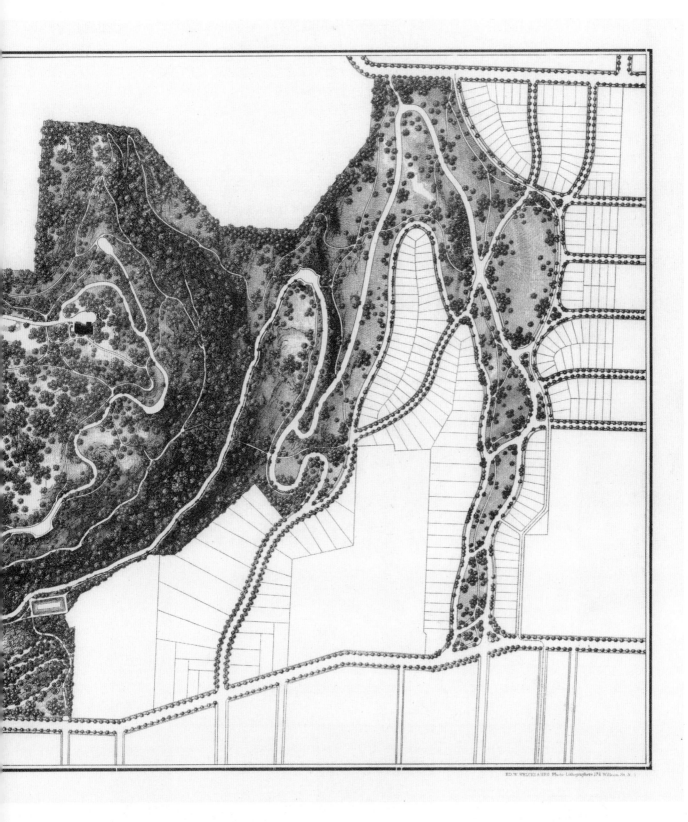

ED. W. WELCKE & BRO. Photo-Lithographers 176 William St. N.Y.

CENTRAL PARK 1858

The Family Tree of The Olmsted Firms

......The seed of the Olmsted Offices germinated in 1858 when Frederick Law Olmsted and Calvert Vaux submitted their "Greensward" plan in competition for the design of New York's Central Park. Since that time there has been a dynamic and dynastic succession of firms bearing the name of Olmsted, and the firm names — together with their dates of activity — are shown as branches of the tree. In the foliage are the names of the principals responsible for carrying on the work of the firms. These Landscape Architects are represented in photographs around the border of the sheet.......

The tree has its roots in Central Park, and at its base are the fruits of over a century of Olmsted design: The National Capitol grounds; the Tower's setting at Mountain Lake in Florida; The Cloisters and Fort Tryon Park in New York; The Cleveland Museum of Art's site; The full landscape development of the National Shrine of the Immaculate Conception — and of the Nation's Jefferson Memorial in the District of Columbia; and the Duke University campus in Durham, North Carolina being the few represented on this document.

CHRONOLOGY

Olmsted and Vaux	1858
Frederick Law Olmsted	1858-1884
F.L. and J.C. Olmsted*	1884-1889
F.L. Olmsted and Company	1889-1893
Olmsted, Olmsted, and Eliot	1893-1897
F.L. and J.C. Olmsted**	1897-1898
Olmsted Brothers	1898-1961
Olmsted Associates***	1961-

* *Father and Son*
** *Brothers*
*** *Partnership 1961-64; Incorporated 1964*

Photograph labels (left border, top to bottom): Artemas P. Richardson; Carl Rust Parker; William Bell Marquis; Edward Clark Whiting; Percival Gallagher; Henry Sargent Codman; John Charles Olmsted

Photograph labels (right border, top to bottom): Joseph G. Hudak; Charles Scott Riley; Leon H. Zach; Henry Vincent Hubbard; James Frederick Dawson; Charles Eliot; Frederick L. Olmsted, Jr.

Photograph labels (bottom center): Frederick Law Olmsted; Calvert Vaux

OLMSTED FIRMS

OLMSTED, VAUX, AND COMPANY
1865–1872

The partnership between landscape architect Frederick Law Olmsted Sr. and English architect Calvert Vaux derived from their meeting through a mutual connection, Andrew Jackson Downing, which led to the collaboration on their 1857 winning entry, the Greensward Plan, for New York's Central Park. Olmsted left that project to head the United States Sanitary Commission during the Civil War, later traveling west to serve as the manager of the Mariposa Estate with its gold mine in Bear Valley, California, where he drafted early management and interpretation strategies for Yosemite Valley, some twenty-five years before the national park was established. After the mine failed, Vaux convinced Olmsted to return to New York and help him lead the budding urban park movement, which had emerged in part because of Central Park's success. The partnership's first commission was the 585-acre Prospect Park in Brooklyn in 1866. Drawing inspiration from the grand parks and boulevards of such European cities as Berlin and Paris, the pair developed the nation's first park and parkway systems in Brooklyn and Buffalo. The partnership's subsequent projects continued to set new precedents, including the creation of one of the country's first major suburban residential communities in Riverside, Illinois. The firm developed the initial plans for Chicago's South Park System in 1869, which included both Washington and Jackson Parks, and the Midway Plaisance. Many of these projects would later be improved upon by Olmsted Sr. in partnership with other landscape architects, including his sons John Charles Olmsted and Frederick Law Olmsted Jr., as well as Henry Codman, architect Daniel Burnham, and others. In 1872, after seven years of collaboration, Olmsted and Vaux dissolved their partnership, although it would not be the last time they would work together. They reunited in 1887 to design the Niagara Reservation, and again two years later in Newburgh, New York, to create Andrew Jackson Downing Memorial Park (now Downing Park). The latter project was developed pro bono in collaboration with their sons, Downing Vaux and John Charles Olmsted, to honor Andrew Jackson Downing, a progenitor of American landscape design and a former colleague of Calvert Vaux.

F. L. AND J. C. OLMSTED
1884–1889, 1897

Originally established by Frederick Law Olmsted Sr. and John Charles Olmsted, the firm was active from 1884 to 1889. The firm name was used again for a short time after the senior Olmsted's retirement, in 1897, with Frederick Law Olmsted Jr. replacing his father.

F. L. OLMSTED AND COMPANY
1889–1893

This was a short-lived iteration. Created when Henry Sargent Codman was added as a partner to the firm of F. L. and J. C. Olmsted, the endeavor was cut short by the tragic death of Codman in 1893, while they were working on the World's Columbian Exposition in Chicago.

OLMSTED, OLMSTED, AND ELIOT
1893–1897

The successor firm to F. L. Olmsted and Company, this office consisted of partners Frederick Law Olmsted Sr., John Charles Olmsted, and Charles Eliot, the latter joining the firm upon Henry Sargent Codman's death in 1893. With Eliot came Boston's Metropolitan Park Commission projects, which he had begun during a decade of independent practice, as well as park planning in Cambridge along the Charles River. He continued to focus on parks in the metropolitan area and was crucial in the development of other park systems, especially that of Hartford, Connecticut.

The firm was involved with numerous projects of various types across the country during its four-year lifespan. They created plans for a number of parks, including Cazenovia and South Parks in Buffalo, New York (1894); the transformation of Chicago's South Park System (Jackson Park, Washington Park, and the Midway Plaisance and parkways) back to parkland after the 1893 Chicago World's Fair (1895); planting plans for the eastern and western sections of Downing Park in Newburgh, New York (1895); West Park in Milwaukee, Wisconsin (1893 and 1895); Morton Park in Newport, Rhode Island (1894 and 1896); and Forest Park in Queens, New York (1896). The firm developed parkway plans for Bay Ridge Parkway in Brooklyn, New York (1893); and for the Mystic Valley Parkway and the Charles River Parkway and its approaches, in Massachusetts (both in 1895). Private commissions included the grounds of the Fogg Memorial Building at the Berwick Academy in South Berwick, Maine (1894); the Cairnwood Estate in Bryn Athyn, Pennsylvania (1895); and the Biltmore Estate in Asheville, North Carolina (1889–1895).

After 1895, Olmsted Sr. no longer actively practiced. Two years later, Eliot died from meningitis, and the remaining partners, John Charles Olmsted and Frederick Law Olmsted Jr., renamed the firm F. L. and J. C. Olmsted for a brief stint in 1897. The following year, the firm became known as Olmsted Brothers.

OLMSTED BROTHERS
1898–1961

After Frederick Law Olmsted Sr.'s retirement, Frederick Law Olmsted Jr. and his older half brother, John Charles Olmsted, formed the Olmsted Brothers firm, a firm that dominated the practice of landscape architecture and planning for decades, providing training for generations of burgeoning practitioners. Olmsted Brothers' canon of diverse work across the nation, and in Canada, Bermuda, and other foreign locales, grew to over five thousand project listings. Both Olmsted Jr. and John Charles Olmsted were stalwart advocates for the emerging profession of landscape architecture, and both were founding members of the American Society of Landscape Architects. The Olmsted Brothers firm designed parks and park systems for several major cities, including Atlanta, Boston, Louisville, and Seattle, among other cities. As the largest landscape architecture practice in the United States in the early twentieth century, the firm managed a portfolio that included exposition grounds, roadways, state capitols, planned communities, libraries, hospitals, and academic campuses.

In 1950, at age 80, Frederick Law Olmsted Jr. became a consultant to the firm, rather than the leading partner. At this time, two new partners were added to the letterhead, Artemas P. Richardson and Charles Scott Riley. Joseph G. Hudak, a landscape architect with notable horticultural skills, also became a partner by 1958.

OLMSTED ASSOCIATES
1961–1979

The firm name of Olmsted Brothers continued even after the death of Frederick Law Olmsted Jr. in 1957. When the firm was renamed in 1961, its partners consisted of the "old guard"—Edward Clark Whiting and William B. Marquis, men who had been trained by one or both of the Olmsted brothers—and the

Members of the Palos Verdes planning team, including surveyors, engineers, and landscape architects, circa 1922. Frederick Law Olmsted Jr. can be seen in the center front.

newer partners: Richardson, Riley, and Hudak. By 1963, Whiting had died, Marquis had retired, and Riley had left the firm, leaving Richardson and Hudak, along with a new partner, Erno J. Fonagy, as the core of Olmsted Associates. By this time, with more skilled practitioners in the profession, the extent and range of the Olmsted firm's practice had greatly changed. While they were still involved in the design for several corporate headquarters, land subdivisions, and some private properties, and continued to be engaged with campus planning for academic institutions (particularly in Mississippi), the practice was diminishing.

Meanwhile, Fairsted—historic home and office of the firm and declared a National Historic Landmark in 1963—was in need of major repairs. Many of the historic files had already been gifted to the Library of Congress, a practice begun by Frederick Law Olmsted Jr. and continued by Artemas Richardson. After several years of negotiations, in 1979 the National Park Service acquired this unique site along with its considerable archives of plans, photographs, and documents (dedicated in 1980). Richardson retained the right to the name, "Olmsted Associates," to continue his landscape practice in New Hampshire.

SELECTED BIOGRAPHIES OF PRINCIPALS AND MEMBERS OF OLMSTED FIRMS

HAROLD HILL BLOSSOM, "HAL" (1879–1935)

Born in Brooklyn, New York, Blossom graduated from the Pratt Institute High School and Amherst College. After graduation, he worked on a fruit farm before continuing his studies at Harvard's Lawrence Scientific School, becoming the first student to graduate with a Master of Landscape Architecture (MLA) in 1907. While at Harvard, he impressed Frederick Law Olmsted Jr., who hired Blossom to work for Olmsted Brothers while he was still a student, a post that he continued after graduation. In 1908 he married Minnie Motley Dawson, sister of his Olmsted colleague James Dawson.

At Olmsted Brothers, Blossom worked under various principals to draft plans and devise planting plans for projects, including South Mountain Reservation in New Jersey. He traveled often on behalf of the firm: he collaborated with James Dawson on the Alaska-Yukon-Pacific Exhibition in Seattle and visited Cuba for the planning of a resort community. In 1911 he represented Olmsted Brothers in planning the 1915 Panama-Pacific Exposition in San Diego. When Olmsted Brothers resigned from that project, Blossom returned to the northeast, working mainly on residential estates, particularly in Newport and on Long Island. In 1919 he left the firm to start his own practice, focusing primarily on the New England area, retaining many of his residential clients. Rheumatic fever in his youth caused Blossom to suffer heart problems all his life. He died in 1935 of cardiac failure at age 56.

HENRY SARGENT CODMAN, "HARRY" (1864–1893)

After graduating from the Massachusetts Institute of Technology in 1884, Harry Codman studied at the Bussey Institution and apprenticed at the Olmsted firm, traveling with the senior Olmsted in 1886 to California to meet with Leland Stanford as the project for that campus began. In 1887 Codman embarked on a European exploration with his uncle, Charles Sprague Sargent, director of the Arnold Arboretum. He stayed abroad for a year, exploring public and private landscapes across the continent and apprenticing with Édouard André, the Parisian park planner. Returning in 1889, he immediately joined the Olmsted firm as a partner, beginning work with the senior Olmsted on the Chicago World's Fair planning. Additionally, he took up several park projects for Milwaukee, Buffalo, Rochester, and Louisville, residential suburb planning in Colorado, and private estate work, especially for Ogden Goelet in Newport.

Codman was respected for his cordiality and skill as a landscape planner, so his unexpected death in January 1893, after an appendectomy, was a personal and professional blow to his Olmsted firm colleagues at a time when numerous major projects were occurring simultaneously. As John Charles Olmsted noted at his death, "We lose a most intimate and warm friend and our profession loses one of its mainstays at a time when it is just struggling for popular recognition . . ."

JAMES FREDERICK DAWSON, "FRED" (1874–1941)

Dawson was born in Boston to a notable horticultural family. His father, Jackson Dawson, superintendent and chief propagator at Arnold Arboretum, was a man reputed to be able to get twigs to grow. Fred Dawson graduated from Harvard University in 1896 having added agriculture and horticulture at the Bussey Institute to his studies. After a European tour, Dawson was chosen by John Charles Olmsted and Frederick Law Olmsted Jr. in 1904 as the first associate partner in the firm of Olmsted Brothers. Dawson spent his entire career with the firm, becoming a full partner in 1922. He supervised projects in Venezuela, Cuba, Canada, and Bermuda, as well as throughout the United States, designing in a wide range of landscape types—arboreta, parks and parkways, expositions, estates, resorts and country clubs, golf courses, and subdivisions.

In his early career, he traveled extensively with his mentor, John Charles Olmsted, who gradually gave him control of many of the public and private projects. Dawson spent significant time on the Pacific coast, developing designs for the park and parkway systems and private estates of Portland, Seattle, and Spokane. His special skill with plant material provided a unique character to the Alaska-Yukon-Pacific Exposition held in 1909 on what was to be further shaped by the Olmsted firm as the University of Washington campus. He worked alongside John Charles in planning the Louisville, Kentucky, park system, which led to numerous private commissions in that area as well as across the country and in Canada. In addition to his work for the Mountain Lake resort in Lake Wales, Florida, he was one of the major planners for the extensive Palos Verdes Estates (where he had a home) and for the British Pacific Properties, named Capilano, in West Vancouver, Canada.

CHARLES ELIOT (1859–1897)

The son of Harvard University's president, Eliot was born into the elite academic environment of Cambridge, Massachusetts. Childhood summers in Mount Desert Island, Maine, spurred a lifelong interest in natural systems. Earning his A.B. (*Artium Baccalaureus*, Latin for Bachelor of Arts) from Harvard in 1882, he continued taking coursework at the Bussey Institute while interning at the F. L. and J. C. Olmsted office in nearby Brookline. Returning from a European tour in 1886, Eliot opened his own office in Massachusetts, handling a wide range of public and private projects. His particular focus was on protecting notable historic properties, for which he initiated the Trustees of (Public) Reservations, a statewide nonprofit organization, to acquire and manage such sites. Similarly, since he was concerned about protection for natural systems, particularly riverine corridors, he recommended parkland rather than development to preserve their banks. Together with journalist Sylvester Baxter, he expanded this thinking to plan for a system of reservations around Boston to protect special scenic land and unique natural features for continuous public enjoyment. This was visionary regional planning, considering land masses regardless of jurisdictional boundaries.

He brought these projects with him when in 1893 he became a partner in the Olmsted office to create Olmsted, Olmsted, and Eliot. Reaching beyond Olmsted Sr.'s original Emerald Necklace linkage of parks, Eliot continued to expand his metropolitan plan for this comprehensive regional system of parks and parkways, incorporating shorefront, rivers, lakes, forests, and areas of sensitive ecology, a first in the nation and a model for other communities. A skilled writer, Eliot is known for his numerous publications, gathered into a tributary volume by his father into *Charles Eliot, Landscape Architect* (1902). Eliot died of spinal meningitis in 1897 while supervising the construction of Hartford's Keney Park. In 1899, Harvard University's landscape architecture program was established in his memory.

PERCIVAL GALLAGHER
(1874–1934)

Born in South Boston, Gallagher studied horticulture at Harvard's Bussey Institute, supplemented by classes in the fine arts program, where he met Frederick Law Olmsted Jr. Graduating in 1894, Gallagher joined Olmsted, Olmsted, and Eliot. Among his projects there was the restoration of the plants on the US Capitol Grounds in Washington, DC. In 1904 he attempted to open a firm with landscape architect James Sturgis Pray, who later became the chairman of the Department of Landscape Architecture at Harvard. Gallagher was ill-suited for the administrative side of running a firm, however, and returned to the Olmsted office after two years, at which point his former firm became Pray, Hubbard, and White.

In 1927 he became a full partner with Olmsted Brothers. Noted for his artistic talent, horticultural knowledge, and generally modest temperament, Gallagher was well suited to collaborative work with colleagues and clients alike. He contributed to the campus design work for Bryn Mawr, Haverford, Swarthmore, Vassar, and Duke University. Gallagher also worked on the design of the park system for Union County, New Jersey, including Rahway River Park, and his most extensive estate work took place around Philadelphia and on Long Island, including Ormston, the George Baker Estate, and the H. H. Rogers Estate. These latter projects show a range of plant palettes and a facility with multiple design styles. His ease with stylistic juxtapositions is well shown at the Oldfields Estate in Indianapolis, now part of the Indianapolis Museum of Art.

GEORGE GIBBS JR.
(1878–1950)

Born in Riverton, Kentucky, Gibbs earned a bachelor's degree in science from the University of Illinois in 1900 and a BSLA (Bachelor of Science, Landscape Architecture) from Harvard University in 1904. Following graduation, Gibbs traveled throughout Europe studying parks and gardens before joining the Olmsted Brothers in 1905. While there, he worked on planning projects across the United States, including parks in Fall River, Massachusetts, and the Denver Mountain Park System. Gibbs departed the Olmsted Brothers firm in 1914 to join the Boston City Planning Board, where he analyzed methods for making the city's North End and East Boston more livable. His results were published in the report *East Boston: A Survey and a Comprehensive Plan*. During World War I, Gibbs served in the Construction Division of the US Army and aided in camp planning. He remained in Europe after the war, overseeing the establishment of American cemeteries for the National Commission of Fine Arts, including the Flanders Field American Cemetery and Memorial. Upon his return to the United States in 1923, Gibbs rejoined the Olmsted Brothers firm in Palos Verdes, California, where he supervised the development of the Palos Verdes Estates, the Pacific Palisades in Los Angeles, and the British Pacific Properties in Vancouver. At the onset of the Great Depression, Gibbs entered the Civilian Conservation Corps and headed the Omaha office of the National Park Service (NPS). He subsequently joined the NPS San Francisco office in 1936, where he developed master plans for sites in Northern California, such as the Redwood Highway and Wild Cat Canyon. After returning to Palos Verdes in 1938, Gibbs opened his own planning practice, continuing to consult with Olmsted Brothers on West Coast projects. Gibbs was named a Fellow of the American Society of Landscape Architects in 1919. He passed away in Palos Verdes at the age of 72.

HENRY VINCENT HUBBARD
(1875–1947)

Born in Taunton, Massachusetts, Hubbard earned an A.B. from Harvard University in 1897 and a master's degree in 1900. In 1901 he became the first student awarded an S.B. (Bachelor of Science) in landscape architecture from Harvard's Lawrence Science School (the program in landscape architecture had been officially established under the leadership of Frederick Law Olmsted Jr. in 1900). Following graduation, Hubbard joined the Olmsted Brothers firm but left in 1906 to cofound the practice Pray, Hubbard, and White with landscape architects H. P. White and James Sturgis Pray. That same year, Hubbard began teaching landscape architecture at Harvard's Graduate School of Applied Science. He was promoted to assistant professor and professor in 1911 and 1921, respectively. Hubbard moved to Washington, DC, in 1917 to work with the US Army's Construction Division. During World War I he served on the Housing Commission of the Council of National Defense, the US Shipping Board, and the US Housing Corporation. Pray, Hubbard, and White closed in 1918, after which Hubbard rejoined Olmsted Brothers, becoming a full partner in 1927. He was responsible for park planning in several cities, including Baltimore, where in 1926 he updated and expanded the earlier Olmsted Brothers firm's comprehensive plan. He designed numerous private landscapes and subdivisions, in particular Colony Hills in Springfield, Massachusetts, where he shaped a number of interior small parks for community meeting places. During his career with the firm, he collaborated with several federal agencies, including the National Park Service and the Tennessee Valley Authority. He was a longstanding and influential member of the National Capital Park and Planning Commission and a planning consultant to numerous cities. Hubbard cofounded the magazine *Landscape Architecture* with Charles Downing Lay and Robert Wheelwright in 1910, and he coauthored the first textbook for the young discipline, *An Introduction to the Study of Landscape Design* (1917) with Theodora Kimball, whom he married in 1924. He would author and contribute to numerous publications throughout his life, including the book *Our Cities To-day, To-morrow: A Survey of Planning and Zoning Progress in the United States* (1929) and the journal *Harvard Planning Studies* (1937). Hubbard was president of the American Society of Landscape Architects from 1931 to 1934. He maintained his employment with Olmsted Brothers until his death.

JOSEPH GEORGE HUDAK
(1927–)

Hudak received a Bachelor of Science in Horticulture and Landscape Architecture from Pennsylvania State College in 1951 and joined the Olmsted Brothers firm in 1953. Mountain Lake Sanctuary in Lake Wales, Florida, was one of the first projects Hudak became involved with, taking over day-to-day project management from William Lyman Phillips. In the 1950s and 1960s Hudak established himself as the firm's planting specialist. In 1963, shortly after the firm was renamed Olmsted Associates, Hudak assumed tenancy of Fairsted, Frederick Law Olmsted Jr.'s home and office in Brookline, Massachusetts, where he introduced new plant materials into the landscape, including azaleas, yews, rhododendrons, and local daylilies. In 1964 Hudak gave up his financial partnership in the firm and his tenancy at Fairsted, though he remained with Olmsted Associates for another fifteen years, eventually becoming vice president in 1978. He worked on campus plans for the University of Mississippi, Mississippi State, and Harvard Business School, and planting plans for numerous projects, including Maryland's Patapsco Tunnel development, Duke University's campus, the Sloan Kettering Institute in Rye, New York, Fort Tryon Park in New York City, and several private estates. Outside of his work with Olmsted Associates, Hudak lectured on horticulture at Harvard University's Graduate School of Design and for the Radcliffe Seminars Program. He wrote extensively on plant identification and garden design. His books, including Gardening with Perennials Month by Month, were accessible to the home gardener, and as a result he formed active relationships with garden clubs around the country. Hudak became a Fellow of the American Society of Landscape Architects in 1992.

PERCY REGINALD JONES, "PA"
(1860–1941)

Born in Cardiff, Glamorgan, Wales, Jones immigrated to Boston, Massachusetts, with his parents in 1884. Although little is known of his early life or education, he began working in the architecture firm of Shepley, Rutan, and Coolidge before joining the Olmsted Brothers firm in 1886 as a draftsman. Diligent and skilled, Jones was to remain with Olmsted Brothers for the rest of his career. He eventually expanded his role beyond draftsman to manage a wide range of projects as a principal assistant. Jones accompanied John Charles Olmsted to review works in progress across the United States, often drafting revisions on the spot and coordinating site work. Heavily involved in the firm's 1903 report on a series of parks and parkways for Seattle, Washington, Jones also worked on the city's Lake Washington Boulevard, Washington Park Arboretum, and Volunteer Park. He also drafted new plans for the Beacon Hill Estate at Newport, Rhode Island, in 1908. With the deteriorating health of John Charles Olmsted in 1917, Jones began to play a larger role in coordinating projects and dealing with myriad clients, especially for the numerous public and private projects in Dayton, Ohio. In 1919, for example, he played a key role in converting the Clifton Estate, in Baltimore, into Clifton Park, which included an eighteen-hole golf course, twenty-seven tennis courts, a three-and-a-half-acre swimming pool, and several athletic fields. He also worked on the twenty-square-mile Palos Verdes peninsula, a vast project near Los Angeles, California, that transformed steep slopes of coastal landscape into several distinct residential neighborhoods. In the early 1930s, Jones's failing eyesight and the economic downturn of the Great Depression slowed his active role in the firm. He eventually moved to Milton, Nova Scotia, Canada, where he remained until his death at the age of 81. He is buried in Milton Cemetery in Queens, Nova Scotia.

HERBERT J. KELLAWAY (1867–1947)

Born in Kent, England, Kellaway moved with his family to Needham, Massachusetts, where he graduated from high school. He began his career in 1892 as a draftsman in the Olmsted office during the period in which the firm was working on its complex plans for Boston's Emerald Necklace park corridor. During his tenure with the Olmsted firm, Kellaway also worked on campus plans for Smith, Amherst, and Middlebury Colleges. He left the firm in 1906 to establish his own office, taking on several projects updating original designs by the Olmsted firm, including the Newton Centre Playground, designed by Olmsted Sr. in 1891. Reflecting the growing popularity of public sports and recreation facilities, Kellaway added basketball courts, a croquet lawn, and archery grounds, as well as rerouting a scenic meandering brook to create additional play areas. He also designed a tree-lined parkway in Brookline, which connected their northern and southern parks, and a plan to improve the waterway systems of Winchester, both in Massachusetts. During World War I, Kellaway was recommended by Frederick Law Olmsted Jr. to serve on a committee of city planners tasked with planning and overseeing

construction of US Army complexes, with Kellaway directing the Fort Devens complex in Ayer, Massachusetts. Kellaway was elected a Fellow of the American Society of Landscape Architects in 1912 and was one of eight landscape architects to incorporate a chapter in Massachusetts. He wrote frequently about the profession, covering topics ranging from suburban home gardening to increasing public attention for land planning. Kellaway retired in 1944, and died in Bath, Maine, in 1947.

HANS J. KOEHLER (1867–1951)

Born in Hoboken, New Jersey, Koehler was raised in Boston, where his father was a curator at the Boston Art Museum. Koehler began working for the Olmsted Brothers firm as a young man in 1905, where he combined his love of nature with his artistic tendencies, becoming a skilled illustrator and designer. During his long career with the Olmsted Brothers firm, Koehler worked on several notable projects, both public parks and private estates. He established himself as the firm's plantsman, with great knowledge about trees, and contributed to the horticultural enrichment of projects such as Branch Brook Park in Newark, New Jersey; parks in the Baltimore system; Washington Park Arboretum in Seattle, Washington; and Fort Tryon Park in New York, where he developed the Heather Garden with James Dawson. His expertise was also an asset to the planning for Bok Tower Sanctuary in Florida and for a number of the Long Island and Newport estates. He helped to rejuvenate many of the plantings around Fairsted, the Olmsted Brothers office in Brookline, Massachusetts. Koehler retired in the 1940s, though he continued to advise the practice on plant materials. Koehler published extensively on horticulture, with a particular focus on trees. He is remembered in Boston for creating nametags for tree species in Boston Common and in Marlboro, Massachusetts, where he made his home. His last years were spent at the Deutsches Altenheim retirement home in West Roxbury, where he died in 1951 at age 85.

WARREN H. MANNING (1860–1938)

Born in Reading, Massachusetts, into a family of renowned nurserymen, Manning tried a variety of tasks before he was hired by Frederick Law Olmsted Sr. from 1888 to 1896, initially as a horticulturist. With a strong interest in conservation, he was influenced by Charles Eliot, working with him in his formative endeavors creating the Boston Metropolitan Park System. He worked in collaboration with John Charles Olmsted on numerous park planning projects, particularly in Louisville, with its challenging climate and topography. On such projects as the Biltmore Estate in Asheville, North Carolina, and the World's Columbian Exposition in Chicago, Manning worked alongside the young Frederick Law Olmsted Jr., expanding the latter's horticultural knowledge. Just as he was leaving the Olmsted firm in 1896 to open his own Boston office, Manning participated in early planning for Vandergrift, Pennsylvania, giving him insight into planning for industrial communities. In his future independent work, Manning would develop a practice of considerable diversity in planning and design nationwide.

WILLIAM BELL MARQUIS, "BILL" (1887–1978)

Born in Rock Island, Illinois, Marquis expressed an interest in botany, forestry, and horticulture from an early age. He graduated with a Bachelor of Arts from Lake Forest College in 1909 and earned a Master of Landscape Architecture from Harvard University in 1912. Upon graduating, Marquis joined the P. J. Berckmans Company in Augusta, Georgia, where he served as an office manager and design supervisor. In this position, he engaged in planning and design projects, including the city plan for North Charleston, South Carolina. During World War I, he joined the Camp Planning Section of the Construction Division of the US Army, alongside Frederick Law Olmsted Jr., where he developed hospitals and encampments across the United States. Upon leaving the army in 1919, Marquis joined the Olmsted Brothers firm in Brookline, Massachusetts, as an associate. During his time there, he worked on a range of projects that spanned the country. In 1926 he designed the Crescent, the first automobile suburb for the city of Charleston, South Carolina, and he also designed Yeamans Hall, the city's first country club community. In the 1930s he partnered with golf course architects Alexander Mackenzie and Bobby Jones to create the Augusta National Golf Club in Georgia. These projects were notable for Marquis's placements of ponds in poorly

drained areas, emphasizing a design philosophy that balanced utility with aesthetic values. He became a partner at Olmsted Brothers in 1937, continuing to work with the firm until 1961. The following year, shortly before his retirement, Marquis and the firm's remaining partners, Edward Clark Whiting, Artemas Richardson, and Joseph Hudak, renamed the firm Olmsted Associates. Outside his practice, Marquis taught design courses at Boston-area institutions, including the Cambridge School of Architecture and the Lowthorpe School of Landscape Architecture. He was named a Fellow of the American Society of Landscape Architects in 1936. Marquis died in Newton, Massachusetts, at the age of 91.

EMANUEL TILLMAN MISCHE, "EMIL" (1870–1934)

Born in Syracuse, New York, Mische worked as a young man at the Missouri Botanic Garden in Saint Louis before studying at the Bussey Institute at Harvard University. In 1896 Mische received a scholarship to study at Kew Gardens in England. In 1898, he returned from England and married Nellie Mae Carpenter. The couple settled in Brookline, Massachusetts, and Mische accepted a position with the Olmsted Brothers firm. With Olmsted Brothers, he was involved in projects including the Essex County Park System in New Jersey and the Biltmore Estate of George W. Vanderbilt in North Carolina. Among his colleagues, he was considered an expert in horticulture. In 1906 John Charles Olmsted recommended Mische to become the first park superintendent Madison, Wisconsin. After two productive years in this post, he was motivated by higher wages to become park superintendent of Portland, Oregon. In Portland, Mische assumed responsibility for the city's street trees, park system, park police, recreation department, engineering, horticulture, and purchasing division. Mische worked with Olmsted Brothers on the completion of their 1903 Park Plan for Portland, while providing designs and planting plans for many of Portland's individual parks, including Sellwood, Columbia, Kenilworth, Peninsula, Laurelhurst, City, Macleay, and Mount Tabor Parks. Additionally, he consulted with John Charles Olmsted on many of the Olmsted firm's private commissions in the area. In 1913 the City of Portland eliminated its park board, and Mische resigned in 1914. He opened a private practice and continued working on the West Coast as a consulting landscape architect on projects including Crater Lake National Park, the estates of Lloyd Frank and Julius Meier, and the Los Angeles city park system. Mische became a Fellow of the American Society of Landscape Architects in 1920. In 1931 he moved to New York City to work with his son Clifford, also a landscape architect, on the Olmsted Brothers firm's Fort Tryon Park project. Mische died in 1934.

FREDERICK LAW OLMSTED JR., "RICK" (1870–1957)

Prior to his 1894 graduation from Harvard, Rick Olmsted had already gained valuable experience, apprenticing in the Chicago office of Daniel Burnham to assist in the World's Columbian Exposition planning. Upon joining the Olmsted office, among his first tasks was the implementation of plans for Biltmore, the 10,000-acre Vanderbilt estate in Asheville, North Carolina. With the unexpected death of Charles Eliot in 1897, Rick also took on the complex reservation planning for the Metropolitan Park System in Boston. In 1898 he joined his brother John Charles in forming Olmsted Brothers, the firm that was to dominate the American landscape architecture profession for decades.

Committed to the protection of natural systems and conversant in the Picturesque style, Olmsted Jr. came of age in the Beaux Arts era of formal estate gardens and City Beautiful urban planning and design. At the behest of President Eliot of Harvard University, in 1899 he set up the first professional university curriculum in landscape architecture, which soon expanded to include city planning. Likewise, in 1900, together with his brother, he was one of the founders of the American Society of Landscape Architects. He was also an early organizer of the National Conference on City Planning in 1909, which ultimately evolved into the American Planning Association. A skilled communicator and prolific writer, Olmsted Jr. was, for over half a century, a preeminent practitioner and spokesman for the professions of landscape architecture and comprehensive planning, emphasizing the interrelationship among aesthetics, practicality, people, and environment.

In 1901 Olmsted was appointed to the Senate Park Improvement Commission for the District of Columbia (commonly known as the McMillan Commission) to renew Pierre Charles L'Enfant's vision for a capital city worthy of the American nation. He steadfastly guarded the McMillan Commission's aesthetic mission, serving on oversight bodies including the Commission of Fine Arts and the National Capital Park and Planning Commission.

As a leading proponent of city planning, Olmsted Jr. produced reports for cities across the United States, including Detroit, Boulder, Pittsburgh, New Haven, Rochester, and Newport, between 1905 and 1915. In the same period, he began to apply comprehensive planning principles to suburban settings, creating master plans for suburbs around Baltimore, New York City, and Los Angeles.

Olmsted devoted the later years of his career to public service, consulting on issues of conservation and preservation of the country's park and wilderness areas. Having drafted key language for the 1916 bill that created the National Park Service, he continued to advise the NPS for thirty years on issues of management, conservation, and scenic resources. His work shaped national parks from coast to coast, including Maine's Acadia National Park, the Florida Everglades, and California's Yosemite National Park; in addition, he worked to develop the California State Park System. Olmsted Jr. remained a partner in Olmsted Brothers until his retirement in 1949, but continued to advise until his death in Malibu, California, in 1957.

FREDERICK LAW OLMSTED SR. (1822–1903)

Frederick Law Olmsted Sr. came to the field, not yet a profession, of landscape planning in the 1850s from a diverse background of experiences. An astute observer of both the natural world and the social conditions around him in his early New England years, various travels broadened his visual and aesthetic horizons and his understanding of differing cultures. Imbued with an abiding commitment to the values and responsibilities of the "American democratic experiment," he advocated throughout his life for the importance of community; for the intended advantages of a free society, including the abolition of slavery; and for public institutions, which he asserted would guarantee these advantages for all. Beyond his early experiments in scientific farming, Olmsted's remarkable forty-year career began with the innovative winning entry in 1857, together with Calvert Vaux, for Central Park's design.

By bringing this concept to reality on the ground with all its multifaceted political, social, and economic implications, Olmsted and Vaux shaped the profession of landscape architecture away from decorative design to comprehensively well-planned endeavors, essential to the development of beneficial and beautiful urban and suburban environments for living and working.

As Olmsted's career expanded, so did his commitment to parks and well-planned park systems as public entities on a grander scale—accessible to all, as respite from urban stress in healthy green surroundings. His experiences managing a gold mine in the Sierra Nevada from 1863 to 1865 motivated his efforts to preserve such extraordinary natural features of this continent as Yosemite and Niagara Falls, by initiating the movement to create public scenic reservations. He also broadened his work into the private realm, creating residential communities as well as large and small estates and grounds for educational and other institutions, all predicated on respect for and working with natural conditions, with consideration of greater community benefits, and with the priority of meeting clients' needs.

The scope of projects throughout Olmsted's career speaks to the breadth of his vision to provide opportunities for all citizens, to enable them to interact with what he saw as the restorative effects of landscape as antidote to urban living. Geographically, his parks and designs stretched from coast to coast and from north to south. Typologically, they ranged from parks, parkways, and systems—in cities such as New York City, Buffalo, Boston, Chicago, Louisville, and Montreal—to institutions such as the US Capitol Grounds; academic campuses such as Stanford University or residential campuses such as the Bloomingdale Asylum; residential communities such as Riverside, Illinois, or Druid Hills, Atlanta; and country estates such as Biltmore in Asheville, North Carolina.

More than Olmsted's canon of nearly 500 implemented projects, he left a lasting legacy by shaping the landscape profession. His offices, whether his early New York City office or Fairsted, his residence and office in Brookline, Massachusetts (which continued as the establishment for all the succeeding Olmsted firms), were lively ateliers for training the next generation of landscape practitioners, as well as places where many diverse professionals—architects, horticulturalists, engineers, and others—collaborated to ensure the best solutions to the problems at hand. Prominent American architects such as Daniel Burnham, Henry Hobson Richardson, Richard M. Hunt,

and Peabody and Stearns; engineers including George Waring, Jr.; and horticulturalists such as Charles Sprague Sargent and O. C. Bullard, all contributed to the effectiveness of significant projects. Some trainees, such as Arthur Shurcliff and Warren Manning, went forth from the firm to establish their own notable practices. Others remained at the Brookline office for their careers, most notably Charles Eliot and the Olmsted brothers, John Charles Olmsted and Frederick Law Olmsted Jr. The continuing practices of these professionals increased the firm's project list to nearly 6000 works, and while expanding the landscape profession in new directions, retained the fundamental aesthetic, social, and philosophical tenets of Frederick Law Olmsted Sr.

JOHN CHARLES OLMSTED, "JCO" (1852–1920)

A founding member and the first president of the American Society of Landscape Architects, John Charles Olmsted was the nephew of Frederick Law Olmsted Sr., becoming his stepson when the senior Olmsted married his brother's widow. Educated at Yale's Sheffield Scientific School, he then apprenticed in his stepfather's New York office, working on the US Capitol Grounds and other park and institutional projects. After the firm moved to Brookline, Massachusetts, Olmsted systematized the office procedures, enabling efficient management of the practice as it expanded from coast to coast. Olmsted joined his stepfather in the planning of the World's Columbian Exposition. In 1898, after the retirement of their father, he and his younger half brother, Frederick Law Olmsted Jr., formed the Olmsted Brothers firm. Exposition work continued, including the 1906 Lewis and Clark Exposition in Portland, Oregon, and the 1909 Alaska-Yukon-Pacific Exposition in Seattle. He terminated the firm's involvement in the 1915 San Diego Exposition rather than despoil the natural landscape of Balboa Park with planned structures inappropriately located. Like his stepfather, he saw expositions as public tastemakers for good design, and comprehensive park system planning as a way of contributing to well-considered residential and civic urban growth to serve expanding populations.

Olmsted was an advocate both for the emerging profession of landscape architecture and for the value of comprehensive planning to develop healthful and attractive cities. During his tenure, the Olmsted firm took on the planning of park systems for numerous cities, including Atlanta, Baltimore, Boston, Hartford, Louisville, Portland, and Seattle. It also gained commissions for subdivisions, private residential work, and institutions. In his more than forty-year career, John Charles Olmsted saw the firm grow from 600 to 3500 commissions, and consistently melded a Picturesque-style aesthetic with pragmatic planning.

CARL RUST PARKER
(1882–1966)

Born in Andover, Massachusetts, Parker graduated from Phillips Academy there in 1901. In lieu of attending college, he began his career working for Olmsted Brothers in Brookline, Massachusetts, serving as a draftsman, planting designer, and construction supervisor. In 1910 he resigned from the firm and opened his own practice in Portland, Maine. There he worked on a range of residential projects, civic spaces, subdivisions, and resorts, sometimes collaborating with architect John Calvin Stevens. At the same time, Parker was active in the community, advocating for the creation of the Portland City Planning Department, serving on the City Planning Committee of the Portland Chamber of Commerce, and delivering a paper titled "Possibilities for Civic Improvement in Maine to the Board of Trade."

During World War I, Parker closed his practice and worked for the United States government in Washington, DC, returning to Maine in 1919 to work for the Olmsted Brothers. His practice expanded to projects in Maine, Mississippi, New Jersey, Ohio, Virginia, and Wisconsin, including the George Washington Masonic Memorial in Alexandria, Virginia; Maine State Capitol Grounds, Augusta, Maine; Kohler Village, Wisconsin; and the National Cash Register Company, Dayton, Ohio. In 1950 Parker became a partner of the firm, retiring in 1961. He was inducted as a Fellow of the American Society of Landscape Architects in 1915.

WILLIAM LYMAN PHILLIPS
(1885–1966)

Born in West Somerville, Massachusetts, Phillips was an early student in Harvard's landscape architecture program, from which he graduated in 1908. By 1911 he joined the Olmsted

Brothers firm, where he worked on the Boston Common. He left the firm after two years to travel, joining the team designing communities along the Panama Canal, then under construction. This began his great appreciation for tropical vegetation. With the termination of that project, he took on various other projects across the country, which included work with the Quartermaster Corps in Puerto Rico and North Carolina. He also worked on a residential development project in Boca Grande, in Florida. In 1925 Phillips moved to Lake Wales, Florida, where he renewed his association with the Olmsted Brothers and spent the rest of his fifty-year career. His work illustrated an understanding of the native Florida landscape—its unique ecosystems and particularly its plants. Working with private clients and for the National Park Service, Civilian Conservation Corps, and Dade County, he created landscapes which have helped define Florida's image. Fairchild Tropical Botanic Garden in Coral Gables is Phillips's best-known work. In twenty years there, he developed tropical plant collections organized by families, arranged along two formal axes, with shaded walks and scenic views. His extensive body of work also includes private estates, cemeteries, public thoroughfares, and campus planning projects, including Greynolds Park, Bok Tower Gardens (with Olmsted Brothers), and McKee Botanic Gardens. Phillips passed away in North Miami, Florida, in 1966.

ARTEMAS PARTRIDGE
RICHARDSON II (1918–2015)

Born in Philadelphia, Pennsylvania, Richardson attended the city's Germantown Friends School and then Williams College, graduating in 1940 with a Bachelor of Fine Arts. He briefly pursued a second bachelor's degree, this time in landscape architecture, at Pennsylvania State College, but left to serve as a naval intelligence officer during World War II. At war's end, Richardson resumed his studies, earning a Bachelor of Science in Landscape Architecture from Iowa State College in 1947. In 1948 he joined Olmsted Brothers in Brookline, Massachusetts, working as a partner from 1950 until 1961. Following the death of Whiting and the retirement of Marquis, both in 1962, Richardson and Hudak formed Olmsted Associates, which lasted until 1979. Richardson then transferred the firm's Brookline headquarters and its vast cache of drawings to the National Park

Service. Moving to Fremont, New Hampshire, he practiced in semiretirement under the name of The Olmsted Office until his death in 2015.

Richardson's forte was site construction. A licensed practitioner in thirteen states, he worked on a great variety and quantity of the Olmsted Brothers firm's ongoing projects, including the Thomas Jefferson Memorial, Rock Creek Park, and the National Cathedral in Washington, DC, as well as the University of Mississippi in Oxford. In 1974 he advised on the recovery of Cherokee Park in Louisville after a devastating tornado, while in the early 1990s he developed a master plan for Crandon Park in Dade County, Florida, after the park suffered damages caused by Hurricane Andrew.

CHARLES SCOTT RILEY
(1909–1966)

Born in Cincinnati, Ohio, Riley graduated from the University of Cincinnati in 1932 before earning his Master of Landscape Architecture from Harvard University. He began his career as a landscape foreman with the Civilian Conservation Corps before starting an independent practice in 1937. In 1947 Riley joined the Olmsted Brothers firm, where he worked on both private and public projects, taking a special interest in the design of campuses, including the University of Mississippi, Sewanee: the University of the South, Millsaps College, and the corporate campuses of National Life Insurance Company and Berkshire Life Insurance Company. Riley became a partner of the firm in 1950 alongside Edward Clark Whiting, Carl Parker, Artemas Richardson, and Joseph Hudak. The partners assumed overall management of the Fairsted estate, the Olmsteds' home and office, and worked to revitalize much of the grounds following a series of hurricanes in the mid-twentieth century. Riley's work on Fairsted included drafting a set of plans that envisioned the possibility of separating the home from the offices, allowing the partners to sell the home. This plan was ultimately rejected by the Brookline Building Commission and the firm retained the entire estate. Riley retired from the Olmsted Brothers in 1961, after which it was renamed Olmsted Associates. Outside of his work with the firm, he served as a founding director of the Hubbard Educational Trust (now Hubbard Educational Foundation), an organization dedicated to fostering education in landscape architecture. Riley died of cancer at the age of 57.

ARTHUR ASAHEL SHURCLIFF
(1870–1957)

A native of Boston, Shurcliff is most noted for his skill in reinterpreting colonial American landscape design. In 1894 Shurcliff completed a Bachelor of Science in Mechanical Engineering from Massachusetts Institute of Technology. Charles Eliot, as both teacher and mentor, then helped him self-design a course of landscape studies at Harvard, resulting in a second B.S. in 1896. Several years later, he would apply this experience in working with Frederick Law Olmsted Jr. to design Harvard's new landscape architecture curriculum.

After eight years with the Olmsted office, Shurcliff opened his own firm in 1904, where he excelled at town planning, dams and reservoirs, park and zoo design, and the restoration of early American town commons. His portfolio included major work, from 1928 to 1941, as the chief landscape architect in the re-creation of Colonial Williamsburg, Virginia (funded by John D. Rockefeller Jr.), and later in working to recapture Old Sturbridge Village in Massachusetts. In his personal quest for historical accuracy, Shurcliff changed his last name (originally Shurtleff) to conform to its ancient spelling.

FREDERICK TODD
(1876–1948)

Born in 1876 in Concord, New Hampshire, Todd attended high school in Andover, Massachusetts, and enrolled at the Massachusetts Agricultural College (a predecessor of the University of Massachusetts, Amherst) before apprenticing with Olmsted, Olmsted, and Eliot in 1896. Near the end of his apprenticeship with the Olmsted firm, Todd was assigned to oversee the completion of work at Montreal's Mount Royal Park. In 1900 he moved to Montreal permanently and established his own practice, purportedly becoming the first resident practitioner in Canada to use the title "Landscape Architect." A proponent of the Picturesque style that he studied under Olmsted Jr., he designed numerous private gardens, city parks, and institutional grounds.

In his independent work, Todd developed a practice of considerable diversity in planning and design throughout Canada. He published on landscape architecture in newspapers, magazines, and journals, and was a fellow of three professional organizations, including the Town Planning Institute of Canada, which he helped found. He died in Montreal at the age of 71.

CALVERT VAUX (1824–1895)

Born in England and trained as an architect, Vaux came to America in 1850 to collaborate with Andrew Jackson Downing on Picturesque-style estate landscape projects. Over his forty-five-year career, Vaux worked collaboratively with many landscape architects, architects, and designers, including Frederick Clarke Withers, Jacob Weidenmann, George K. Radford, Samuel Parsons Jr., and his son, Downing Vaux. His best-known partnership, with Frederick Law Olmsted Sr., began in 1857 with their Greensward plan for the competition for Central Park. Other significant collaborative projects with Olmsted Sr. include Brooklyn's Prospect Park, parks and park systems for Brooklyn and Buffalo, South Park in Chicago, and the New York State Reservation at Niagara. The pair collaborated on a wide range of projects from estate landscapes and cemeteries to campuses and planned communities. After the 1872 dissolution of the Olmsted, Vaux, and Company firm, Vaux continued to work both as an architect and in landscape design. He continued working with established client the Metropolitan Museum of Art, as well as taking on projects that included New York City's Grace Church and its grounds, Trinity Cemetery, and Cemetery of the Evergreens in Brooklyn; Bryn Mawr College, Pennsylvania; and the Wisner Estate in Summit, New Jersey (now the Reeves-Reed Arboretum). Vaux served as landscape architect for the New York Department of Public Parks. His chosen title, "landscape architect," was first used in the early 1860s to describe the work of Olmsted and Vaux at Central Park.

EDWARD CLARK WHITING, "TED" (1881–1962)

Born in Brooklyn, New York, Whiting graduated with a bachelor's degree from Harvard University in 1903. Following a further year of study at Harvard in landscape architecture, he joined the Olmsted Brothers in 1905 and would spend his entire professional career with the firm, extending into its final iteration,

Olmsted Associates. He worked as a draftsman, an assistant engineer, and a general designer before finally becoming a partner in 1920. In published articles and private correspondence, Whiting defined landscape architecture as a fine art composed of nature, climate, topography, and living materials. He worked on many types of projects throughout his long career, including park and city planning, subdivisions, institutional grounds, private estates, and cemeteries. He worked alongside John Charles Olmsted on park systems in Essex and Union Counties in New Jersey, and with Frederick Law Olmsted Jr. on Fort Tryon Park in Manhattan, Rock Creek Park in Washington, DC, and on city plans for Pittsburgh and Newport. A specialist in subdivision planning, Whiting designed Oyster Harbor in Osterville, Massachusetts; Khakum Wood in Greenwich, Connecticut; Munsey Gardens in Manhasset, New York; and Indian Hills and Cherokee Gardens, both in Louisville, Kentucky. He also worked on many private estates, including the Davis Estate in Marstons Mills on Cape Cod; J. E. Aldred's Ormston (today known as St. Josaphat's Monastery) alongside Percival Gallagher in Nassau County, New York; and the George Cluett Estate, later incorporated into Williams College in Williamstown, Massachusetts. Whiting's designs also included institutional grounds, such as Catholic University (now Catholic University of America) and Trinity College (now Trinity Washington University) in Washington, DC. He was named a Fellow of the American Society of Landscape Architects in 1930.

FREDERICK CLARKE WITHERS (1828–1901)

Born in Somerset, England, Withers was educated at the Sherborne School, in Dorsetshire. After a five-year apprenticeship with architect and builder Edward Mondey, he joined the London office of architect Thomas Henry Wyatt in 1849. In February 1852, Withers immigrated to the United States, beckoned by Andrew Jackson Downing to join his practice in Newburgh, New York. After Downing's untimely death later that year, Withers formed Vaux and Withers with architect and former Downing collaborator Calvert Vaux, a partnership that lasted until 1856.

Withers enlisted in the Union Army in 1861 but resigned his commission in 1862 after falling ill. He moved his practice to New York City and by December 1863 had once again joined

Vaux in a partnership that lasted until 1872. During this period, Withers designed buildings for several projects for which Olmsted, Vaux and Company designed the landscapes. These include the Hudson River State Hospital; the president's house and several faculty buildings at the Columbia Institution for the Deaf and Dumb (now Gallaudet University) in Washington, DC; and the chapel and a commercial block for the newly planned suburban community of Riverside, Illinois.

LEON HENRY ZACH
(1895–1966)

The son of a respected Austrian violist and conductor, Zach was born in Jamaica Plain, Massachusetts, and graduated from Roxbury Latin School. He entered Harvard College in 1914 but left in 1918 to serve in the First World War. A stint in Richelieu, France, exposed Zach to the landscaped gardens of nearby châteaux, and he returned to Harvard in 1919 to study in the School of Landscape Architecture. After a European tour in 1921, Zach found employment with Olmsted Brothers, where he stayed for over twenty years. Zach was a competent artist, but his real talent lay in project administration. Zach supervised numerous simultaneous projects funded by John D. Rockefeller Jr. including the Fort Tryon, Cloisters, and Claremont Park constructions in New York, and for several components of the Rockefeller-funded Acadia National Park in Maine. He also supervised numerous concurrent projects for the Bok family in various locales. In the 1920s and 1930s, he oversaw construction throughout Alabama for parks, educational institutions, and the state capitol at Montgomery.

Zach was made a partner of Olmsted Brothers in 1938. In 1941 he was offered the chance to set up the Site Planning Unit in the Construction Division of the Quartermaster General's Office in Washington, DC. Finding the planning of military cantonments, internment camps, and hospitals of great interest, he never returned to Olmsted Brothers. Zach retired in 1965 as Chief of the Planning Branch, Engineering Division of the US Army. He died in 1966.

SELECTED BIBLIOGRAPHY

WRITINGS BY FREDERICK LAW OLMSTED SR.

Olmsted, Frederick Law. *Civilizing American Cities: Writings on City Landscapes*. Edited by S.B. Sutton. New York: Da Capo Press, 1997.

Olmsted, Frederick Law. *Forty years of Landscape Architecture: Central Park*. Edited by Frederick Law Olmsted Jr. and Theodora Kimball. Cambridge: MIT Press, 1973.

Olmsted, Frederick Law. "Notes of the Plan of Franklin Park and Related Matters." *Bulletins 3 and 4 of the Franklin Park Coalition*. November 1978 and January 1979.

Olmsted, Frederick Law. *Walks and Talks of an American Farmer in England*. Introduction by Charles C. McLaughlin. Reprint of 1852 edition. Amherst: Library of American Landscape History, 2002.

Olmsted, Frederick Law. *Writings on Landscape, Culture, and Society*. Edited by Charles E. Beveridge. New York: Library of America, 2015.

Olmsted Frederick Law. *Yosemite and the Mariposa Grove: A Preliminary Report, 1865*. Yosemite National Park: Yosemite Association, 1995.

Olmsted, Vaux & Co. *Preliminary Report Upon the Proposed Suburban Village at Riverside Near Chicago*. Chicago: Wicklander Printing Corp., 1982. (reprint of 1868 ed.)

Olmsted, Frederick Law. *The Papers of Frederick Law Olmsted* (vols. 1–12). Edited by Charles Capen McLaughlin, Charles E. Beveridge, et al. Baltimore: The Johns Hopkins University Press, 1977–2020.

Supplementary Series to *The Papers of Frederick Law Olmsted*. Beveridge, Charles E., Lauren Meier, and Irene Mills, eds. *Volume II Frederick Law Olmsted: Plans and Views of Public Parks*. Baltimore: Johns Hopkins University Press, 2015.

Supplementary Series to *The Papers of Frederick Law Olmsted*. Beveridge, Charles E., Lauren Meier, and Irene Mills, eds. *Volume III Frederick Law Olmsted: Plans and Views of Communities and Private Estates*. Baltimore: Johns Hopkins University Press, 2020.

BIOGRAPHIES AND STUDIES OF FREDERICK LAW OLMSTED SR.

Beveridge, Charles, and Paul Rocheleau. *Frederick Law Olmsted: Designing the American Landscape*. New York: Rizzoli, 1995.

Fein, Albert. *Frederick Law Olmsted and the American Environmental Tradition*. New York: George Braziller, 1972.

Fisher, Irving. *Frederick Law Olmsted and the City Planning Movement in the United States*. Ann Arbor: University of Michigan Research Press, 1986.

Roper, Laura Wood. *FLO: A Biography of Frederick Law Olmsted*. Baltimore: Johns Hopkins University Press, 1973.

Rybczynski, Witold. *A Clearing in the Distance: Frederick Law Olmsted and America in the Nineteenth Century*. New York: Scribner, 1999.

Stevenson, Elizabeth. *Park Maker: A Life of Frederick Law Olmsted*. New York: Macmillan, 1977.

OLMSTED FIRMS, GENERAL

Lawliss, Lucy, Caroline Loughlin, and Lauren Meier, eds. *The Master List of Design Projects of the Olmsted Firm 1857–1979*. Washington D.C.: the National Association for Olmsted Parks, the National Park Service, and the Frederick Law Olmsted National Historic Site, 2008.

Note: The Olmsted firm assigned each of its projects a job number by which the company organized all documents, plans, and images for a project. This volume organizes the projects geographically and by typology, also providing the critical job number.

UNPUBLISHED MATERIALS AND PHOTOGRAPHS

Library of Congress, Manuscript Division. "Frederick Law Olmsted Papers." Accessed November 10, 2021. https://www.loc.gov/collections/frederick-law-olmsted-papers.

Harvard University, Graduate School of Design. Frances Loeb Library, The John Charles Olmsted Papers.

National Association for Olmsted Parks. "Olmsted Online: Projects of the Olmsted Firm." Accessed November 10, 2021. https://olmstedonline. org.

Note: Olmsted Online provides multifaceted information. Searchable by job number, it provides direct links to: 1) the digitized plans and photographs from the Flickr site of the Frederick Law Olmsted National Historic Site; 2) the major Olmsted project correspondence files from the Library of Congress Manuscript Division; 3) the National Register Nomination documents for appropriate projects; and 4) information in select other repositories or websites, such as The Cultural Landscape Foundation and soon to include Olmsted projects found in the Archives of American Gardens of the Smithsonian Institute. In addition, Olmsted Online enables locating the various projects by job number on a national map, revealing the clusters of projects in each locale.

National Park Service. "Olmsted Archives, Frederick Law Olmsted National Historic Site." Accessed November 10, 2021. https://www.flickr.com/ photos/olmsted_archives/albums.

Olmsted Research Guide Online. Accessed November 10, 2021. http://ww2. rediscov.com/olmsted.

OLMSTED FIRMS, INDIVIDUALS

Alex, William. *Calvert Vaux: Architect and Planner*. New York: Ink, Inc. 1994.

Birnbaum, Charles, and Robin Karson, eds. *Pioneers of American Landscape Design*. Volume 1. New York: McGraw Hill, 2000.

Birnbaum, Charles A, and Stephanie S. Foell. *Shaping the American Landscape: New Profiles from the Pioneers of American Landscape Design Project*. Charlottesville: University of Virginia Press, 2009.

Cushing, Elizabeth Hope. *Arthur A. Shurcliff: Design, Preservation, and the Creation of the Colonial Williamsburg Landscape*. Amherst: University of Massachusetts Press in association with the Library of American Landscape History, 2014.

Eliot, Charles W. *Charles Eliot, Landscape Architect*. Introduction by Keith N. Morgan. Amherst: University of Massachusetts Press in association with the Library of American Landscape History, 1999.

Karson, Robin, Jane Brown, and Sarah Allaback, eds. *Warren Manning: Landscape Architect and Environmental Planner*. Amherst: University of Massachusetts Press in association with the Library of American Landscape History, 2015.

Kowsky, Francis. *Country, Park, and City: The Architecture and Life of Calvert Vaux*. New York: Oxford University Press, 1998.

Morgan, Keith N. *Charles Eliot, Landscape Architect: A Research Guide*. Jamaica Plain, MA: Institute for Cultural Landscape Studies, Arnold Arboretum of Harvard University, 1999.

NEW ENGLAND

Connecticut

Alexopoulus, John. *The Nineteenth Century Parks of Hartford, a Legacy to the Nation*. Hartford: Hartford Architecture Conservancy, 1983.

Maine

Holtwijk, Theo, and Earle G. Shuttleworth Jr. *Bold Vison: The Development of the Parks of Portland, Maine*. Portland: Greater Portland Landmarks, 1999.

Mattor, Theresa, and Lucie Teegarden. *Designing the Maine Landscape*. Camden: Down East Books and the Maine Olmsted Alliance for Parks and Landscapes, 2009.

Roberts, Anne Rockefeller. *Mr. Rockefeller's Roads: The Story Behind Acadia's Carriage Roads*. Camden: Down East Books, 2012.

Shuttleworth, Earle G., and Scott T. Hanson. *The Architecture of Cushing Island*. Portland, ME: Cushing Island Association, 2012.

Massachusetts

Anderson, Nola. *Immersion: Living and Learning in an Olmsted Garden*. Bologna, Italy: Damiani, 2021.

Arrison, Julie. *Images of America: Franklin Park*. Charleston: Arcadia, 2009.

Haglund, Karl. *Inventing the Charles River*. Cambridge: MIT Press, 2003.

Morgan, Keith N., Elizabeth Hope Cushing, and Roger G. Reed. *Community by Design: The Olmsted Firm and the Development of Brookline, Massachusetts*. Amherst: University of Massachusetts Press in association with the Library of American Landscape History, 2013.

Sinclair, Jill. *Fresh Pond: The History of a Cambridge Landscape*. Cambridge: MIT Press, 2009.

Zaitzevsky, Cynthia. *Fairsted: A Cultural Landscape Report, Volume 1: Site History*. Afterword by Mac Griswold. Boston: Olmsted Center for Landscape Preservation, National Park Service, and US Department of the Interior, 1997.

Zaitzevsky, Cynthia. *Frederick Law Olmsted and the Boston Park System*. Cambridge: Harvard University Press, 1982.

Rhode Island

Levee, Arleyn A. *The Blue Garden: Recapturing an Iconic Newport Landscape*. Lewes, UK: The Hamilton Family Charitable Trust, 2019.

Olmsted, Frederick Law (Jr.). *Proposed Improvements for Newport*. Cambridge, Mass: The University Press, 1913.

Vermont

Lipke, William C., ed. *Shelburne Farms: The History of an Agricultural Estate*. Burlington: Robert Hull Fleming Museum and the University of Vermont, 1979.

MID-ATLANTIC

Maryland

Olmsted Brothers. *Development of Public Grounds for Greater Baltimore*. Baltimore: Friends of Maryland's Olmsted Parks and Landscapes, 1987. (reprint of 1904 ed.)

Waesche, James F. *A History of the Roland Park-Guildford-Homeland District*. Baltimore: Maclay & Associates, 1987.

New Jersey

Kelsey, Frederick W. *The First County Park System: A Complete History of the Inception and Development of the Essex County Parks of New Jersey*. New York: J.S. Ogilvie Publishing Company, 1905.

Kolva, Jeanne. *Olmsted Parks in New Jersey*. Atglen, PA: Schiffer Publishing, 2011.

New York City and environs

Colley, David P. *Prospect Park: Olmsted and Vaux's Brooklyn Masterpiece*. New York: Princeton Architectural Press, 2013.

Heckscher, Morrison H. *Creating Central Park*. New Haven: Yale University Press, 2011.

Klaus, Susan. *A Modern Arcadia: Frederick Law Olmsted Jr. and the Plan for Forest Hills Gardens*. Amherst: University of Massachusetts Press in association with the Library of American Landscape History, 2004.

Miller, Sarah Cedar. *Central Park: An American Masterpiece*. New York: Abrams, 2003.

Rogers, Elizabeth Barlow. *Saving Central Park: A History and a Memoir*. New York: Knopf, 2018.

Simpson, Jeffrey, and Mary Ellen Hern, eds. *Art of the Olmsted Landscape: His Works in New York City*. New York: New York City Landmarks Preservation Commission, 1981.

New York State

Buscaglia-Castellani Art Gallery. *The Distinctive Charms of Niagara Scenery: Frederick Law Olmsted and the Niagara Reservation*. Niagara Falls: Niagara University, 1985.

Conklin, Edgar C. *Frederick Law Olmsted's Point Chautauqua, the Story of a Historic Lakeside Community*. Buffalo: Cansius College Press, 2001.

Kowsky, Francis R. *The Best Planned City in the World: Olmsted, Vaux, and the Buffalo Park System*. Amherst: University of Massachusetts Press and the Library of American Landscape History, 2013.

MacKay Robert B. et al. *Long Island Country Houses and Their Architects, 1860–1940*. New York: Norton, 1997.

McKelvey, Blake. *A Growing Legacy: An Illustrated History of Rochester's Parks*. Rochester: Parks Centennial Committee, 1999.

Pennsylvania

Mosher, Ann E. *Capital's Utopia: Vandergrift, PA 1855–1916*. Baltimore: The Johns Hopkins University Press, 2004.

Washington, DC

Allen, William C. *History of the United States Capitol: A Chronicle of Design, Construction and Politics*. Honolulu: University Press of the Pacific, 2005.

Kohler, Sue A. *The Commission of Fine Arts: A Brief History, 1910–1995*. Washington DC: US Commission of Fine Arts, 1996.

Kohler, Sue A., and Pamela Scott, eds. *Designing the Nation's Capitol: The 1901 Plan for Washington D.C.* Washington DC: US Commission of Fine Arts, 2006.

Luebke, Thomas E., ed. *Civic Art: A Centennial History of the US Commission of Fine Arts*. Washington DC: US Commission of Fine Arts, 2013.

SOUTH

White, Dana and Victor A. Kramer. *Olmsted South, Old South Critic, New South Planner*. Westport: Greenwood Press, 1979.

Alabama

Tipton, Katherine M. and Marjorie L. White, eds. *Hand Down Unharmed: Olmsted Files on Birmingham Parks, 1920–1925*. Birmingham: Birmingham Historical Society, 2008.

White, Marjorie L., and Heather McArn. *The Olmsted Vision: Parks for Birmingham*. Birmingham: Birmingham Historical Society, 2006.

Florida

Ceo, Rocco J., and Joanna Lombard. *Historic Landscapes of Florida*. Miami: The Deering Foundation and the University of Miami School of Architecture, 2001.

Georgia

Hartle, Robert Jr. *Atlanta's Druid Hills: A Brief History*. Charleston: The History Press, 2008.

Lawliss, Lucy. "Residential Work of the Olmsted Firm in Georgia, 1893–1937." *Magnolia Essays: Occasional Papers of the Southern Garden History Society*. no. 1, Spring 1993.

Richardson, Jennifer J. et al. *Druid Hills*. Mt. Pleasant: Arcadia Press, 2019.

Louisiana

Lake, Douglas. *Public Spaces, Private Gardens: A History of Designed Landscapes in New Orleans*. Baton Rouge: Louisiana State University Press, 2011.

Logdson, Joseph, and L. Ronald Forman. *Audubon Park: An Urban Eden*. Baton Rouge: Friends of the Zoo, 1985.

North Carolina

Covington, Howard E. *Lady on the Hill: How Biltmore Estate Became an American Icon*. Hoboken: Wiley, 2006.

Messer, Pamela Lynn. *Biltmore Estate: Frederick Law Olmsted's Landscape Masterpiece*. Asheville: World Comm, 1993.

Schenck, Carl Alwin. *The Biltmore Story: Recollections of the Beginning of Forestry in the United States*. St. Paul: American Forest History Foundation, 1955.

MIDWEST

Tishler, William. *Midwestern Landscape Architecture*. Urbana: University of Illinois Press in association with the Library of American Landscape History, 2000.

Illinois

Bachman, Julia Sniderman. *The City in a Garden: A Photographic History of Chicago's Parks*. Santa Fe: Center for American Places, 2001.

Bassman, Herbert J. *Riverside Then and Now: A History of Riverside, Illinois*. Riverside: Riverside Historical Commission, 1995.

Ranney, Victoria. *Olmsted in Chicago*. Boston: R.R. Donnelley & Sons, 1972.

Michigan

Anderson, Janet. *Island in the City: Detroit's Beautiful Island: How Belle Isle Changed Detroit Forever*. Detroit: Heitman-Garland, 2001.

Rodriguez, Michael, and Thomas Featherstone. *Detroit's Belle Isle: Island Park Gem*. Chicago: Arcadia Press, 2003.

Missouri

Grove, Carol. *Henry Shaw's Victorian Landscapes: The Missouri Botanical Garden and Tower Grove Park*. Amherst: University of Massachusetts Press in association with the Library of American Landscape History, 2005.

Loughlin, Caroline, and Catherine Anderson. *Forest Park, St Louis Missouri*. Columbia: Junior League of St. Louis in association with the University of Missouri Press, 1986.

ROCKY MOUNTAINS

Colorado

Etter, Carolyn, and Don Etter. *City of Parks: The Preservation of Denver's Park and Parkway System*. Denver: Denver Public Library, 2006.

Olmsted, Frederick Law Jr. *The Improvement of Boulder, Colorado: Report to the City Improvement Association*. Boulder: Boulder City Improvement Association, 2010. (reprint of 1910 ed.)

PACIFIC NORTHWEST

Hockaday, Joan. *Greenscapes: Olmsted's Pacific Northwest*. Pullman: Washington State University Press, 2009.

Johnson, Catherine Joy, and Friends of Seattle's Olmsted Parks. *Olmsted in the Pacific Northwest: Private Estates and Residential Communities 1873–1959: An Inventory*. Seattle: Friends of Seattle's Olmsted Parks, 1997.

Oregon

Hawkins, William J. III. *The Legacy of Olmsted Brothers in Portland, Oregon*. Seattle: William J. Hawkins III, 2014.

Washington

Olmsted Brothers. *First Annual Report of the Board of Park Commissioners, Seattle, Washington 1884–1904*. Seattle: Friends of Seattle's Olmsted Parks, 1997. (reprint of 1903 ed.)

Ott, Jennifer. *Olmsted in Seattle: Creating a Park System for a Modern City*. Seattle: History Link and Documentary Media, 2019.

Stein, Alan J., and Paula Becker. *Alaska–Yukon–Pacific Exposition: Washington's First World's Fair*. Seattle: History Link in association with the University of Washington Press, 2009.

WEST

California

Berkeley Architectural Heritage Association. *Piedmont Way and the Berkeley Property Tract: Frederick Law Olmsted's Berkeley Legacy*. Berkeley: Berkeley Architectural Heritage Association, 1995.

Brandi, Richard. *San Francisco's St. Francis Wood*. San Francisco: St. Francis Homes Association, 2012.

Engbeck, Joseph H. Jr. *State Parks of California from 1864 to the Present*. Portland: C.H. Belding, 1980.

Hise, Greg, and William Francis Deverell. *Eden by Design: the 1930 Olmsted-Bartholomew Plan for the Los Angeles Region*. Berkeley: University of California Press, 2000.

Morgan, Delane. *The Palos Verdes Story*. Palos Verdes: Review Publications, 1982.

Olmsted Brothers and Ansel F. Hall. *Report on Proposed Park Reservation for East Bay Cities*. Forward by East Bay Park District Association. Berkeley: December 1930.

CANADA

Beveridge, Charles E. *Mount Royal in the Works of Frederick Law Olmsted*. Montreal: Entente sur le Developement Cultural de Montreal, 2002

McCann, Larry. *Imagining Uplands: John Olmsted's Masterpiece of Residential Design*. Victoria: Brighton Press, 2016.

PHOTOGRAPHY AND ILLUSTRATION CREDITS

Kmiragaya, page 70
Lerka555, page 212
Lopitechco, page 190
Paulbradyphoto, page 121
Robhainer, page 89
Sampete, page 211
Starharper, page163
Trekandshoot, pages 40–41
Vividimpressions, page 14
Wolterk, page 101
Elkulak, page 288
Jacoby Elrod, page 84
James Ewing Photography, page 231
Jennifer Franklin, page 111
Felicity Frisbie, page 202
Nancy Fuentes, page 169
Josh Graciano, page 176
Robin Grussling, page 295
Steve Guttman, page 293
Billy Hathorn, page 268
Asher Heimermann, page 299
Kristina D. C. Hoeppner, page 305
iStock
    Alex Potemkin, page 204
    AlexPro9500, page 209
    AppalachianViews, page 74
    BrookePierce, page 212
    eurobanks, pages 63, 74
    Fotoluminate LLC, page 116
    Gary Kavanagh, page 288
    sshepard, page 122
    Terraxplorer, page 216
    traveler1116, page 106
Jasperdo, page 311
Josh S. Jackson, page 205
Tom Klein, pages 139, 152
Knowlesgallery, page 95
Jennifer Kowatch, page 256
Courtesy of Lawrenceville School,
    page 186
Leslee, page 137
Joe Mabel, page 294
Maduarte, page 259
Scott McDonough, page 184

mk97007, page 246
Barbara Merrill, page 145
Andreas Metz/Amz Photography, page 183
Fred Moore, page 26
Orah Moore, page 278
Courtesy of New York City Parks and Recreation,
    page 206
Anthony T. Nigrelli, page 236
Courtesy of Olmsted Parks Conservancy
    Dimo Petrov, page 109
    Layla George, page 108
Erin O'Toole, page 147
John Roger Palmour, page 85
Daniell Penfield, page 221
Peter, page 246
Phillip Ennis Photography, page 218
Radio Raheem, page 242
Daniel Ramirez, page 29
Rchappo2002, page 222
Bill Reynolds, page 245
Beau Rogers, page 25
ME Sanseverino, page 306
Courtesy of Seattle Parks Department, page 288
Thomas Shahan, page 26
Leslie Sherr, page 213
Shutterstock
    George Wirt, page 181
Courtney Spearman, page 80, 230
Stanford Historical Photograph Collection,
    page 31
SteveKC, page 172
Courtesy of Stonehurst Friends, page 159
Corey Templeton, page 123, 124
Brian Thomson, page 45
TIA International Photography, pages 288, 290,
    291
Matthew Traucht, page 281
Sarah Vance, page 262
Regan Vercruysse, page 185
Aniko Nagyne Vig, page 219
Courtesy of Washington State Department of
    Transportation, page 285
Ted Wathen, page 109
Marshall Webb, page 277

Courtesy of Weequahic Park, page 178
Liz West, page 158
Wikimedia
    Made available under the Creative Com-
        mons CC0 1.0 Universal Public Domain,
        Daderot, pages 106, 159
    Used under a Creative Commons Attribu-
        tion-Share Alike 3.0 Unported License,
        Prashkan90
    Used under a Creative Commons Attribu-
        tion-Share Alike 4.0 International License,
        Kenneth C. Zirkel, page 56; Alston Jenkins,
        page 255, page 91; Luciof, page 137
    Public Domain on Wikimedia Commons,
        Sgerbic, page 37
Courtesy of Williams College, page 160
Christian Zimmerman, page 202

INDEX

A

Abele, Julian, 231
academic campus design. *See also* quadrangles
  addressing future growth, 122
  aspects critical to campus design, 31
  English campus system, 186
  ovals, 32, 58, 111, 112
  paving student-created paths, 101
  Regents Plan (University of Washington, Seattle), 293
  school-town relationships, 174–175
  surrounding neighborhoods, 32, 152, 174–175
  University of Idaho, Moscow, 95–96
  University of Louisville, 111–112
  University of Maine, Orono, 122
  University of Mississippi, Oxford, 169
  University of North Alabama, Florence, 19–20
  University of Washington, Seattle, 293–294
  "village" approach, 122
  Williams College, Williamstown, 160
Adams, Herbert (James Scott Memorial Fountain), 163
advocacy and stewardship, 15, 54, 128, 204, 263
"aesthetic forestry", 184–185
Ahwahnee Hotel, Yosemite National Park, 28
Alabama landscapes, 17–21
  Birmingham, 17–18
  Florence, 19–20
  Montgomery, 21
Alaska-Yukon-Pacific Exposition, 293, 317
allées, 70, 98, 102, 115, 121, 122
All Hallows Guild, 74
Amateis, Edmond (*Great Frieze*), 171
American park movement, 178

American Society of Landscape Architects, founding of, 314
Ames Memorial Hall, North Easton, 158
amphitheaters, 19, 20, 43, 44, 47, 117, 195, 222, 298
Angel of the Waters (Stebbins), 209
arboretums
  Arnold Arboretum, Boston, 146, 148
  Bayard Cutting Arboretum State Park, New York, 219
  Bernheim Arboretum, Clermont, 105
  Highland Park, Rochester, 222
  scientific, 229
  Thomas Kiel Arboretum, Manhattan, 211
  Washington Park Arboretum, Seattle, 292–293
arches, 63, 146, 183, 202, 216, 260
architecture firms, collaborating, 19, 141, 171, 204, 207, 260
Arnold, Bion, 221
Art Deco style, 58, 300, 305
Art Out-Of-Doors (Van Rensselaer), 10
Ashland Park, Lexington, 107
Atterbury, Grosvenor, 217
Audubon Park, New Orleans, 114–115

B

Back Bay Fens, Boston, 115, 123–124, 146, 147, 148
Bacon, Henry
  Carl Schurz Memorial, 211
  Lincoln Memorial Grounds, 70
Baltimore parks and parkways system, 126–128
  creation of parkways, 127–128
  parks plan, 1924, 126
  "Report Upon the Development of Public Grounds for Baltimore", 1904, 127
balustrades, 79, 121, 202

Barnard, George Grey (*Let There Be Light*), 105
Bartholdi, Frédéric-Auguste, 211
Barton Hills, Ann Arbor, 164
Baxter, Sylvester, 136
Beach, Chester (*Fountain of the Waters*), 237
Beadle, Chauncey, 229
Beardsley, James, 51
Beardsley Park, Bridgeport, 51
Beaux Arts style, 46, 68, 143, 163, 171, 254, 260, 272
Beaver Lake, Montreal, 309
Belle Isle Park, Detroit, 162
belvederes, 211, 302
Bennett, Edward, 98, 247
Bethesda Water Terrace, 209
bicycle paths, 205, 291
Billings, Cornelius K. G., 215, 216
Biltmore estate, Asheville, 228–230
Biltmore Forest School, 229
bird sanctuaries, 81, 143
Birmingham city parks plan, 17–18
  areas held in trust, 18
  Linn Park, 17
  A System of Parks and Playgrounds for Birmingham: Preliminary Report, 1925, 17
Birmingham Park and Recreation Board plea to citizens, 17
Bitter, Karl (Carl Schurz Memorial), 211
Black community, 109–110
Blackstone Boulevard, Providence, 263
Black Sun (Noguchi), 291
Blossom, Harold Hill, "Hal" (1879-1935), 261, 316
Blue Hills Reservation, 138
bluffs, 260
Bodega Bay, 25
Bok Tower Gardens, Lake Wales, 81
Boulder Civic Improvement Association, 43
Boulder Creek banks and washes, 43
Boulder park system, 43–44
  Chautauqua Park, 44
  Sunrise Amphitheater, 44

"The Improvement of Boulder Colorado", 1910, 43
boulders, use in design and construction, 158, 159, 208, 209, 213
Bouton, Edward, 129, 132
Bradley, William C., 92
Bradley Olmsted Garden, Columbus, Georgia, 92–93
Branch Brook Park, Newark, 179–181
Brandywine Park, Wilmington
Bratenahl, Florence Brown, 74
bridges
  accommodating traffic above and pedestrians below, 179
  Erie Canal disruption solution, 223
  pedestrian, 199, 210, 223, 300
  small individually designed, 180
  unobtrusive blending of, 120
  variety in Central Park, 210
bridges, specific
  Boulder Bridge, 65
  Branch Brook Park, 179
  Bunnell's Pond, 51
  Charles Eliot Memorial Bridge, 136
  Goat Island pedestrian bridge, 199
  Lion Bridge, 300, 302
  Lions Gate Bridge, 305
  Riverway, 147
bridle paths, 73, 205, 219, 229, 239, 256
Brooklyn Botanic Garden, 207–208
Brooklyn park and parkway system, 200–208
  about, 200
  Brooklyn Botanic Garden, 207–208
  Fort Greene Park, 204
  Long Meadow, 204
  Ocean and Eastern Parkways, 205–206
  Prospect Park, 201–203
Brunner, Arnold, 213, 221, 242
Buck, Charles, 82

Buffalo Olmsted Parks Conservancy, 195
Buffalo park and parkway system, 195–197
   Buffalo interconnected parks and parkways (map), 197
   Cazenovia Park, 196
   Delaware Park, 195
   South Park, 196
   "The Parade", 195
building codes, 259
Bulfinch, Charles, 121
Bullard, Oliver C., 51, 323
Burnham, Daniel H., 67, 97, 141, 313, 322, 323
Burr, Alfred, complications of memorial to, 56–57
Bushnell Park and Connecticut State Capitol Grounds, Hartford, 56–57, 62

C
Cadwalader Park, Trenton, 187–188
California Department of Parks and Recreation, 23
California landscapes, 23–41
   Los Angeles, 40–41
   Oakland, 29–30
   Palo Alto, 31–33
   Palos Verdes, 37–39
   San Francisco, 34–35
   State Route 1, 26
   Yosemite National Park and Mariposa Grove, 27–28
California State Parks and Historical Monuments (map), 24
California State Park System, 23–27
   about, 23–24
   Bodega Bay, Lake Tahoe and Humboldt Redwoods, 25
   Camp Curry (now Curry Village), 27
   Castle Crags and Point Lobos, 26
Canada landscapes, 304–311
   Montreal, 309–311
   Vancouver, 304–306
   Victoria, 307–308
Caparn, Harold, 207, 208
Capilano Estates, Vancouver, 304–305
Capitol Square, Raleigh, 233–234
Carillon Historical Park, Dayton, 239, 240
carillon towers, 81, 239, 240

Carl Schurz Memorial (Bacon and Bitter), 211
Castle Crags, 26
Cazenovia Park, Buffalo, 196
cemeteries
   on Gold Coast estate properties, 219
   Hillside Cemetery, Torrington, 60
   Mountain View Cemetery, Oakland, 29–30
   Swan Point Cemetery arrival experience, 263
   Washtenong Memorial Park, Ann Arbor, 165
cemetery "rooms", 218
Central Park, Manhattan, 209–210
Central Park Conservancy, 11, 12, 210
Central Park Mall, 209
Charles River Esplanade, 136
Château-sur-Mer, 262
Chautauqua Park, Boulder, 44
Cheney, Charles, 37
Cherry Esplanade, 208
Chicago World's Fair (1893) planners, 67. See also World's Columbian Exposition
children's play areas
   Noguchi-designed, 91
   as park amenities, 225–226
   recommendation for placement of, 43, 287
   in tenement neighborhoods, 98
Church, Frederic, 198–199
City Beautiful movement, 45, 47, 67, 127, 224
Civic Center Park, Denver, 45
Civilian Conservation Corps (CCC)
   advancing the Olmsted firm's vision, 43, 73
   firm members' work experience with, 318, 324, 325
   labor provided by, 43, 44, 47, 73, 119, 185, 268
civil rights role of Lincoln Memorial grounds, 70
Civil War Memorial, 158
Civil War reparation funds, 106
Clas Alfred C., 302
Cleveland, H. W. S., 263
Cleveland Museum of Art, Fine Arts Garden, 236–237
climate-specific design, 31
Cloisters, Fort Tryon Park, 215

Codman, Henry Sargent, "Harry" (1864–1893), 97, 317
colleges and universities
   Alcorn State University, Alcorn, 167–168
   Amherst College, Amherst, 140–141
   Denison University, Granville, 241–242
   Duke University, Durham, 231
   Fisk University, Nashville, 271–272
   Harvard University, Cambridge, 151–152
   Huntingdon College, Montgomery, 21
   Indiana University, Bloomington, 101
   Johns Hopkins University, Baltimore, 133–134
   Louisiana State University, Baton Rouge, 114–117
   Stanford University, Palo Alto, 31–33
Colonial Revival style, 154, 167
Colorado landscapes, 43–49
   Boulder, 43–44
   Denver, 45–49
Connecticut landscapes, 51–60
   Bridgeport, 51
   Hartford, 52–57
   New Britain, 58
   New Canaan, 59
   Torrington, 60
Connecticut State Capitol Grounds and Bushnell Park, Hartford, 56–57, 62
Corbett, Harvey Wiley (Masonic Memorial to George Washington), 281
Corbin Park, Spokane, 295
Corning Fountain, 56
Cotterill, George, 291
Cranford Rose Garden, 208

D
Dambo, Thomas (Forest Giants in a Giant Forest), 105
Dawson, James Frederick, "Fred" (1874–1941)
   arboretums, 105, 292–293
   biography and overview of projects, 317
   campus planning, 293
   garden design, 286

park design, 215, 317
residential communities and commissions, 34, 37, 270, 304–305, 308, 317
DeBoer, S. R., 45, 46, 47
deed restrictions, 129, 130, 307
Deeds, Edward Andrew, 239, 240
Delaware landscapes (Wilmington), 76–77
Denver mountain parks system, 47–49
   Denver's Proposed Mountain Parks (map), 48–49
   Lariat Trail Scenic Mountain Drive, 47
   Red Rocks Park, 47
Denver park and parkway system, 45–46
   Civic Center Park, 45
   Olmsted firm's implementation of parkways, 45–46
   Speer Boulevard, 46
District of Columbia landscapes, 62–74
   Lincoln Memorial grounds, 70
   McMillan Plan, 67–68, 71
   National Cathedral Grounds, 74
   Rock Creek Park, 65–66
   Theodore Roosevelt Island National Memorial, 72
   Thomas Jefferson Memorial, 68–69
   US Capitol Grounds, 62–63
   Washington Monument, 71
   White House Grounds (President's Park), 13, 64
diversity, horticultural, 81, 186, 188, 292
Downing, Andrew Jackson, 71, 313
Downing Park, 194, 313
drainage solutions, 115, 256, 321
Druid Hills, Atlanta, 84–87
Duncan, John, 295
Dunn, Arthur, 286
Dunn Gardens, Seattle, 286

E
Eagle Rock Reservation, West Orange-Verona-Montclair, 182, 183
Eastern Parkway, Brooklyn, 12
Eberle, Abastenia St. Leger, 59
Echo Lake Park, Mountainside, 190–191

Eliot, Charles (1859-1897), 136–137, 178, 317–318

Elk Rock Garden at the Bishop's Close, Portland, Oregon, 244–245

Ellicott Arch, 146

"elsewhere", idea of, 207–208

Emerald Necklace Conservancy, 147

Emerald Necklace Park System, Boston, 146–148
  Arnold Arboretum, 146, 148
  Back Bay proposed improvements, 148
  Ellicott Arch, 146
  Franklin Park, 146, 148
  Jamaica Pond, 146
  linking parkways, 146–147
  Marine Park, 148
  Riverway, 147
  "Sanitary Improvement of the Muddy River", 1881, 146

entrance drives and approaches
  estates, 144, 150, 219, 230, 255, 260, 283
  residential communities, 165
  Victorian-style park entrance, 115

environmental considerations
  ecologically driven design, 23, 43, 115, 127, 139, 146, 188
  flood control, 127, 188, 256
  impact of hydroelectric power, 198
  landscape rehabilitation, 65, 283
  river dredging and bank restoration, 147

Erie Canal site disruption, 223

esplanades, 123, 136, 137, 208, 211, 213, 228

Essex County Park System, New Jersey, 178–185
  about, 178–179
  Branch Brook Park, 179–181
  Eagle Rock Reservation, 182, 183
  Passaic River Park, 185
  South Mountain Reservation, 184–185

estate properties
  Arthur Curtiss James estate, 261, 262
  Biltmore, 228–230
  Château-sur-Mer, 262
  F. W. Vanderbilt estate, 260
  Gold Coast estates, 218–219
  Harbor Court, 261

Harold Pratt Estate (now Welwyn Preserve), 219
  Moraine Farm, 144
  Newport estates, 260–262
  Ochre Court, 260
  Oldfields, 102
  Otto Kahn Estate (now Oheka Castle, 218
  Rough Point, 260
  Stonehurst, 159
  Stoneleigh, 254–255
  Thornewood, 283–284
  William Coe Estate, 218

F

Fairsted
  acquisition by National Park Service, 150, 315
  archive, 11
  Hudak's tenancy and plantings, 319
  improvements, 319, 320, 325

Fall River parks, 155–156

Farrand, Beatrix, 119

Favretti, Rudy, 82

FDR Park, Philadelphia, 250–251

The Fens, Boston, 115, 123–124, 146, 147, 148

Fine Arts Garden, Cleveland Museum of Art, 236–237

firsts
  country's first bicycle path, 205
  country's first regional agency to acquire and manage land, 205
  first central government to set aside land for nonutilitarian purposes, 27
  first designed parkway, 12, 263
  first planned shopping center, 129
  landscape architect, first use of term, 326

Flagg, Ernest, 242, 285

F. L. and J. C. Olmsted (1884-1889, 1897), 259, 313

F. L. Olmsted and Company (1889-1893), 141, 314

Florida landscapes, 79–82
  Jacksonville, 79
  Lake Wales, 80–82

Forest Giants in a Giant Forest (Dambo), 105

Forest Hills Gardens, Queens, 217

formal gardens, 236–237, 247, 284

formal landscape elements, 59, 102, 228, 255, 296. See also allées

Fort Greene Park, Brooklyn, 204

Fort Greene Park Conservancy, 204

Fort Tryon Park, Manhattan, 213, 215–216

Fountain of the Waters (Beach), 237

fountains
  Bethesda Fountain (Mould), 209
  Corning Fountain, 56
  Drumheller Fountain, 293
  Fountain of the Waters (Beach), 237
  James Scott Memorial Fountain (Gilbert and Adams), 163
  Neptune Fountain, 37
  Seligman Fountain (Walter), 211
  at St. Francis Wood, 34–35

Frederick Law Olmsted National Historic Site (FLONHS), Brookline. See Fairsted

French, Prentiss, 29

Freshwater Land Trust, 18

Friends of Keney Park, 54

Friends of Maryland's Olmsted Parks and Landscapes, 128

Friends of Pope Park, 55

Friends of Seattle's Olmsted Parks, 287

Friends of the Olmsted Landscape at Moraine Farm, 144

Frink Park, Seattle, 287, 288

funding
  bonds, 18, 23
  Civil War reparation funds, 106
  consortium of federal, state, and local, 147
  fractions of trolley fares, 127
  fund-raising, 171
  New Deal money, 188
  plea for citizen cooperation in funding, 17
  World War II effects on park maintenance budgets, 52, 115, 156

G

Gallagher, Percival (1874-1934)
  academic campus design, 175, 231, 271–272
  biography and overview of projects, 318
  cemetery landscaping, 60
  environmental concerns, 283
  estate properties, design, 102, 255

park planning, 181, 184–185, 188
  residential commissions, 261

garden clubs, 237, 284, 292, 319

Garden History of Georgia, 1733–1933 (Peachtree Garden Club), 93

garden rooms, 59, 144, 160, 219, 283, 284

gardens
  Bok Tower Gardens, Lake Wales, 81
  Brooklyn Botanic Garden, 208
  Dunn Gardens, Seattle, 286
  formal, 236–237, 247, 284
  Japanese Hill-and-Pond Garden, 208
  lily pond, 57
  rose gardens, 59, 64, 208, 261
  sunken, 102, 144, 283, 285
  water garden, 284
  woodland, 102, 286

Gardner, James T., 198

Gardner, William, 307, 308

Genesee Valley Park, Rochester, 223

Georgia landscapes, 84–93
  Atlanta, 84–91
  Columbus, 92–93

Gibbs, George, Jr. (1878-1950), 142, 154, 164, 318

Gilbert, Cass (James Scott Memorial Fountain), 163

Gold Coast estates, North Shore of Long Island, 218–219

Goodwin, William, 123–124

Goodwin Park, Hartford, 53

Gothic style, 21, 29, 60, 216, 231

Gould, Carl, 293

grading
  in campus design, 101
  creating border mounds, 54
  gentle grades to accommodate automobiles, 47
  manipulating to resolve site issues, 157, 214, 255

Graves, Bibb, 19

Great Depression, 298

Great Frieze (Amateis), 171

Great New England Hurricane of 1938, 57, 188

Green, Andrew Haswell, 211

Green Lake Park, Seattle, 288

Greensward Plan, 1858, 194, 209

greenways, 99, 146, 200

Guilford Park, Baltimore, 131

H

handicapped accessibility, 309
Hare and Hare, 171
Harmony (Perry), 57
Hartford parks system, 52–55
    about, 52
    Goodwin Park, 53
    Keney Park, 54
    Pope Park, 55
health, promotion of, 43, 56, 127,
    155, 178, 210, 296
H. H. Richardson Historic District,
    158
Highland Park, Rochester, 222
Hills and Dales MetroPark, Dayton, 240
Hillside Cemetery, Torrington, 60
Hoban, James, 64
Hog Island. *See* Belle Isle Park,
    Detroit
Homeland Park, Baltimore, 132
Honor the Mountain Monument,
    226
Howard, John Galen, 34–35, 293
Hubbard, Henry Vincent
    (1875–1947)
    academic campus design, 122,
        151–152
    biography and overview of projects, 318–319
    monument and memorial landscapes, 68–69, 71, 72–73,
        268–269
    park design, 128, 215–216
    road design, 119
    site solutions, 157
Hubbard Educational Foundation,
    14, 325
Hudak, Joseph George (1927–), 319
Humboldt Redwoods, 25
Hunt, Richard Morris, 228, 260

I

Idaho landscapes (Moscow), 95
Illinois landscapes, 97–99
    Chicago, 97–98
    Riverside, 99
Indiana Landscapes, 101–103
    Bloomington, 101
    Indianapolis, 102–103
Indigenous peoples
    burial cairns, 308
    cultural practices of Songhees
        First Nation, 307

Lenape Indigenous peoples, 183,
    184, 207, 208, 215
Lenni-Lenape peoples, 183
Narragansett nation, 260
infrastructure considerations, 37,
    43, 120, 131
Interlaken Park, Seattle, 288
Ireys, Alice, 208
Italianate-Mediterranean style,
    37–39
Italian Renaissance style, 34–35, 208

J

Jamaica Pond, Boston, 146
Japanese Hill-and-Pond Garden,
    208
Jirouch, Frank (*Night Passing the
    Earth to Day*), 237
Jones, Percy Reginald "Pa" (1860–
    1941), 180, 239, 319–320

K

Kellaway, Herbert J. (1867–1947), 320
Keney Park, Hartford, 54
Kenilworth Park, Portland, 246
Kennedy Park, Fall River, 156
Kentmere Parkway, Wilmington, 76
Kentucky landscapes, 105–112
    Clermont, 105
    Frankfort, 106
    Lexington, 107
    Louisville, 108–112
Kentucky State Capitol Grounds,
    Frankfort, 106
Kerr, Peter, 244
Kessler, George E., 45, 129, 171
Kirby Park, Wilkes-Barre, 256
Koehler, Hans J. (1867–1951), 320
Kohler, Walter, Sr., 12, 298
Kohler, Wisconsin, 298–299

L

Lake Park, Milwaukee, 302
Lake Tahoe, 25
Lake Washington Boulevard, Seattle, 291–292
lampposts, US Capitol, 63
land
    acquisition campaigns, 47–49, 182
    associated with Indigenous peoples, 183, 184, 215, 307, 308
    considering masses regardless
        of jurisdictional boundaries, 317
    desert land, 23

Eliot's five categories, 136
    first regional agency to acquire
        and manage land, 136
    Freshwater Land Trust, 18
    government setting aside for
        nonutilitarian purposes, 27
    lot sizes, 253
    Morrill Act of 1862 land grants,
        122
land-grant colleges, 122, 167
land reservations
    changing attitudes toward, 185
    land acquisition to develop as,
        183, 184–185
    for "perpetual use and refreshment", 18
    removing previous incursions
        upon, 184, 198
    The Trustees of Reservations
        (The Trustees), 137, 139, 317
landscape architect, first use of
    term, 326
landscape architecture profession,
    10, 323
landscape rehabilitation, 65, 88,
    150, 283
Laura Spelman Rockefeller Memorial, Gatlinburg, 268–269
Laurelhurst Park, Portland, 246
Lawrenceville Academy, Lawrenceville, 186
Lay, Charles Downing, 213, 215, 319
L'Enfant, Pierre, 64, 67, 71, 322
Let There Be Light (Barnard), 105
Lewis, E.G., 37
Liberty Memorial, Kansas City,
    171–172
Lincoln Memorial Grounds, 70
Linn Park, Birmingham, 18
Lions Gate Bridge, Vancouver, 305
Long Meadow, Prospect Park, 203
Louisiana landscapes, 114–117
    Baton Rouge, 116–117
    New Orleans, 114–115
Louisville parks and parkways system, 109–110
    accent elements in parks, 108, 110
    Chickasaw Park, 109–110
    parkways, 110
    residential subdivisions, 110

M

MacArthur Bridge, 163
Magonigle, Harold Van Buren, 58,
    171–172

Maine landscapes, 119–124
    Augusta, 119–120, 121
    Mount Desert, 119–120
    Orono, 122
    Portland, 123–124
Maine State Capitol Grounds,
    Augusta, 121
Manito Park, Spokane, 296
Manning, A. Chandler, 59
Manning, Warren H. (1860–1938),
    133, 176, 232, 237, 256,
    320–321
Manship, Paul, 72, 73, 269
Mariposa Grove, 27–28
Marquis, William Bell, "Bill" (1887–
    1978), 57, 92, 265, 314, 321
Maryland landscapes (Baltimore),
    126–134
Masonic Memorial to George
    Washington, Alexandria
    (Corbett), 280–281
Massachusetts landscapes, 136–160
    Amherst, 140–141
    Andover, 142–143
    Beverly, 144–145
    Boston, 136–138, 146–148
    Brookline, 149–150
    Cambridge, 151–152
    Concord, 153–154
    Fall River, 155–156
    Hingham, 139
    Newton, 157
    North Easton, 158
    Waltham, 136
    Williamstown, 160
McDowell, Jr., Henry Clay, 107
McDuffie, Duncan, 34
McKim, Charles Follen, 67, 141
McKim, Mead, and White, 141,
    204, 207, 260
McMillan Commission, 72, 322
McMillan Plan, 67–68, 70, 71, 72
McMurtry, George, 252, 253
Mead, William Rutherford, 141
Mellon, Rachel Lambert, 64
Memorial Park, Jacksonville, 12, 79
Metropolitan Museum of Art, 215
Metropolitan Park Commission,
    Boston, 136–138, 314
    Beaver Brook Reservation, 137, 138
    Blue Hills Reservation, 137, 138
    Charles River Esplanade, 137, 138
    Hemlock Gorge, 137, 138
    reservation acquisitions, 137
    Revere Beach, 137

Miantonomi Hill, Newport, 260
Michigan landscapes, 162–165
    Ann Arbor, 164–165
    Detroit, 162–163
Middlesex School, Concord,
    153–154
Mische, Emanuel Tillman, "Emil"
    (1870-1934), 244, 247, 248,
    321–322
Mississippi landscapes, 167–169
    Alcorn, 167–168
    Oxford, 169
Missouri landscapes (Kansas City),
    171–172
monadnock, 308–309
Moorish influences, 82
Moraine Farm, Beverly, 144–145
Morelli, Patrick (9/11 memorial),
    183
Morningside Park, Manhattan,
    211–212
Moses, Robert, 202, 206, 213
mosquitos, 162, 163, 185
Mould, Jacob Wrey, 209, 210, 211
Mountain Lake, Lake Wales, 80
Mountain View Cemetery, Oak-
    land, 29–30
Mount Desert Island, 119
Mount Royal, Montreal, 308,
    309–311
Mount Tabor Park, Portland, 246
music pavilions, 180, 291, 302

N

National Association for Olmsted
    Parks, 11
National Capital Park Commis-
    sion, 68
National Cathedral Bishop's Gar-
    den, 74
National Cathedral Grounds, 74
National Historic Landmarks, 12
National Mall, 67–68, 70–71
national parks
    Acadia National Park, 119–120
    establishment of, 27–28
    Great Smoky Mountains
        National Park, 268
    Yosemite and the Mariposa Grove:
        A Preliminary Report, 1865,
        27
    Yosemite National Park and
        Mariposa Grove, 27–28
National Park Service, 27, 150, 268,
    315, 322

National Register of Historic
    Places, 12
native plants
    academic campus landscapes, 33
    in "aesthetic forestry", 185
    Bradley Olmsted Garden, 92–93
    Brooklyn Botanic Garden collec-
        tion, 207
    memorial and monument
        grounds, 72–73
    National Cathedral Grounds, 74
    Pacific Northwest, 244
    perimeter plantings, 82
    preservation of, 76, 77, 92, 259
    recommended use of, 13, 106,
        183
    restoring with, 73, 283
    scientific arboretum of, 229
"Nature Theater", 299
NCR (National Cash Register) Cor-
    poration Projects, Dayton,
    238–240
Neoclassical style, 68, 70, 106, 208,
    293
Neo-Gothic style, 95, 101
New Hampshire landscapes
    (Exeter), 174–176
New Jersey landscapes, 178–192
    Elizabeth, 189–190
    Essex County, 178–185
    Lawrenceville, 186
    Mountainside, 190–192
    Newark, 179–181
    Rahway, 190, 191
    Trenton, 187
    Union County, 188–192
    West Orange, 184–185
    West Orange-Verona-Montclair,
        182–183
Newport City Plan, 13, 258–259
Newport estates, 260–262
Newton City Hall, 157
New York landscapes, 195–226
    Brooklyn, 12, 200–208
    Buffalo, 195–197
    Long Island, 218–219
    Manhattan, 209–216
    Niagara Falls, 198–199
    Queens, 217
    Rochester, 220–224
    Watertown, 225–226
Niagara Falls Hydraulic Power and
    Manufacturing Company,
    199
Niagara Falls viewpoint, 199

Niagara Reservation, Niagara Falls,
    198–199
Nichols, William, 169
Night Passing the Earth to Day (Jir-
    ouch), 237
9/11 memorial (Morelli), 183
Noguchi, Isamu (*Black Sun*), 291
North Carolina landscapes,
    228–234
    Ashville, 228–230
    Durham, 231
    Pinehurst, 232
    Raleigh, 233–234
North Carolina State Capitol
    Grounds, 233–234
North Carolina Veterans Monu-
    ment, 233
North Easton Railroad Station, 158
North Easton Town Complex, 158

O

Ocean and Eastern Parkways,
    Brooklyn, 200, 205–206
Ohio landscapes, 236–242
    Cleveland, 236–238
    Dayton, 239–240
    Granville, 241–242
Oldfields, Indianapolis, 102–103
Old River Park, Dayton, 240
Olmsted, Frederick Law, Jr., "Rick"
    (1870-1957)
    academic campus design, 21,
        116–117, 151–152, 242
    approach to city as cultural land-
        scape, 259
    biography and overview of proj-
        ects, 322
    Bok Tower Gardens, 81
    A City Plan for Rochester, 1911, 221
    defense of "park values", 213
    drafting of language for National
        Park Service bill, 322
    "The Improvement of Boulder
        Colorado", 1910, 43
    land acquisition as a landscape
        tenet, 65
    memorial and monument
        grounds, 68–73
    National Cathedral grounds, 74
    Palos Verdes planning team, 315
    on park and playground place-
        ment, 43, 287
    parks, planning and design,
        23–24, 43–44, 65–66,
        126–128, 240, 256

Proposed Improvements to Newport,
    1913, 259, 261
"Report Upon the Development
    of Public Grounds for Bal-
    timore", 1904, 127
residential communities, 37, 80,
    260–262, 315
    White House Grounds, 64
Olmsted, Frederick Law, Sr.
    (1822-1903)
    academic campus design, 31–32,
        122, 141, 186
    biography and role in landscape
        profession, 322
    cemetery design, 29–30
    concerns about commercializa-
        tion, 198–199
    design characteristics of residen-
        tial communities, 130
    domestic landscape ideals, 149–150
    estate properties, design, 144,
        159, 228–230
    farm-forest-park plan, 277
    forest lodge concept, 159
    Greensward Plan, 1858, 194, 209
    home (Fairsted), 149–150
    national park development, role
        in, 27–28, 323
    "open-air apartment" concept,
        144, 159
    parks, planning and design, 155–
        156, 162–163, 204, 209–210,
        211–212, 213–214, 223–224,
        300–302
    park systems, 52, 97–98, 109–110,
        146–148, 200–201, 220
    parkways, 205–206
    Picturesque style and design
        principles, 91
    residential communities, 84, 99,
        130, 260, 309–311
    resource knowledge base, 11–12
    on scenery, 13
    significant collaborative projects
        with Vaux, 326
    South Park water feature, 196
    town complex, 158
    United States Capitol Grounds,
        62–63
    use of organically shaped bodies
        of water, 309
    World's Columbian Exposition,
        1893, 97–98
    Yosemite and the Mariposa Grove: A
        Preliminary Report, 1865, 27

Olmsted, John Charles, "JCO" (1852-1920)
　academic campus design, 95, 153–154, 242, 285, 293
　"aesthetic forestry" concept, 184–185
　biography and projects overview, 323–324
　boulevard design, 263
　A Comprehensive System of Parks and Parkways, 1925, 287
　estate properties, design, 283–284
　gardens, 244
　parks, planning and design, 51, 55, 88, 98, 115, 124, 156, 225–226, 290
　park systems, 147, 178–185, 195, 246–248
　The Portland Park Plan of 1903, 246–247, 248
　residential communities, 307–308
　state capitol grounds, 56, 106, 274–275, 285
　town plan, 252
Olmsted, Olmsted, and Eliot (1893-1897), 314
Olmsted, Vaux, and Company (1865-1872), 313
Olmsted Associates, (1961-1979), 314–315
Olmsted Brothers (1898-1961)
　firm profile and overview of projects, 314
　Genesee Valley Park site disruption, 223
　guiding of land acquisition campaign, 182
　Olmsted General Plan of Campus, 1929, 19
　parkways, 45–46
　A System of Parks and Playgrounds for Birmingham: Preliminary Report, 1925, 17
Olmsted firms. *See also* F. L. and J. C. Olmsted; F. L. Olmsted and Company; Olmsted, Olmsted, and Eliot; Olmsted, Vaux, and Company; Olmsted Associates; Olmsted Brothers
　biographies and project overviews, 316–327
　family tree, 312

landscape typologies invented by, 12
　resource knowledge base, 11–12
Olmsted Parks and Parkways Thematic Resources, Buffalo, 195
Olmsted Woods, 74
"open-air apartment" concept, 144, 159
Open Space and Mountain Parks preserves, Boulder, 43
"open valley" landscape rehabilitation, 65
Oregon landscapes (Portland), 244–248
overlooks, scenic, 18, 145, 179, 216, 224, 226, 310

P
pagoda, 128
Palos Verdes Estates, 36, 37
Palos Verdes Parkway, Los Angeles, 40–41
Palos Verdes planning team, 315
Palos Verdes Syndicate, Palos Verdes, 37–39
Panic of 1873, 309
park construction boom, Detroit, 163
Parker, Carl Rust (1882-1966), 21, 122, 239–240, 280–281, 324
parkland acquisition tenets, 65
park planning values
　connectivity, 102, 110, 188, 195
　equitable distribution of access, 13, 296
　Olmsted's "American democratic experiment", 322
　park and playground placement recommendations, 43, 287
　promotion of health, 43, 56, 127, 155, 178, 210, 296
　specific goals, 66, 188, 210, 287
parks, accent elements, 108, 110
parkways
　accompanying stream corridors, 127–128
　Buffalo interconnected parks and parkways (map), 197
　coining of term, 200
　first designed, 12, 263
　linking Boston parks, 146–147
　Louisville, 110
　Ocean and Eastern Parkways, Brooklyn, 200, 205–206

Olmsted firm's legacy contribution, 45–46
　Seattle, 287
　Terwilliger Parkway, Portland, 248
Parsons, Samuel, Jr., 210, 213
parterres, 59, 296
Passaic River Park, 185
pastoral landscapes
　ensuring a pastoral setting, 130
　idea of "elsewhere", 207–208
　impingements upon, 187–188, 190
Patterson Park, Baltimore, 128
pedestrians
　bridges, 199, 210, 223, 300
　buffer from vehicular traffic, 76
　coastal access, 259
Peninsula Park, Portland, 247
Pennsylvania landscapes, 250–256
　Philadelphia, 250–251
　Vandergrift, 252–253
　Villanova, 254–255
　Wilkes-Barre, 256
pergolas, 108, 110, 255
Perry, Charles (*Harmony*), 57
Phillips, William Lyman (1885-1966), 82, 319, 324
Phillips Academy, Andover, 142–143
Phillips Exeter Academy, Exeter, 174–175
Picturesque style
　Fairsted landscape and home, 149–150
　garden, 244
　H. H. Richardson's conception of, 159
　in parks, 46, 90　91, 220, 222, 251
Piedmont Park, Atlanta, 90
Pilát, Ignatz, 210
Pillars, Charles Adrian (*Spiritualized Life*), 79
Pinchot, Gifford, 229
Pinehurst Village, North Carolina, 232
Pinewood Estate, Lake Wales, 82
Pinnacle Hill, Watertown, 225, 226
plans and drawings. *See also* planting plans
　ACADEMIC CAMPUSES:
　　Alcorn campus development plan, 168
　　Denison University campus plan, 1918, 241

Fisk University campus expansion, 271
Harvard University buildings and walkways, 151
Johns Hopkins University, 133
Leland Stanford Jr. University, 32–33
Louisiana State University campus proposal, 117
Middlesex School green, 153
quadrangles, 133, 294
University of North Alabama, Florence, 20
University of Washington, 294
BRIDGES:
　Charles Eliot Memorial Bridge, 136
　Genesee Valley Park's barge canal pedestrian bridges, 223
CEMETERIES:
　Mountain View Cemetery, Oakland, 30
CITIES AND TOWNS:
　Boone Square (Louisville), 108
　"Nature Theater", 299
　Newport improvements, 258
　Vandergrift general plan, 253
ESTATES:
　Biltmore grounds, 229
　Fairsted, 149
　NCR (National Cash Register) Corporation Plaza, 1937, 238
ORNAMENTAL FARMS:
　Shelburne Farms' functions, 277
PARKS:
　Back Bay Fens improvement plan, 148
　Beardsley Park, 51
　Belle Isle Park, 162
　Cadwalader Park plan, 187
　Cazenovia Park plan, 196
　Denver's Proposed Mountain Parks plan, 48–49
　Eagle Rock Reservation, 182
　Eastern Promenade, Portland, 123
　entrance and shelter structures, 115
　FDR Park, 250
　Fort Tryon Park, 216

PARKS (CONT):
Grant Park, 88
greater Boston parkland,
1897, 136
Lake Park plan, 302
Maine State Park, 121
Mount Royal design, 310–311
Niagara Reservation, 198
South Park (now Kennedy
Park), 154–155
"Study for Barless Enclosure
for Bears", 115
Theodore Roosevelt Island,
72
The Uplands plan, 306
Victorian-style park entrance,
115
Volunteer park plan, Seattle,
289
Walnut Hill Park, New Brit-
ain, 58
Washtenong Memorial Park
approach, 165
PARK SYSTEMS:
Baltimore parks expansion,
126
Birmingham park system,
17
Hartford park network, 52
interconnected parks and
parkways, Buffalo, 197
Seattle parks plan, 287
Union County interconnected
public parks, 189
PARKWAYS:
Exeter Shore Parkway, 1929,
175
RESIDENTIAL COMMUNITIES:
Capilano Golf and Country
Club, 305
Crescent development plan,
Charleston, 266
Druid Hills, 86–87
Forest Hills Gardens 1910,
217
Palos Verdes Estates, 36
Riverside residential commu-
nity, 99
St. Francis Wood, 34, 35
The Uplands plan, 306
Yeamans Hall Club home-
sites, 265
planting plans
base of Bok Tower planting
study, 81

Dunn Gardens planting plan,
286
Elk Rock Garden cut-flower
garden, 245
espalier fruit trees, 262
formal gardens and tree placement, 284
Japanese flowering cherries
extent, 181
Keney Park plantings, 54
Lawrenceville Academy planting
plan, 1886, 186
rose gardens, 59, 261
Thomas Jefferson Memorial
plantings, 68–69
Thompson Park planting plan,
225
Washington Monument planting study, 71
Washington Park Arboretum,
293
planting schemes. See also native
plants
blue color scheme, 262
espalier fruit trees, 262
"garden suburb" appeal, 38
groupings by species, 293
naturalistic, 81, 88, 213
pale to darker colors,
283–284
Picturesque-style garden,
244
planting for screening, 29, 53,
54, 56, 59, 150, 156
Platt, Charles, 129, 143, 265
play areas. See children's play
areas
plazas, 37, 298
Point Lobos, California, 26
Pope, John Russell, 68, 72
Pope Park, Hartford, 55
Portland Parks (Maine), Eastern
and Western Promenades,
123–124
Portland (Oregon) park system,
246–247
eighteen-point plan, 247
Firwood Lake, 246
Kenilworth Park, 246
Laurelhurst Park, 246
Mount Tabor Park, 246
Peninsula Park, 246, 247
The Portland Park Plan of 1903,
246–247, 248
Sellwood Park, 246

Potomac River, 72
Prellwitz, E. M., 171
Prospect Park, Brooklyn, 201–203
Prospect Park Alliance, 202
public-private partnerships, 91, 210
Puryear, G. A., Jr., estate land, 270

Q
quadrangles
axes, 33, 143, 169, 241, 293
in campus design, 31–33, 116–117,
133–134, 143, 160, 169, 174,
231, 241–242, 293–294
plans and drawings, 133, 294
Queen Victoria Park, 199

R
Rahway River Parks, Rahway,
190–191
Raynor, Seth, 265
recreation
balancing old world aesthetic
with recreational needs,
215–216
changing priorities, 156, 202
children's play areas, 43, 91, 98,
225–226, 287
recreational amenities, 37, 55,
130, 162, 184, 219
refectories, 187, 302
residential communities
covenants, restrictive, 129, 130,
307
design characteristics, 130
residential communities, locations
Atlanta, 84–87
residential community locations
Baltimore, 129–132
Dayton, 239–240
Lexington, 107
Louisville subdivisions, 110
Mountain Lake, 80
Nashville, 270
Palos Verdes, 36–39
Queens, 217
Riverside, 99
San Francisco, 34–35
Victoria, British Columbia,
307–308
Rhode Island landscapes, 258–263
Newport, 258–259, 258–262
Providence, 263
Richardson, Artemas Partridge,
II (1918-2015), 10, 314,
324–325

Richardson, H. H. (Henry Hobson),
147, 158, 159
Riley, Charles Scott (1909-1966), 325
Riverside Community, Riverside, 99
Riverside Park, Manhattan, 213–214
Riverway, Boston, 147
Rochester parks system, 220–221
Genesee Valley Park, 221
Lower Falls in Maplewood Park,
220
Rock Creek Park, 65–66
Rockefeller, Laura Spelman, memo-
rial, 268–269
Rockery, 158
Roland Park, Baltimore, 129
rotundas, 112, 251
Russell Sage Homes Foundation,
217

S
Saint Francis Wood, San Francisco,
34–35
Saint-Gaudens, Augustus, 67, 141
scenery
designing for, 53, 54, 66, 209–
210, 259
enhancing natural assets, 60,
259
historic / scenic values vs. public
demand, 199
Olmsted Sr. on enjoyment of, 13
preservation and protection of,
18, 115, 198–199, 259
scenic overlooks, 18, 145, 179, 216,
224, 226, 310
schist outcroppings, 209, 215
Schwagerl, Edward, 290
Seattle Garden Club, 292
Seattle Parks and Boulevard System, 289–293
about, 289
Frink Park, 289–288
Green Lake Park, 288
Interlaken Park and Boulevard,
288
Lake Washington Boulevard, 291
Seward Park, 290
Volunteer Park, 289, 290–291
Washington Park Arboretum,
292–293
Seligman Fountain (Walter), 211
Sellwood Park, Portland, 246
Seneca Park, Rochester, 224
Seward Park, Seattle, 290
shadow studies, 74

Shelburne Farms, Burlington, 277

Shepley, Rutan, and Coolidge, 31, 222, 319

Shiota, Takeo, 208

Shipman, Ellen, 79, 231

shopping center, first planned, 129

shovels, manufacture of, 158

Shurcliff, Arthur Asahel (1870-1957), 115, 147, 151–152, 325

Soergel, Kenneth, 281

Soldiers and Sailors Arch at Grand Army Plaza, 202

South Carolina landscapes (North Charleston / Charleston), 265–266

South Mountain Reservation, West Orange, 184–185

South Park, Buffalo, 196

South Park (now Kennedy Park), Fall River, 155–156

South Park system, Chicago, 97–98
    McKinley Park, 98
    Midway Plaisance, 97, 98
    planned spaces for active uses, 98
    Washington Park, 97, 98

Speer, Robert, 45

Speer Boulevard, Denver, 46

Spiritualized Life (Pillars), 79

Spokane park system, 295–296
    about, 295
    Corbin Park, 295
    Manito Park, 296

State Capitol grounds, 45, 56–57, 106, 121, 233–234, 274–275, 285

Stebbins, Emma (Angel of the Waters), 209

Stonehurst, Waltham, 159

Stoneleigh, Villanova, 254–255

streets and roads
    for automobiles, 47, 119
    boulevards, 46, 263, 291–292
    carriage roads, 119, 139
    circulation systems, 76, 132, 139, 199, 222, 231, 300, 309
    convergence at US Capitol, 63
    curvilinear street pattern, 130, 165, 167, 188, 217, 307
    departure from grid pattern, 307
    directing sightlines along, 120
    planned along existing contours, 37
    recommendations based on traffic counts, 43

sinking of transverse, 209

street hierarchy, 132

unobtrusive blending of scenic roadways, 120

subdivisions. *See* residential communities

Sudbrook Park residential community, Baltimore, 130

Summerhouse, US Capitol, 63

sunken gardens, 102, 144, 283, 285

Sunrise Amphitheater, 44

Swan Point Cemetery, Providence, 263

Swasey Parkway, Exeter, 176

swimming pools, 219, 224

T

Taylor, Alfred, J. T., 304

Tennessee landscapes, 268–272
    Gatlinburg, 268–269
    Nashville, 270–272

terraces, 63, 68, 106, 121, 216, 268, 269

Terwilliger Parkway, Portland, 248

Theodore Roosevelt Island National Memorial, 72

Theodore Roosevelt Memorial Association, 72

"The Parade" , Buffalo, 195

The Three Graces replica, 102

The Trustees of Reservations (The Trustees), 137, 139, 144, 317

Thomas Jefferson Memorial, 68–69

Thompson, Stanley, 305

Thompson Park, Watertown, 225–226

Thornewood, American Lake, 283–284

Todd, Frederick G. (1876-1948), 309, 325–326

tourism and public demand, 199

transportation considerations, 37, 51, 120

tree-clogging notch intervention, 138

tree-massing plan, 71

trees. *See also* arboretums
    allées, 70, 98, 102, 115, 121, 122
    canopy in campus design, 143
    cherry, 68, 69, 181, 208, 294
    Douglas firs, 246, 286
    evergreens, 232
    Garry oak trees ecosystem, 307
    Joshua tree, 23
    live oaks, 29, 81, 82, 115, 265

living "museum of botany and dendrology", 186

native, 73, 106, 232

pines, 82, 232, 309

quincunx planting of tulip poplars, 62

Waverly Oaks (white oaks), 136, 137, 138

Trumbauer, Horace, 231

Tudor Revival style, 255

Tudor style, 260, 283

U

Union County park system, New Jersey, 188–192
    about, 188–189
    Echo Lake Park, Mountainside, 190–191
    Rahway River Parks, Rahway, 190–191
    Warinanco Park, Elizabeth, 189–190
    Watchung Reservation, Mountainside, 192

United States Capitol Grounds, 62–63

United States Civil Rights Trail, 272

universities. *See* colleges and universities

The Uplands, Victoria, 307–308

urns, 202

US Commission of Fine Arts, 68, 70

Utah State Capitol Grounds, Salt Lake City, 274–275

V

"Vale of Cashmere" (Prospect Park), 201

Vanderbilt, F. W., 260

Vanderbilt, George W., estate. *See* Biltmore

Vandergrift Town Plan, 252–253

Vanderlip, Frank, 37

Van Rensselaer, Schuyler, Mrs. (*Art Out-Of-Doors*), 10

Vaux, Calvert (1824-1895)
    biography and projects overview, 326
    Buffalo park and parkway system, 195
    Central Park, 209–210
    Greensward Plan, 1858, 194, 209
    Niagara Reservation public use amenities, 199

Olmsted-Vaux design intent, 205–206

significant collaborative projects with Olmsted Sr., 326

South Park, Fall River, 155–156

Vermont landscapes (Burlington), 277–278

Victorian style, 114, 115, 252, 253, 262

Virginia landscapes (Alexandria), 280–281

Volunteer Park, Seattle, 289, 290–291

W

walls
    retaining, 62, 121, 211, 212, 216, 280–281
    sitting, 145

Walnut Hill Park, New Britain, 58

Walter, Edgar, Seligman Fountain, 211

Warinanco Park, Elizabeth, 189

Waring, George E., 210

war memorials. *See* World War I

Warren, H. Langford, 21

Warren, Knight, and Davis, 19

Washington landscapes, 283–296
    American Lake, 283–284
    Olympia, 285
    Seattle, 286–294
    Spokane, 295–296

Washington Monument (Baltimore), 127

Washington Monument (Washington DC), 71

Washington Park, Milwaukee, 300–301

Washington Park Arboretum, Seattle, 292–293

Washington State Capitol, Olympia, 285

Washtenong Memorial Park, Ann Arbor, 165

Watchung Reservation, Mountainside, 192

water tower, Riverside, 99

Waveny Park, New Canaan, 59

Waverly Oaks, 136, 138

Weidenmann, Jacob, 53, 56

Welwyn Preserve, 219

"West Side Improvement" plan, Manhattan, 213

White, Aubrey, 295–296

White, Stanford, 202
"White City" remaining building, 97
White House Grounds (President's Park), 13, 64
Whiting, Edward Clark "Ted" (1881-1962)
    academic campus design, 111–112, 143, 160, 242
    biography and projects overview, 326
    Connecticut State Capitol Grounds, 56–57
    Fine Arts Garden, Cleveland Museum of Art, 237
    Hillside Cemetery, 60
    Rock Creek Park assessment report, 65–66
    stone entry gates, 164
Whittemore, Harlow Olin, 165
Wight and Wight, 171
Williston, David, 271–272
Wirth, Theodore, 52
Wisconsin landscapes, 298–302
    Kohler, 298–299
    Milwaukee, 300–302
    West Park-Washington Park plan, Milwaukee, 301
Wisedell, Thomas, 62, 63

Withers, Frederick Clarke (1828-1901), 326–327
Woodmont Estates, Nashville, 271
(WPA) Works Progress Administration, 101, 115, 185, 202, 208, 213
World's Columbian Exposition, 1893, 68, 97
World's End, Hingham, 139–140
World War I
    effects on transportation development, 37
    memorials, 58, 79, 171
World War II, effects on park maintenance budgets, 52, 115, 256
Wright Brothers Memorial, 239–240

Y

Yeamans Hall Club, North Charleston, 265
Yosemite National Park and Mariposa Grove, 27–28

Z

Zach, Leon Henry (1895-1966), 237, 327
zoological garden, 115